Judging Executive Power

Judging Executive Power

Sixteen Supreme Court Cases That Have Shaped the American Presidency

Edited by
Richard J. Ellis

ROWMAN & LITTLEFIELD PUBLISHERS, INC.
Lanham • Boulder • New York • Toronto • Plymouth, UK

ROWMAN & LITTLEFIELD PUBLISHERS, INC.

Published in the United States of America
by Rowman & Littlefield Publishers, Inc.
A wholly owned subsidiary of The Rowman & Littlefield Publishing Group, Inc.
4501 Forbes Boulevard, Suite 200, Lanham, Maryland 20706
www.rowmanlittlefield.com

Estover Road
Plymouth PL6 7PY
United Kingdom

British Library Cataloguing in Publication Information Available

Library of Congress Cataloging-in-Publication Data:

Judging executive power : sixteen Supreme Court cases that have shaped the
American presidency / edited by Richard J. Ellis.
    p. cm.
 Includes bibliographical references and index.
 ISBN-13: 978-0-7425-6512-8 (cloth : alk. paper)
 ISBN-10: 0-7425-6512-2 (cloth : alk. paper)
 ISBN-13: 978-0-7425-6513-5 (pbk. : alk. paper)
 ISBN-10: 0-7425-6513-0 (pbk. : alk. paper)
 eISBN-13: 978-0-7425-6514-2
 eISBN-10: 0-7425-6514-9
 1. Executive power—United States Cases. 2. Constitutional law—United
States—Cases. 3. United States. Supreme Court. I. Ellis, Richard (Richard J.)
 KF5050.J83 2009
 342.73'06—dc22   2008043438

Printed in the United States of America

⊗™ The paper used in this publication meets the minimum requirements of
American National Standard for Information Sciences—Permanence of Paper for
Printed Library Materials, ANSI/NISO Z39.48-1992.

Contents

II. War Powers and Diplomacy

The "Sole Organ" of Foreign Relations

Wartime and Emergency Powers

The Civil War

World War II

The Korean War and the Cold War

The War on Terror

Preface

Bringing the Courts Back In

The first time I taught the presidency in the fall of 1990 I organized the course around five themes: (1) public evaluations of the president and attitudes toward the presidency, (2) the relationship between the president and Congress, (3) the president's relationship with his cabinet members and the federal bureaucracy, (4) the president's relationship with his political party, and (5) the role of personality in explaining presidential behavior. The course reflected my training in graduate school during the 1980s, where the central organizing concepts in the study of the presidency were things like presidential character, political skill, presidential popularity, presidential rhetoric, congressional support, and decision-making style. A year-long graduate field seminar in American politics that I took in 1983 included three books on the presidency—Richard Neustadt's *Presidential Power*, James David Barber's *Presidential Character*, and Fred Greenstein's *Hidden-Hand Presidency*—each of which focused on the personal attributes, political skills, and leadership style of individual presidents.

That first course I taught in 1990, like my graduate field seminar in 1983, included nothing on the courts or the legal system. I gave the Constitution no more thought in my first presidency class than most of my teachers had given it in the courses I took as a graduate student. The political scientists I knew were keenly interested in explaining political behavior but quite happy to leave the interpretation of legal doctrine to the lawyers and teachers of constitutional law; public law, in this view, was something entirely separate from the study of American politics. This strict separation of law and politics seemed natural to me at first but I gradually grew uncomfortable with it; leaving out the Constitution, I came to see, was not a satisfactory way to teach about the presidency. By the end of the decade I was not only requiring my students to read the standard Federalist essays by Alexander Hamilton (typically Federalist 69 and 70) but plunging them directly into the spirited debates over presidential power at the Constitutional Convention. In 1999, in an effort to bring the Constitution back into the teaching of the presidency, I published *Founding the American Presidency*, an edited collection of the Framers' debates about the presidency.

The Bush administration's aggressive assertion of presidential power, particularly after September 11, 2001, made it even more difficult to teach the presidency without studying the intersection of law and politics. Formal, constitutionally prescribed (or at least claimed) powers seemed to matter more than the public's approval of a president's job performance. Influence in Congress still mattered, of course, but at least as impressive was a president's ability to act on his own, without explicit congressional approval. My students wanted to talk most not about Bush's approval ratings or his support scores in Congress but about his use of signing statements, recess appointments, military tribunals, and executive orders. Outraged students wanted to know why he was allowed to do these things. Why didn't judges stop him? What, they wanted to know, did the courts have to say about Bush's claims and actions? In other words, they wanted to talk about the very aspects of presidential power that had been generally left out of my own education.

Their questions pushed me to read the court cases that I had never been asked to read in graduate school. I do not pretend to be a pioneer in this area. Indeed I am embarrassed to admit just how much of a Johnny-come-lately I am. A number of scholars have been toiling in this vineyard for years, including Louis Fisher, Richard Pious, Robert Spitzer, and David Adler. Fisher is particularly prolific; among his recent works are first-rate studies of the Nazi saboteur case (*Ex parte Quirin*) and the Cold War era state secrets case (*United States v. Reynolds*) as well as an award-winning study of military tribunals in American history. Spitzer has written, among many other things, penetrating accounts of the legal challenges to the line-item veto that culminated in *Clinton v. City of New York*. These and other exemplary works of scholarship have illuminated the enduring importance of the legal debate over presidential powers, but I also wanted my students to wrestle directly with the arguments made by the justices of the Supreme Court. And here I found no good options.

Of course, each of the Supreme Court cases that I was interested in was available on the Internet. But rare is the undergraduate who can navigate his or her way through an unedited Supreme Court opinion. There are constitutional law readers that include a wide variety of cases of presidential powers—including Fisher and Adler's reader in *American Constitutional Law*—but these cases make up only a small segment of these massive (and expensive) textbooks. Closer to what I had in mind is Michael Genovese and Robert Spitzer's more focused collection of cases, *The Presidency and the Constitution*. But while their collection of fifty presidency-related cases is a wonderful sourcebook, it is not a practical option for the teacher who does not wish to devote an entire course to the legal and constitutional foundations of presidential power.

Although I believe that an analysis of the intersection between law and politics is a vital part of the study of the presidency, I am not willing to forgo altogether the study of presidential character and behavior, political bargaining and rhetoric, public opinion, and legislative influence. This book, then, is for those teachers, like myself, who wish to expose their students to many of the most important Supreme Court cases that have shaped presidential power but who also still wish to leave time to explore the more personal and behavioral aspects of the presidency as well.

In composing this book, I have followed one guiding principle: to edit the opinions of the Supreme Court cases in ways that make them more accessible to undergraduate students while leaving the interpretation of those opinions squarely in the hands of students (and teachers). I have therefore purposely avoided a general introduction to the text that advances my interpretation of the Supreme Court's role in constraining or promoting presidential power. In addition, in the short introductions I have written for each case, I have not summarized what the Court argued. As a teacher I have always found it unhelpful when editors pen introductions that essentially provide a *CliffsNotes'* version of the chosen document. Not only does this make it far too easy for students, but it destroys the drama inherent in a court case. I have therefore crafted introductions that contextualize the case without recapping the judicial opinions or interpreting their meaning. The test of a good introduction, in my view, is that it leaves the reader wanting to read the document and to find out what the justices had to say about the case. I have tried in each of the introductions to give students space to wrestle with the arguments on their own terms and also to give teachers the room to teach cases in their own distinctive ways. Both students and teachers, I am confident, will find that, now more than ever, these historic cases deserve the careful thought and attention of American citizens.

I

DOMESTIC POWERS

The Removal Power

1

Myers v. United States (1926)

The delegates at the Constitutional Convention in 1787 argued strenuously about the appointment power yet did not once discuss the power of removal. Cabinet members were to be appointed by the president with the advice and consent of the Senate.[1] But the Constitution was silent about who would remove them from office. They could be impeached, of course, but was that the only grounds for removal? Did they serve during good behavior, like judges? Did they serve at the pleasure of the president or the Senate or both? As the first Congress set about establishing the Department of Foreign Affairs, legislators were forced to confront these unresolved matters.

One group, which included former constitutional delegates Elbridge Gerry and Roger Sherman, argued that just as the department heads could be appointed only with the consent of the Senate so department heads could only be removed with the Senate's approval. In support of their position they could point to the assurances of Alexander Hamilton in Federalist 77 that "the consent of [the Senate] would be necessary to displace as well as to appoint." On the House floor, James Madison pressed the opposing theory: removal of officers was an executive function and the Constitution clearly vested the executive power in the president. The president, Madison maintained, only shared his executive powers when the Constitution specified an exception, as it did in the case of appointments. Madison's argument, however, rested not only on constitutional grounds but on policy grounds as well: allowing the Senate to block the removal of officers would erode executive responsibility and debilitate the presidency. Others agreed with Madison that it was wise to vest the power of removal in the president but rejected Madison's constitutional theory. This group argued that Congress was free to vest the power of removal wherever it chose. Without reaching agreement on the constitutional questions, the House agreed—by a vote of 29 to 22—to exclude the Senate from the removal process. The following month the Senate concurred, though only after Vice President John Adams cast the deciding vote.

Throughout the nineteenth century, Congress and the president continued to spar over the power of removal. In 1833, for instance, Andrew Jackson fired his secretary of the treasury for failing to comply with the president's order to remove all government deposits from the national bank, prompting the Senate to censure Jackson (in 1837, after Democrats regained control of the Senate, the censure resolution was expunged). The most famous nineteenth-century showdown over the removal power came as a result of the Tenure of Office Act of 1867, which the Republicans passed to prevent President Andrew Johnson from removing any officials that had been appointed with the consent of the Senate. Johnson's subsequent attempt to remove Secretary of War Edwin Stanton precipitated impeachment proceedings against Johnson. Johnson's Republican successors complained bitterly about the act, but not until 1887, during Grover Cleveland's administration, did Congress repeal it.

One act that Congress did not rescind was an 1876 statute passed by Congress—and signed by President Ulysses S. Grant—that provided that "Postmasters of the first, second, and third classes shall be appointed and may be removed by the President with the advice and consent of the Senate." It's difficult in the twenty-first century to appreciate the significance of the postmaster in the nineteenth-century and early twentieth-century polity. The postmaster of a town was one of the plum patronage positions, a reward for party loyalty and a job one could expect to hold for only as long as one's party or faction remained in power.

In 1917, Frank S. Myers had been rewarded for his loyalty to the Democratic Party when President Woodrow Wilson named him a first-class postmaster in Portland, Oregon. Myers's term was for four years, but after a little less than three years in the job Wilson requested Myers's resignation. Myers refused and was then fired. He subsequently took the president to court, arguing that since the Senate had not approved of his dismissal, Wilson's actions were in violation of the law. He requested that the government pay him the eight thousand dollars he would have received had he finished his term.

The courts had generally tried, successfully, to steer clear of fights between Congress and the president over the power of removal. The court of claims that heard Myers's case continued that pattern of avoiding the contested constitutional and legal questions by siding with the government on the narrow grounds that Myers had waited too long to file the suit. Myers then appealed his case to the Supreme Court. By the time the Court heard oral arguments in April 1925 Myers had died, but his widow continued the case. The Court took nearly a year and a half before announcing its verdict in favor of Myers.

Writing for the Court was Chief Justice William Howard Taft, who had walked in presidential shoes in a way that no other Supreme Court justice ever has. For, of course, he was the president of the United States until Woodrow Wilson defeated him in 1912. During his four-year term as president, Taft had the opportunity to appoint an extraordinary five justices to the Supreme Court (only George Washington and Franklin Roosevelt have appointed more), though only one (William Devanter) was still on the bench by the time *Myers* reached the Court. Although Taft is often remembered for the restrained conception of presidential power he articulated in his postpresidential battle of words with his political mentor Theodore Roosevelt, in *Myers* he offered an expansive reading of presidential power that would have made Roosevelt proud. Joining Taft's opinion were Devanter and the four justices who had joined the Court during the previous five years (three were Harding appointees and one a Coolidge appointee).

Three judges were not persuaded by Taft's reasoning, and each felt the need to write a dissenting opinion. The longest of these, weighing in at sixty-two pages, was authored by one of two Wilson appointees on the Court, Justice James Clark McReynolds. The other Wilson appointee, Louis Brandeis, penned a fifty-six-page dissent. Briefest of the three dissenters was eighty-five-year-old Oliver Wendell Holmes, who required only three short paragraphs to explain why he believed the Court had got it wrong.

*   *   *   *   *   *

Mr. Chief Justice Taft delivered the opinion of the Court.

This case presents the question whether, under the Constitution, the President has the exclusive power of removing executive officers of the United States whom he has appointed by and with the advice and consent of the Senate. . . .

The debates in the Constitutional Convention indicated an intention to create a strong Executive, and, after a controversial discussion, the executive power of the Government was vested in one person and many of his important functions were specified so as to avoid the humiliating weakness of the Congress during the Revolution and under the Articles of Confederation.

Mr. Madison and his associates in the discussion in the House [of Representatives in 1789] dwelt at length upon the necessity there was for construing Article II to give the President the sole power of removal in his responsibility for the conduct of the executive branch, and enforced this by emphasizing his duty expressly declared in the third section of the Article to "take care that the laws be faithfully executed."

The vesting of the executive power in the President was essentially a grant of the power to execute the laws. But the President, alone and unaided, could not execute the laws. He must execute them by the assistance of subordinates. . . . As he is charged specifically to take care that they be faithfully executed, the reasonable implication, even in the absence of express words, was that, as part of his executive power, he should select those who were to act for him under his direction in the execution of the laws. The further implication must be, in the absence of any express limitation respecting removals, that as his selection of administrative officers is essential to the execution of the laws by him so must be his power of removing those for whom he cannot continue to be responsible. . . .

It is quite true that, in state and colonial governments at the time of the Constitutional Convention, power to make appointments and removals had sometimes been lodged in the legislatures or in the courts, but such a disposition of it was really vesting part of the executive power in another branch of the Government. In the British system, the Crown, which was the executive, had the power of appointment and removal of executive officers, and it was natural, therefore, for those who framed our Constitution to regard the words "executive power" as including both. . . .

Under section 2 of Article II . . . the power of appointment by the Executive is restricted in its exercise by the provision that the Senate, a part of the legislative branch of the Government, may check the action of the Executive by rejecting the officers he selects. Does this make the Senate part of the removing power? . . .

The history of the clause by which the Senate was given a check upon the President's power of appointment makes it clear that it was not prompted by any desire to limit removals. . . . The important purpose of those who brought about the restriction was to lodge in the Senate, where the small States had equal representation with the larger States, power to prevent the President from making too many appointments from the larger States. . . .

A veto by the Senate—a part of the legislative branch of the Government—upon removals is a much greater limitation upon the executive branch and a much more serious blending of the legislative with the executive than a rejection of a proposed appointment. . . . The rejection of a nominee of the President for a particular office does not greatly embarrass him in the conscientious discharge of his high duties in the selection of those who are to aid him, because the President usually has an ample field from which to select for office, according to his preference, competent and capable men. The Senate has full power to reject newly proposed appointees whenever the President shall remove the incumbents. Such a check enables the Senate to prevent the filling of offices with bad or incompetent men or with those against whom there is tenable objection.

The power to prevent the removal of an officer who has served under the President is different from the authority to consent to or reject his appointment. When a nomination is made, it may be presumed that the Senate is, or may become, as well advised as to the fitness of the nominee as the President, but, in the nature of things, the defects in ability or intelligence or loyalty in the administration of the laws of one who has served as an officer under the President are facts as to which the President, or his trusted subordinates, must be better informed than the Senate, and the power to remove him may, therefore, be regarded as confined, for very sound and practical reasons, to the governmental authority which has administrative control. The power of removal is incident to the power of appointment, not to the power of advising and consenting to appointment, and when the grant of the executive power is enforced by the express mandate to take care that the laws be faithfully executed, it emphasizes the necessity for including within the executive power as conferred the exclusive power of removal. . . .

In the discussion in the First Congress fear was expressed that such a constitutional rule of construction . . . would expose the country to tyranny through the abuse of the exercise of the power of removal by the President. Underlying such fears was the fundamental misconception that the President's attitude in his exercise of power is one of opposition to the people, while the Congress is their only defender in the government, and such a misconception may be noted in the discussions had before this court. This view was properly contested by Mr. Madison in the discussion. . . . The President is a representative of the people, just as the members of the Senate and of the House are, and it may be at some times, on some subjects, that the President, elected by all the people, is rather more representative of them all than are the members of either body of the Legislature, whose constituencies are local and not country wide, and as the President is elected for four years, with the mandate of the people to exercise his executive power under the Constitution, there would seem to be no reason for construing that instrument in such a way as to limit and hamper that power beyond the limitations of it, expressed or fairly implied. . . .

It could never have been intended [by the Framers of the Constitution] to leave to Congress unlimited discretion to vary fundamentally the operation of the great independent executive branch of government, and thus most seriously to weaken it. It would be a delegation by the Convention to Congress of the function of defining the primary boundaries of another of the three great divisions of government. . . .

It is reasonable to suppose also that, had it been intended to give to Congress power to regulate or control removals in the manner suggested, it would have been included among the specifically enumerated legislative powers in Article I, or in the specified limitations on the executive power in Article II. The difference between the grant of legislative power under Article I to Congress, which is limited to powers therein enumerated, and the more general grant of the executive power to the President under Article II, is significant. The fact that the executive power is given in general terms, strengthened by specific terms where emphasis is appropriate, and limited by direct expressions where limitation is needed, and that no express limit is placed on the power of removal by the executive, is a convincing indication that none was intended. . . .

It is argued that the denial of the legislative power to regulate removals in some way involves the denial of power to prescribe qualifications for office, or reasonable classification for promotion, and yet that has been often exercised. We see no conflict between the latter power and that of appointment and removal, provided, of course, that the qualifications do not so limit selection and so trench upon executive choice as to be, in effect, legislative designation. As Mr. Madison said in the First Congress:

> The powers relative to offices are partly Legislative and partly Executive. The Legislature creates the office, defines the powers, limits its duration, and annexes a compensation. This done, the Legislative power ceases. They ought to have nothing to do with designating the man to fill the office. That I conceive to be of an Executive nature.

Mr. Madison and his associates pointed out with great force the unreasonable character of the view that the Convention intended, without express provision, to give to Congress or the Senate, in case of political or other differences, the means of thwarting the Executive in the exercise of his great powers and in the bearing of his great responsibility, by fastening upon him, as subordinate executive officers, men who, by their inefficient service under him, by their lack of loyalty to the service, or by their different views of policy, might make his taking care that the laws be faithfully executed most difficult or impossible. As Mr. Madison said in the debate in the First Congress:

> Vest this power in the Senate jointly with the President, and you abolish at once that great principle of unity and responsibility in the Executive department which was intended for the security of liberty and the public good. If the President should possess alone the power of removal from office, those

who are employed in the execution of the law will be in their proper situation, and the chain of dependence be preserved, the lowest officers, the middle grade, and the highest, will depend, as they ought, on the President, and the President on the community. . . .

Made responsible under the Constitution for the effective enforcement of the law, the President needs as an indispensable aid . . . the disciplinary influence upon those who act under him of a reserve power of removal. But it is contended that executive officers appointed by the President with the consent of the Senate are bound by the statutory law, and are not his servants to do his will, and that his obligation to care for the faithful execution of the laws does not authorize him to treat them as such. The degree of guidance in the discharge of their duties that the President may exercise over executive officers varies with the character of their service as prescribed in the law under which they act. The highest and most important duties which his subordinates perform are those in which they act for him. In such cases, they are exercising not their own but his discretion. This field is a very large one. It is sometimes described as political. Each head of a department is and must be the President's alter ego in the matters of that department where the President is required by law to exercise authority. . . .

In all such cases, the discretion to be exercised is that of the President in determining the national public interest and in directing the action to be taken by his executive subordinates to protect it. In this field, his cabinet officers must do his will. He must place in each member of his official family, and his chief executive subordinates, implicit faith. The moment that he loses confidence in the intelligence, ability, judgment or loyalty of anyone of them, he must have the power to remove him without delay. To require him to file charges and submit them to the consideration of the Senate might make impossible that unity and coordination in executive administration essential to effective action.

The duties of the heads of departments and bureaus in which the discretion of the President is exercised and which we have described are the most important in the whole field of executive action of the Government. There is nothing in the Constitution which permits a distinction between the removal of the head of a department or a bureau, when he discharges a political duty of the President or exercises his discretion, and the removal of executive officers engaged in the discharge of their other normal duties. The imperative reasons requiring an unrestricted power to remove the most important of his subordinates in their most important duties must, therefore, control the interpretation of the Constitution as to all appointed by him.

But this is not to say that there are not strong reasons why the President should have a like power to remove his appointees charged with other duties than those above described. The ordinary duties of officers prescribed by statute come under the general administrative control of the President by virtue of the general grant to him of the executive power, and he may properly supervise and guide their construction of the statutes under which they act in order to secure that unitary and uniform execution of the laws which Article II of the Constitution evidently contemplated in vesting general executive power in the President alone. Laws are often passed with specific provision for the adoption of regulations by a department or bureau head to make the law workable and effective. The ability and judgment manifested by the official thus empowered, as well as his energy and stimulation of his subordinates, are subjects which the President must consider and supervise in his administrative control. Finding such officers to be negligent and inefficient, the President should have the power to remove them. Of course, there may be duties so peculiarly and specifically committed to the discretion of a particular officer as to raise a question whether the President may overrule or revise the officer's interpretation of his statutory duty in a particular instance. Then there may be duties of a *quasi*-judicial character imposed on executive officers and members of executive tribunals whose decisions after hearing affect interests of individuals, the discharge of which the President cannot in a particular case properly influence or control. But even in such a case, he may consider the decision after its rendition as a reason for removing the officer, on the ground that the discretion regularly entrusted to that officer by statute has not been, on the whole, intelligently or wisely exercised. Otherwise, he does not discharge his own constitutional duty of seeing that the laws be faithfully executed. . . .

We come now to consider an argument advanced and strongly pressed on behalf of the complainant, that this case concerns only the removal of a postmaster; that a postmaster is an inferior officer; that such an office was not included within the legislative decision of 1789, which related only to superior officers to be appointed by the President by and with the advice and consent of the Senate. . . .

The power to remove inferior executive officers, like that to remove superior executive officers, is an incident of the power to appoint them, and is in its nature an executive power. The authority of Congress given by the excepting clause [that is, the clause in Article II, section 2 that reads: "but the Congress may by Law vest the Appointment of such inferior Officers, as they think proper, in the Presidents alone, in the Courts of Law, or in the Heads of Departments"] to vest the appointment of such inferior officers in the heads of departments carries with it authority incidentally to invest the heads of departments with power to remove. It has been the practice of Congress to do so and this Court has recognized that power. The Court also has recognized . . . that Congress, in committing the appointment of such inferior officers to the heads of departments, may prescribe incidental regulations controlling and restricting the latter in the exercise of the power of removal. But the Court never has held, nor reasonably could hold, although it is argued to the contrary on behalf of the appellant, that the excepting clause enables Congress to draw to itself, or to either branch of it, the power to remove or the right to participate in the exercise of that power. To do this would be to go beyond the words and implications of that clause and to infringe the constitutional principle of the separation of governmental powers.

Assuming then the power of Congress to regulate removals as incidental to the exercise of its constitutional power to vest appointments of inferior officers in the heads of departments, certainly so long as Congress does not exercise that power the power of removal must remain where the Constitution places it, with the President, as part of the executive power, in accordance with the legislative decision of 1789. . . .

What, then, are the elements that enter into our decision of this case? We have first a construction of the Constitution made by a Congress which was to provide by legislation for the organization of the Government in accord with the Constitution which had just then been adopted, and in which there were, as representatives and senators, a considerable number of those who had been members of the Convention that framed the Constitution and presented it for ratification. It was the Congress that launched the Government. It was the Congress that rounded out the Constitution itself by the proposing of the first ten amendments, which had, in effect, been promised to the people as a consideration for the ratification. It was the Congress in which Mr. Madison, one of the first in the framing of the Constitution, led also in the organization of the Government under it. It was a Congress whose constitutional decisions have always been regarded, as they should be regarded, as of the greatest weight in the interpretation of that fundamental instrument. This construction was followed by the legislative department and the executive department continuously for seventy-three years. . . .

We are now asked to set aside this construction, thus buttressed, and adopt an adverse view because the Congress of the United States did so during a heated political difference of opinion between the then President and the majority leaders of Congress over the reconstruction measures adopted as a means of restoring to their proper status the States which attempted to withdraw from the Union at the time of the Civil War. The extremes to which the majority in both Houses carried legislative measures in that matter are now recognized by all who calmly review the history of that episode in our Government, leading to articles of impeachment against President Johnson, and his acquittal. Without animadverting on the character of the measures taken, we are certainly justified in saying that they should not be given the weight affecting proper constitutional construction to be accorded to that reached by the First Congress of the United States during a political calm and acquiesced in by the whole Government for three-quarters of a century, especially when the new construction contended for has never been acquiesced in by either the executive or the judicial departments. . . . When, on the merits, we find our conclusion strongly favoring the view which prevailed in the First Congress, we have no hesitation in holding that conclusion to be correct, and it therefore follows that the Tenure of Office Act of 1867, insofar as it attempted to prevent the President from removing executive officers who had been appointed by him by and with the advice and consent of the Senate, was invalid, and that subsequent legislation of the same effect was equally so.

For the reasons given, we must therefore hold that the provision of the law of 1876, by which the unrestricted power of removal of first class postmasters is denied to the President, is in violation of the Constitution, and invalid.

*   *   *   *   *   *

Mr. Justice Brandeis, dissenting.

May the President, having acted under the statute insofar as it creates the office and authorizes the appointment, ignore, while the Senate is in session, the provision which prescribes the condition under which a removal may take place?

It is this narrow question, and this only, which we are required to decide. We need not consider what power the President, being Commander in Chief, has over officers in the Army and the Navy. We need not determine whether the President, acting alone, may remove high political officers. We need not even determine whether, acting alone, he may remove inferior civil officers when the Senate is not in session. It was in session when the President purported to remove Myers, and for a long time thereafter. All questions of statutory construction have been eliminated by the language of the Act. It is settled that, in the absence of a provision expressly providing for the consent of the Senate to a removal, the clause fixing the tenure will be construed as a limitation, not as a grant, and that, under such legislation, the President, acting alone, has the power of removal. But, in defining the tenure, this statute used words of grant. Congress clearly intended to preclude a removal without the consent of the Senate. . . .

Continuously for the last fifty-eight years, laws comprehensive in character, enacted from time to time with the approval of the President, have made removal from the great majority of the inferior presidential offices dependent upon the consent of the Senate. Throughout that period these laws have been continuously applied. We are requested to . . . overturn this long established constitutional practice.

The contention that Congress is powerless to make consent of the Senate a condition of removal by the President from an executive office rests mainly upon the clause in § 1 of Article II which declares that "The executive Power shall be vested in a President." The argument is that appointment and removal of officials are executive prerogatives; that the grant to the President of "the executive Power" confers upon him, as inherent in the office, the power to exercise these two functions without restriction by Congress, except insofar as the power to restrict his exercise of them is expressly conferred upon Congress by the Constitution; that, in respect to appointment, certain restrictions of the executive power are so provided for; but that, in respect to removal, there is no express grant to Congress of any power to limit the President's prerogative. The simple answer to the argument is this: the ability to remove a subordinate executive officer, being an essential of effective government, will, in the absence of express constitutional provision to the contrary, be deemed to have been vested in some person or body. But it is not a power inherent in a chief executive. The President's power of removal from statutory civil inferior offices, like the power of appointment to them, comes immediately from Congress. It is true that the exercise of the power of removal is said to be an executive act, and that, when the Senate grants or withholds consent to a removal by the President, it participates in an executive act. But the Constitution has confessedly granted to Congress the legislative power to create offices, and to prescribe the tenure thereof, and it has not in terms denied to Congress the power to control removals. To prescribe the tenure involves prescribing the conditions under which incumbency shall cease. For the possibility of removal is a condition or qualification of the tenure. When Congress provides that the incumbent shall hold the office for four years unless sooner removed with the consent of the Senate, it prescribes the term of the tenure. . . .

To imply a grant to the President of the uncontrollable power of removal from statutory inferior executive offices involves an unnecessary and indefensible limitation upon the constitutional power of Congress to fix the tenure of inferior statutory offices. That such a limitation cannot be justified on the ground of necessity is demonstrated by the practice of our governments, state and national. In none of the original thirteen States did the chief executive possess such power at the time of the adoption of the Federal Constitution. In none of the forty-eight States has such power been conferred at any time since by a state constitution, with a single possible exception. In a few States, the legislature has granted to the governor, or other appointing power, the absolute power of removal. The legislative practice of most States reveals a decided tendency to limit, rather than to extend, the governor's power of removal. . . .

The practice of Congress to control the exercise of the executive power of removal from inferior offices is evidenced by many statutes which restrict it in many ways besides the removal clause here in question. Each of these restrictive statutes became law with the approval of the President. Every President who had held office since 1861, except President Garfield, approved one or more of such statutes. Some of these statutes, prescribing a fixed term, provide that removal shall be made only for one of several specified causes. Some provide a fixed term, subject generally to removal for cause. Some provide for removal only after hearing. Some provide a fixed term, subject to removal for reasons to be communicated by the President to the Senate. Some impose the restriction in still other ways. . . .

The historical data submitted present a legislative practice, established by concurrent affirmative action of Congress and the President, to make consent of the Senate a condition of removal from statutory, inferior, civil, executive offices to which the appointment is made for a fixed term by the President with such consent. They show that the practice has existed, without interruption, continuously for the last fifty-eight years; that, throughout this period, it has governed a great majority of all such offices; that the legislation applying the removal clause specifically to the office of postmaster was enacted more than half a century ago, and that recently the practice has, with the President's approval, been extended to several newly created offices. The data show further that the insertion of the removal clause in acts creating inferior civil offices with fixed tenure is part of the broader legislative practice, which has prevailed since the formation of our Government, to restrict or regulate in many ways both removal from and nomination to such offices. A persistent legislative practice which involves a delimitation of the respective powers of Congress and the President, and which has been so established and maintained, should be deemed tantamount to judicial construction in the absence of any decision by any court to the contrary.

The persuasive effect of this legislative practice is strengthened by the fact that no instance has been found, even in the earlier period of our history, of concurrent affirmative action of Congress and the President which is inconsistent with the legislative practice of the last fifty-eight years to impose the removal clause. Nor has any instance been found of action by Congress which involves recognition in any other way of the alleged uncontrollable executive power to remove an inferior civil officer. The action taken by Congress in 1789 after the great debate does not present such an instance. The vote then taken did not involve a decision that the President had uncontrollable power. It did not involve a decision of the question whether Congress could confer upon the Senate the right, and impose upon it the duty, to participate in removals. It involved merely the decision that the Senate does not, in the absence of legislative grant thereof, have the right to share in the removal of an officer appointed with its consent, and that the President has, in the absence of restrictive legislation, the constitutional power of removal without such consent. Moreover, as Chief Justice Marshall recognized, the debate and the decision related to a high political office, not to inferior ones. . . .

The separation of the powers of government did not make each branch completely autonomous. It left each in some measure dependent upon the others, as it left to each power to exercise, in some respects, functions in their nature executive, legislative and judicial. Obviously the President cannot secure full execution of the laws if Congress denies to him adequate means of doing so. Full execution may be defeated because Congress declines to create offices indispensable for that purpose. Or because Congress, having created the office, declines to make the indispensable appropriation. Or because Congress, having both created the office and made the appropriation, prevents, by restrictions which it imposes, the appointment of officials who in quality and character are indispensable to the efficient execution of the law. If, in any such way, adequate means are denied to the President, the fault will lie with Congress. The President performs his full constitutional duty, if, with the means and instruments provided by Congress and within the limitations prescribed by it, he uses his best endeavors to secure the faithful execution of the laws enacted.

Checks and balances were established in order that this should be "a government of laws, and not of men." As [Alexander] White said in the House in 1789, an uncontrollable power of removal in the Chief Executive "is a doctrine not to be learned in American governments." Such power had been denied in Colonial Charters, and even under Proprietary Grants and Royal Commissions. It had been denied in the thirteen States before the framing of the Federal Constitution. The doctrine of the separation of powers was adopted by the convention of 1787 not to promote efficiency, but to preclude the exercise of arbitrary power. The purpose was not to avoid friction but, by means of the inevitable friction incident to the distribution of the governmental powers among three departments, to save the people from autocracy. In order to prevent arbitrary executive action, the Constitution provided . . . that presidential appointments be made with the consent of the Senate, unless Congress should otherwise provide. . . . Limiting further executive prerogatives customary in monarchies, the Constitution empowered Congress to vest the appointment of inferior officers, "as they think proper, in the President alone, in the Courts of Law, or in the Heads of Departments." Nothing in support of the claim of uncontrollable power can be inferred from the silence of the Convention of 1787 on the subject of removal. For the outstanding fact remains that every specific proposal to confer such uncontrollable power upon the

President was rejected. In America, as in England, the conviction prevailed then that the people must look to representative assemblies for the protection of their liberties. And protection of the individual, even if he be an official, from the arbitrary or capricious exercise of power was then believed to be an essential of free government.

*   *   *   *   *   *

Mr. Justice Holmes, dissenting.

My brothers McReynolds and Brandeis have discussed the question before us with exhaustive research, and I say a few words merely to emphasize my agreement with their conclusion. . . .

We have to deal with an office that owes its existence to Congress, and that Congress may abolish tomorrow. Its duration and the pay attached to it while it lasts depend on Congress alone. Congress alone confers on the President the power to appoint to it, and at any time may transfer the power to other hands. With such power over its own creation, I have no more trouble in believing that Congress has power to prescribe a term of life for it free from any interference than I have in accepting the undoubted power of Congress to decree its end. I have equally little trouble in accepting its power to prolong the tenure of an incumbent until Congress or the Senate shall have assented to his removal. The duty of the President to see that the laws be executed is a duty that does not go beyond the laws or require him to achieve more than Congress sees fit to leave within his power.

NOTE

1. Article II, section 2 of the Constitution says that the president "shall nominate, and by and with the Advice and Consent of the Senate, shall appoint Ambassadors, other public Ministers and Consuls, Judges of the Supreme Court, and all other Officers of the United States, whose Appointments are not herein otherwise provided for, and which shall be established by Law; but the Congress may by Law vest the Appointment of such inferior Officers, as they think proper, in the President alone, in the Courts of Law, or in the Heads of Departments."

The Removal Power

2

Humphrey's Executor v. United States (1935)

The Federal Trade Commission (FTC) was created in 1914 and charged with investigating and prohibiting "unfair methods of competition." The FTC embodied the Progressive idea that a capitalist economy needed an impartial umpire to ensure that powerful corporations did not combine and collude in ways that hurt consumers and small producers. By endowing the commissioners with seven-year terms, Progressives hoped the FTC would rise above everyday political bickering and act instead in the public interest. In addition, the statute stipulated that no more than three of the five commissioners could be of the same party and that they could be removed by the president for "inefficiency, neglect of duty, or malfeasance in office." Each commissioner was to be appointed by the president with the advice and consent of the Senate.

Although Progressives hailed the FTC as a "historic political and constitutional reform," business groups were generally wary. When the FTC went after the meat packers in 1919 for profiteering and unlawful restraint of trade, conservatives in Congress rallied around the meat packers, derailing the case before eventually transferring jurisdiction to the Agriculture Department. In their 1920 platform, Republicans signaled their intentions by charging the commission of "unfair persecution of honest business." After 1920, the FTC found its regulatory efforts consistently blocked not only by Congress but also by the courts, which insisted on defining "unfair methods" in the most narrow of terms. Emboldened by legislative and judicial resistance, business showed an increasing willingness to defy the commission's directives and requests for information. Up until 1925, however, the commission generally did try to pursue its regulatory mandate—that is, until the appointment of William Ewart Humphrey.

Humphrey had served in the House of Representatives from 1903 to 1917, during which time he earned a reputation as one of the most strident pro-business conservatives in the nation. Nebraska senator George Norris called Humphrey "the greatest reactionary of the country," and a newspaper from Humphrey's home state of Washington called him "a noisy, ill-mannered, narrowly-partisan, always carping critic." A noisy and narrow partisan, however, is exactly what President Calvin Coolidge was looking for as he sought to make the FTC friendlier to business interests. Humphrey made an immediate impact on the commission, not only because of his forceful pro-business views but also because his appointment gave the pro-business forces on the commission a 3–2 majority. From the moment Humphrey's appointment was confirmed, the FTC became a partner working with and protecting corporations rather than the regulatory oversight body the Progressives had intended. In 1931 President Herbert Hoover nominated Humphrey for a second term, and six months later the Senate confirmed by a vote of 53 to 28.

When Franklin Roosevelt became president in 1933, his attention quickly turned to the FTC. The nation's catastrophic economic collapse had discredited the old economic orthodoxy, and an anxious nation now looked to Washington for economic answers. FDR believed that his election was a popular mandate for a new set of economic policies that would transform the relationship between business and the government. The new president was understandably concerned that an FTC—which had administrative jurisdiction over several important New Deal programs—that was avowedly hostile to his goals could undermine the coherence of the recovery effort. As luck would have it, though, two commissioners had recently died, thereby creating two vacancies for Roosevelt to fill. With those two appointments FDR was able to forge a commission sympathetic to his policy aims: his two new Democratic appointees would join a North Carolina Democrat and liberal Minnesota Republican. Still Roosevelt worried that Humphrey, as the most senior and most stridently ideological of the commissioners, might weaken the resolve or disrupt the workings of the FTC. And so, in July 1933, he asked Humphrey for his resignation. "The work of the Commission," FDR explained to Humphrey, "can be carried out most effectively with personnel of my own selection."

Humphrey refused to resign. Roosevelt tried again: "You will, I know, realize that I do not feel that your mind and my mind go along together on either the policies or the administering of the Federal Trade Commission, and frankly, I think it best for the people of this country that I should have full confidence." Humphrey dug in his heels still further. If FDR wanted rid of the "contentious commissioner," he would have to fire him. Roosevelt's confidants assured the president that he had the legal authority to do so in light of the Supreme Court's sweeping affirmation of the president's power of removal in *Myers*. Indeed Taft's opinion had explicitly said that the president's authority of removal extended to independent commissions. On October 7, the president sent Humphrey a note informing him of his dismissal.

Humphrey was furious, though in a letter of protest he blamed "certain insurgent Republicans" for having poisoned the president's mind. "They come with slanderous and polluted lips and spew their putrid filth upon you," wrote Humphrey. These "sanctified experts of expediency," Humphrey ranted, "are mental perverts who glorify treachery and intellectual dishonesty." Humphrey had no intention of giving these "cowards" the satisfaction of seeing him walk away from a fight. On December 28, he filed suit in the U.S. Court of Claims, claiming he had been illegally fired. Humphrey demanded restitution and back salary. Six weeks later, the irascible Humphrey dropped dead from a stroke. His executor, however, carried on the legal fight.

The court of claims requested that the Supreme Court answer two questions. First, did the act establishing the FTC limit dismissal of commissioners to the grounds specified in the statute, namely, "inefficiency, neglect of duty, or malfeasance in office"? Second, if the act did so limit the president's power of removal, were those limits constitutional? The Supreme Court agreed to take the case and scheduled oral arguments for May 1, 1935.

The Roosevelt administration's legal team believed that the Court's recent opinion in *Myers* made the case a slam dunk. So confident was the administration that when advised by Attorney General Homer Cummings to be sure to start out on a winning foot, the new solicitor general—whose job it is to argue the government's case before the Court—carefully picked out *Humphrey's Executor* as his maiden assignment. In *Myers* the Court took sixteen months before issuing its judgment; in *Humphrey's* the verdict came less than a month after the oral arguments. And whereas the *Myers* court had been badly split, the *Humphrey's* decision was unanimous. The outcome, however, was a stunning setback for the administration. Justice George Sutherland, a determined foe of the New Deal, wrote the Court's opinion.

*   *   *   *   *   *

Mr. Justice Sutherland delivered the opinion of the Court.

The question first to be considered is whether, by the provisions of Section 1 of the Federal Trade Commission Act . . . the President's power is limited to removal for the specific causes enumerated therein. . . .

The commission is to be nonpartisan, and it must, from the very nature of its duties, act with entire impartiality. It is charged with the enforcement of no policy except the policy of the law. Its duties are neither political nor executive, but predominantly *quasi*-judicial and *quasi*-legislative. Like the Interstate Commerce Commission, its members are called upon to exercise the trained judgment of a body of experts "appointed by law and informed by experience."

The legislative reports in both houses of Congress clearly reflect the view that a fixed term was necessary to the effective and fair administration of the law. . . .

The debates in both houses demonstrate that the prevailing view was that the commission was not to be "subject to anybody in the government, but . . . only to the people of the United States"; free from "political domination or control" or the "probability or possibility of such a thing"; to be "separate and apart from any existing department of the government—not subject to the orders of the President.". . . While the general rule precludes the use of these debates to explain the meaning of the words of the statute, they may be considered as reflecting light upon its general purposes and the evils which it sought to remedy.

Thus, the language of the act, the legislative reports, and the general purposes of the legislation as reflected by the debates all combine to demonstrate the Congressional intent to create a body of experts who shall gain experience by length of service—a body which shall be independent of executive authority except in its selection, and free to exercise its judgment without the leave or hindrance of any other official or any department of the government. To the accomplishment of these purposes it is clear that Congress was of opinion that length and certainty of tenure would vitally contribute. And to hold that, nevertheless, the members of the commission continue in office at the mere will of the President might be to thwart, in large measure, the very ends which Congress sought to realize by definitely fixing the term of office.

We conclude that the intent of the act is to limit the executive power of removal to the causes enumerated, the existence of none of which is claimed here, and we pass to the second question.

To support its contention that the removal provision of Section 1, as we have just construed it, is an unconstitutional interference with the executive power of the President, the government's chief reliance is *Myers v. United States*. That case has been so recently decided, and the prevailing and dissenting opinions so fully review the general subject of the power of executive removal, that further discussion would add little of value to the wealth of material there collected. These opinions examine at length the historical, legislative and judicial data bearing upon the question, beginning with what is called "the decision of 1789" in the first Congress and coming down almost to the day when the opinions were delivered. . . . Nevertheless, the narrow point actually decided was only that the President had power to remove a postmaster of the first class without the advice and consent of the Senate as required by act of Congress. In the course of the opinion of the court, expressions occur which tend to sustain the government's contention, but these are beyond the point involved, and, therefore do not come within the rule of *stare decisis.* Insofar as they are out of harmony with the views here set forth, these expressions are disapproved. . . .

The office of a postmaster is so essentially unlike the office now involved that the decision in the *Myers* case cannot be accepted as controlling our decision here. A postmaster is an executive officer restricted to the performance of executive functions. He is charged with no duty at all related to either the legislative or judicial power. The actual decision in the *Myers* case finds support in the theory that such an officer is merely one of the units in the executive department, and, hence, inherently subject to the exclusive and illimitable power of removal by the Chief Executive, whose subordinate and aid he is. Putting aside dicta, which may be followed if sufficiently persuasive but which are not controlling, the necessary reach of the decision goes far enough to include all purely executive officers. It goes no farther; much less does it include an officer who occupies no place in the executive department, and who exercises no part of the executive power vested by the Constitution in the President.

The Federal Trade Commission is an administrative body created by Congress to carry into effect legislative policies embodied in the statute in accordance with the legislative standard therein prescribed, and to perform other specified duties as a legislative or as a judicial aid. Such a body cannot in any proper sense be characterized as an arm or an eye of the executive. Its duties are performed without executive leave, and, in the contemplation of the statute, must be free from executive control. In administering the provisions of the statute in respect of "unfair methods of competition"—that is to say, in filling in and administering the details embodied by that general standard—the commission acts in part *quasi*-legislatively and in part *quasi*-judicially. In making investigations and reports thereon for the information of Congress under section 6, in aid of the legislative power, it acts as a legislative agency. Under section 7, which authorizes the commission to act as a master in chancery under rules prescribed by the court, it acts as an agency of the judiciary. To the extent that it exercises any executive function—as distinguished from executive power in the constitutional sense—it does so in the discharge and effectuation of its *quasi*-legislative or *quasi*-judicial powers, or as an agency of the legislative or judicial departments of the government.

If Congress is without authority to prescribe causes for removal of members of the trade commission and limit executive power of removal accordingly, that power at once becomes practically all-inclusive in respect of civil officers with the exception of the judiciary provided for by the Constitution. The Solicitor General, at the bar, apparently recognizing this to be true, with commendable candor, agreed that his view in respect of the removability of members of the Federal Trade Commission necessitated a like view in respect of the Interstate Commerce Commission and the Court of Claims. We are thus confronted with the serious question whether not only the members of these *quasi*-legislative and *quasi*-judicial bodies, but the judges of the legislative Court of Claims, exercising judicial power, continue in office only at the pleasure of the President.

We think it plain under the Constitution that illimitable power of removal is not possessed by the President in respect of officers of the character of those just named. The authority of Congress, in creating *quasi*-legislative or *quasi*-judicial agencies, to require them to act in discharge of their duties independently of executive control cannot well be doubted, and that authority includes, as an appropriate incident, power to fix the period during which they shall continue in office, and to forbid their removal except for cause in the meantime. For it is quite evident that one who holds his office only during the pleasure of another cannot be depended upon to maintain an attitude of independence against the latter's will.

The fundamental necessity of maintaining each of the three general departments of government entirely free from the control or coercive influence, direct or indirect, of either of the others has often been stressed, and is hardly open to serious question. So much is implied in the very fact of the separation of the powers of these departments by the Constitution, and in the rule which recognizes their essential coequality. The sound application of a principle that makes one master in his own house precludes him from imposing his control in the house of another who is master there. . . .

The power of removal here claimed for the President falls within this principle, since its coercive influence threatens the independence of a commission which is not only wholly disconnected from the executive department, but which, as already fully appears, was created by Congress as a means of carrying into operation legislative and judicial powers, and as an agency of the legislative and judicial departments. . . .

The result of what we now have said is this: whether the power of the President to remove an officer shall prevail over the authority of Congress to condition the power by fixing a definite term and precluding a removal except for cause will depend upon the character of the office; the *Myers* decision, affirming the power of the President alone to make the removal, is confined to purely executive officers, and, as to officers of the kind here under consideration, we hold that no removal can be made during the prescribed term for which the officer is appointed except for one or more of the causes named in the applicable statute.

To the extent that, between the decision in the *Myers* case, which sustains the unrestrictable power of the President to remove purely executive officers, and our present decision that such power does not extend to an office such as that here involved, there shall remain a field of doubt, we leave such cases as may fall within it for future consideration and determination as they may arise. . . .

*   *   *   *   *   *

POSTSCRIPT

The Court's decision in *Humphrey's* dealt the administration an embarrassing political black eye because it made the administration appear as if it had "flouted the Constitution" in firing Humphrey. But the case also produced uncertainty about how to reconcile the decision the Court had reached in *Humphrey's* with its prior decision in *Meyers*. Sutherland argued that the proper distinction was between administrative officials who exercised purely executive powers and those who discharged quasi-judicial or quasi-legislative duties. The former could be discharged at the president's pleasure, but if an agency official had rulemaking or adjudication functions then Congress could legislate the conditions under which an officer could be removed.

But what about when Congress did not specify how an official should be removed? Could the president then remove an officer at his own discretion? President Dwight Eisenhower thought so, and after his election in 1952 he promptly asked for the resignations of all three members of the War Claims Commission, which had been set up by Congress in 1948 to adjudicate claims filed by prisoners of war, internees, and religious organizations that had "suffered personal injury or property damage at the hands of the enemy in connection with World War II." One of the commission members, Myron Wiener, refused to resign and took the Eisenhower administration to court. The court of claims agreed with the government that the president had the right to dismiss Weiner since Congress had not specified the grounds of removal, but a unanimous Supreme Court reversed. Since the war claims commissioners exercised quasi-judicial functions, the president could not ask him to resign simply because he wanted someone of his own party or choice. Even if Congress had not specified grounds for removal, the president needed cause to dismiss an agency official who had adjudication or rulemaking functions.

The Court's unanimous ruling in *Wiener v. United States* clarified the legal terrain, but it hardly settled the political contest over the removal power. It did not prevent presidents from asking for resignations, and the president could still dismiss agency officials so long as they were careful about the reasons they offered for the dismissal. Congress, meanwhile, could constrain the president's removal power by endowing an agency official with quasi-legislative or quasi-judicial functions. The continuing political tug-of-war over the power of removal between the president and Congress wound up back in court in a very public fight over the Office of Independent Counsel, which the Congress had created in the late 1970s in reaction to executive abuses during Watergate.

The office was born out of a belief that the executive branch could not be trusted to investigate its own wrongdoing. The attorney general, after all, was often a close confidant of the president: John Mitchell had been Nixon's campaign manager before he was selected as attorney general, and John Kennedy had picked his own brother to be attorney general. The independent counsel would be independent of the president and the attorney general and would therefore be able to investigate and prosecute high administration officials without fear or favor. Congress stipulated that an independent counsel would be selected by a panel of three federal judges and could only be removed from office by the president for "good cause." The Reagan administration challenged the independent counsel law in court, arguing—among other things—that prosecution was a purely executive function and so the president should be free to dismiss the independent counsel for any reason.

The case *Morrison v. Olson* (1988), exposed the limitations of the Court's earlier distinction between executive functions on the one hand and quasi-legislative or quasi-judicial functions on the other. The Court conceded that the independent counsel exercised executive functions "in the sense that they are law enforcement functions that typically have been undertaken by officials within the Executive Branch," but argued that the real test was whether the removal provisions prevented the president from carrying out his constitutionally prescribed duty to see that the laws are faithfully executed. By empowering the executive branch to remove an independent counsel for "good cause," the law preserved the executive's ability to "perform his constitutionally assigned duties," particularly since, unlike a cabinet member or agency head, the independent counsel had a narrow jurisdiction and only a negligible impact on government policy. Therefore, the Court concluded, the law's removal provision was constitutional.[1]

But what constitutes "good cause"? If an officer is entrusted to carry out the president's priorities would disagreement with the administration's policies constitute good cause? Does an executive branch official who disagrees with or resists implementing the president's agenda thereby prevent the president from performing his constitutional duties and undermine democratic accountability? Construed broadly in this manner, cause becomes indistinguishable from serving at the president's pleasure. Or should "good cause" be construed narrowly to encompass only misconduct or neglect of duties? Is there a danger that if the president's power of removal is construed narrowly that the president will drum up false charges against those he wants to remove, claiming malfeasance when the president really just wants to appoint somebody who shares views that are more in line with his own?

Something like that seems to have occurred when the administration of George W. Bush fired seven federal prosecutors in December 2006. The firings created a political firestorm, as critics assailed the administration for politicizing the Department of Justice. The Bush administration defended its actions by insisting that the removals—or at least all but one—were for "performance-related" issues. But that only intensified the outrage; the fired attorneys insisted that the real reasons were political and that the administration was slandering their professional reputations in order to save face. If federal attorneys exercise exclusively executive powers then is the president free to fire them at his pleasure, and was Bush's only mistake that he tried to dress up political removals in the guise of firings for cause? That was certainly the consensus among the administration's defenders, who saw the removals as political bungling of the highest order but not a constitutional violation. New presidents, after all, upon entering office, have often asked for the resignation of federal attorneys so that they can put their own people in these places. President Clinton, for instance, asked for the resignation of every federal attorney but one when he entered office in 1993. The Bush administration's mistake, on this reading, had been in not openly avowing that the attorneys had been fired for purely political reasons.

Unlike the decisions that are made by an independent counsel, the decisions of a federal attorney to pursue some types of cases more aggressively than others—say drug smuggling rather than hate crimes—clearly play a significant part in the execution of an administration's objectives. Moreover, an attorney's jurisdiction and legal discretion is far broader than that of an independent counsel. And whereas Congress had specified the conditions of removal for the independent counsel, it had fixed only the term of office for federal attorneys. But could Congress, if it wished, prescribe the terms under which a federal attorney could be fired? Does Congress have an interest in ensuring that the officials entrusted with wielding the enormous power of prosecutorial discretion pursue cases based on an adherence to law and evidence rather than political imperatives and partisan pressures?[2] Would a law that required the president to show cause before firing a federal attorney be unconstitutional? It is a question well worth pondering and debating.

NOTES

1. Although the independent counsel law survived this legal challenge, it failed to survive the subsequent political challenges. Republicans had long complained about the law, and in 1999, after Democrats watched in dismay as Independent Counsel Kenneth Starr zealously pursued the impeachment of President Clinton, the law was allowed to expire.

2. Prior to 2005, the law had required that when a vacancy occurred in the middle of a term, the attorney general could select an interim replacement to serve for 120 days. However, after those 120 days if the president had not appointed and the Senate had not approved a permanent replacement then a federal judge was empowered to fill the vacancy until the permanent replacement had been named. In 2005, however, when the Patriot Act was being renewed, the Justice Department persuaded a Senate Judiciary Committee aide to slip into the act a provision that removed the 120-day limit on the president's interim appointments. The president could thus select an "interim" appointment who could serve until the end of the president's term and without Senate confirmation. When the ramifications of this change became evident in the wake of the "Firegate" scandal, Congress promptly voted to restore the original requirements.

Executive Privilege

3

United States v. Nixon (1974)

Before becoming a candidate for president, a television star, and a U.S. senator, Fred Thompson was the chief counsel for the Republicans on the select committee charged with investigating the Watergate break-in. On July 16, 1973, before a nationally televised audience, Thompson popped the question that prompted the answer that would lead eventually to the resignation of the president of the United States. He asked the witness, Alexander Butterfield, whether he was aware of any listening devices in the Oval Office. Butterfield said that indeed he was.[1] In fact he had been the person charged by Richard Nixon's chief of staff with seeing that the taping system was installed back in February 1971.

Butterfield's admission made it apparent to everybody that it should now be possible to answer the question that had been posed during the hearings repeatedly by Thompson's boss, Tennessee's Republican senator Howard Baker: "What did the president know, and when did he know it?" Most especially, what did President Nixon know about the break-in at the Democratic National Committee (DNC) headquarters (housed in an office complex called Watergate) in Washington, D.C., in June 1972; what did he know about the attempt to bug DNC phones; what did he know about the bribes paid to purchase the silence of the men who had been arrested in the break in; and what did he know about the efforts to cover up the White House's involvement? The answers were surely in the tapes.

Archibald Cox, who had been appointed special prosecutor in May 1973, directed the president to hand over the tapes. Nixon refused, citing executive privilege. Cox turned to the courts for help, and the courts backed him up. Nixon agreed to release summaries of the taped conversations but that did not satisfy Cox, who insisted on receiving the actual tapes. Nixon then ordered Attorney General Elliot Richardson to fire Cox. Richardson refused and resigned, as did his deputy William Ruckelshaus. Finally the order was carried out by the solicitor general, Robert Bork, who fifteen years later would be nominated by President Ronald Reagan to serve on the Supreme Court, only to be turned down by the Senate in one of the most bruising confirmation hearings in American history.

The public outcry against the so-called Saturday Night Massacre compelled Nixon to appoint another special prosecutor. This time he tapped Leon Jaworski, a Texas Democrat who had been a close friend of President Lyndon Johnson and had supported Nixon's reelection in 1972. Although Nixon hoped, and his critics feared, that Jaworski would be more sympathetic to presidential claims of privilege, Jaworski quickly showed his independence by insisting that Nixon turn over sixty-four tapes that had conversations that related to Watergate. Like Cox, Jaworski insisted he needed to listen to these tapes in order to carry out the criminal prosecution of Nixon's former aides. Once again Nixon refused, though he tried to mollify the independent counsel by giving Jaworski twenty edited tapes, one of which contained a famous eighteen-and-a-half-minute gap that led to accusations that the tape had been doctored. The legal wrangling continued, but Nixon still refused to comply with the court orders. Finally Jaworski asked the Supreme Court to intervene, which it agreed to do.

On July 8, 1974, a month after its regular term had finished, the Court heard oral arguments in *United States v. Nixon*. While the Court was hearing the legal arguments, the House was drawing up articles of impeachment against a president who by now was intensely unpopular (fewer than one in four voters approved of his job performance by this point) and could count few steadfast friends in Congress. It took the Court only two weeks to reach its decision, and announce its unanimous opinion, written by Chief Justice Warren Burger, a lifelong Republican who had been elevated to his post by Nixon in 1969.

*　　*　　*　　*　　*　　*

Mr. Chief Justice Burger delivered the opinion of the Court.

We turn to the claim that the subpoena should be quashed because it demands "confidential conversations between a President and his close advisors that it would be inconsistent with the public interest to produce." The first contention is a broad claim that the separation of powers doctrine precludes judicial review of a President's claim of privilege. The second contention is that if he does not prevail on the claim of absolute privilege, the court should hold as a matter of constitutional law that the privilege prevails over the subpoena. . . .

In the performance of assigned constitutional duties each branch of the Government must initially interpret the Constitution, and the interpretation of its powers by any branch is due great respect from the others. The President's counsel, as we have noted, reads the Constitution as providing an absolute privilege of confidentiality for all Presidential communications. Many decisions of this Court, however, have unequivocally reaffirmed the holding of *Marbury v. Madison* (1803) that "it is emphatically the province and duty of the judicial department to say what the law is."

No holding of the Court has defined the scope of judicial power specifically relating to the enforcement of a subpoena for confidential Presidential communications for use in a criminal prosecution, but other exercises of power by the Executive Branch and the Legislative Branch have been found invalid as in conflict with the Constitution. . . . Since this Court has consistently exercised the power to construe and delineate claims arising under express powers, it must follow that the Court has authority to interpret claims with respect to powers alleged to derive from enumerated powers.

Notwithstanding the deference each branch must accord the others, the "judicial Power of the United States" vested in the federal courts by Art. III, §1, of the Constitution can no more be shared with the Executive Branch than the Chief Executive, for example, can share with the Judiciary the veto power, or the Congress share with the Judiciary the power to override a Presidential veto. Any other conclusion would be contrary to the basic concept of separation of powers and the checks and balances that flow from the scheme of a tripartite government. We therefore reaffirm that it is the province and duty of this Court "to say what the law is" with respect to the claim of privilege presented in this case.

In support of his claim of absolute privilege, the President's counsel urges two grounds, one of which is common to all governments and one of which is peculiar to our system of separation of powers. The first ground is the valid need for protection of communications between high Government officials and those who advise and assist them in the performance of their manifold duties; the importance of this confidentiality is too plain to require further discussion. Human experience teaches that those who expect public dissemination of their remarks may well temper candor with a concern for appearances and for their own interests to the detriment of the decision-making process. Whatever the nature of the privilege of confidentiality of Presidential communications in the exercise of Art. II powers, the privilege can be said to derive from the supremacy of each branch within its own assigned area of constitutional duties. Certain powers and privileges flow from the nature of enumerated powers; the protection of the confidentiality of presidential communications has similar constitutional underpinnings.

The second ground asserted by the President's counsel in support of the claim of absolute privilege rests on the doctrine of separation of powers. Here it is argued that the independence of the Executive Branch within its own sphere insulates a President from a judicial subpoena in an ongoing criminal prosecution, and thereby protects confidential Presidential communications.

However, neither the doctrine of separation of powers, nor the need for confidentiality of high-level communications, without more, can sustain an absolute, unqualified Presidential privilege of immunity from judicial process under all circumstances. The President's need for complete candor and objectivity from advisers calls for great deference from the courts. However, when the privilege depends solely on the broad, undifferentiated claim of public interest in the confidentiality of such conversations, a confrontation with other values arises. Absent a claim of need to protect military, diplomatic, or sensitive national security secrets, we find it difficult to accept the argument that even the very important interest in confidentiality of Presidential communications is significantly diminished by production of such material for *in camera* inspection with all the protection that a district court will be obliged to provide.

The impediment that an absolute, unqualified privilege would place in the way of the primary constitutional duty of the Judicial Branch to do justice in criminal prosecutions would plainly conflict with the function of the courts under Art. III. In designing the structure of our Government and dividing and allocating the sovereign power among three co-equal branches, the Framers of the Constitution sought to provide a comprehensive system, but the separate powers were not intended to operate with absolute independence.

> While the Constitution diffuses power the better to secure liberty, it also contemplates that practice will integrate the dispersed powers into a workable government. It enjoins upon its branches separateness but interdependence, autonomy but reciprocity. *Youngstown Sheet & Tube Co. v. Sawyer* (Jackson, J., concurring).

To read the Art. II powers of the President as providing an absolute privilege as against a subpoena essential to enforcement of criminal statutes on no more than a generalized claim of the public interest in confidentiality of nonmilitary and nondiplomatic discussions would upset the constitutional balance of "a workable government" and gravely impair the role of the courts under Art. III.

Since we conclude that the legitimate needs of the judicial process may outweigh Presidential privilege, it is necessary to resolve those competing interests in a manner that preserves the essential functions of each branch. The right and indeed the duty to resolve that question does not free the Judiciary from according high respect to the representations made on behalf of the President.

The expectation of a President to the confidentiality of his conversations and correspondence, like the claim of confidentiality of judicial deliberations, for example, has all the values to which we accord deference for the privacy of all citizens and, added to those values, is the necessity for protection of the public interest in candid, objective, and even blunt or harsh opinions in Presidential decision making. A President and those who assist him must be free to explore alternatives in the process of shaping policies and making decisions and to do so in a way many would be unwilling to express except privately. These are the considerations justifying a presumptive privilege for Presidential communications. The privilege is fundamental to the operation of Government and inextricably rooted in the separation of powers under the Constitution. . . .

But this presumptive privilege must be considered in light of our historic commitment to the rule of law. This is nowhere more profoundly manifest than in our view that "the twofold aim [of criminal justice] is that guilt shall not escape or innocence suffer." We have elected to employ an adversary system of criminal justice in which the parties contest all issues before a court of law. The need to develop all relevant facts in the adversary system is both fundamental and comprehensive. The ends of criminal justice would be defeated if judgments were to be founded on a partial or speculative presentation of the facts. The very integrity of the judicial system and public confidence in the system depend on full disclosure of all the facts, within the framework of the rules of evidence. To ensure that justice is done, it is imperative to the function of courts that compulsory process be available for the production of evidence needed either by the prosecution or by the defense. . . .

In this case the President challenges a subpoena served on him as a third party requiring the production of materials for use in a criminal prosecution; he does so on the claim that he has a privilege against disclosure of confidential communications. He does not place his claim of privilege on the ground they are military or diplomatic secrets. As to these areas of Art. II duties the courts have traditionally shown the utmost deference to Presidential responsibilities In *C. & S. Air Lines v. Waterman S.S. Corp.* (1948), dealing with Presidential authority involving foreign policy considerations, the Court said:

> The President, both as Commander-in-Chief and as the Nation's organ for foreign affairs, has available intelligence services whose reports are not and

ought not to be published to the world. It would be intolerable that courts, without the relevant information, should review and perhaps nullify actions of the Executive taken on information properly held secret.

In *United States v. Reynolds* (1953), dealing with a claimant's demand for evidence in a Tort Claims Act case against the Government, the Court said:

> It may be possible to satisfy the court, from all the circumstances of the case, that there is a reasonable danger that compulsion of the evidence will expose military matters which, in the interest of national security, should not be divulged. When this is the case, the occasion for the privilege is appropriate, and the court should not jeopardize the security which the privilege is meant to protect by insisting upon an examination of the evidence, even by the judge alone, in chambers.

No case of the Court, however, has extended this high degree of deference to a President's generalized interest in confidentiality. Nowhere in the Constitution . . . is there any explicit reference to a privilege of confidentiality, yet to the extent this interest relates to the effective discharge of a President's powers, it is constitutionally based.

The right to the production of all evidence at a criminal trial similarly has constitutional dimensions. The Sixth Amendment explicitly confers upon every defendant in a criminal trial the right "to be confronted with the witnesses against him" and "to have compulsory process for obtaining witnesses in his favor." Moreover, the Fifth Amendment also guarantees that no person shall be deprived of liberty without due process of law. It is the manifest duty of the courts to vindicate those guarantees, and to accomplish that it is essential that all relevant and admissible evidence be produced.

In this case we must weigh the importance of the general privilege of confidentiality of Presidential communications in performance of the President's responsibilities against the inroads of such a privilege on the fair administration of criminal justice. The interest in preserving confidentiality is weighty indeed and entitled to great respect. However, we cannot conclude that advisers will be moved to temper the candor of their remarks by the infrequent occasions of disclosure because of the possibility that such conversations will be called for in the context of a criminal prosecution.

On the other hand, the allowance of the privilege to withhold evidence that is demonstrably relevant in a criminal trial would cut deeply into the guarantee of due process of law and gravely impair the basic function of the courts. A President's acknowledged need for confidentiality in the communications of his office is general in nature, whereas the constitutional need for production of relevant evidence in a criminal proceeding is specific and central to the fair adjudication of a particular criminal case in the administration of justice. Without access to specific facts a criminal prosecution may be totally frustrated. The President's broad interest in confidentiality of communications will not be vitiated by disclosure of a limited number of conversations preliminarily shown to have some bearing on the pending criminal cases.

We conclude that when the ground for asserting privilege as to subpoenaed materials sought for use in a criminal trial is based only on the generalized interest in confidentiality, it cannot prevail over the fundamental demands of due process of law in the fair administration of criminal justice. The generalized assertion of privilege must yield to the demonstrated, specific need for evidence in a pending criminal trial. . . .

*   *   *   *   *   *

POSTSCRIPT

Three days after the Supreme Court announced its verdict, the House Judiciary Committee approved its first article of impeachment, which charged Nixon with obstruction of justice. The committee then approved a second article charging Nixon with abuse of power and a third accusing him of contempt of Congress. What little support Nixon had among Republicans—only about a third of the seventeen Republicans on the House Judiciary Committee voted in favor of the first two articles of impeachment and just two voted for the third article—evaporated when the nation heard Nixon, on the tapes released by order of the Supreme Court, instructing his chief of staff, H. R. Haldeman, to call the Federal Bureau of Investigation and have them halt the investigation into the Watergate break-in. A few days later, on August 9, 1972, Nixon announced his resignation from the presidency, the first and so far only time a president has resigned from office.

NOTE

1. Thompson already knew that this would be Butterfield's response because three days earlier, in a closed session, Butterfield had revealed the same information to the committee, under questioning from Don Sanders, Thompson's deputy. Thompson does, however, deserve credit for Butterfield's bombshell, but not in the straightforward way it might appear from the dramatic public hearing. As the chief counsel on the Republican side, Thompson was in close communication with the Nixon White House and he had written a memo that summarized

a series of the White House's "attack points," including lengthy quotations from the president. After seeing this memo, the Democratic investigator, Scott Armstrong, was prompted to ask Butterfield about the long quotations from Nixon. Who wrote down the president's exact words? Did the president dictate them? No, said Butterfield. Several hours later, Sanders picked up the dangling thread and asked Butterfield whether conversations in the president's office were recorded. Only then, after a long and deliberate pause, did Butterfield reveal that there was a recording system in the White House.

Executive Immunity

4

Nixon v. Fitzgerald (1982)

On November 4, 1969, the U.S. Air Force announced it had abolished the position of deputy for management systems. The occupant of that position, A. Ernest Fitzgerald, was accordingly relieved of his duties. Why had the air force decided it no longer needed a deputy for management systems? According to the air force, the reason was simply "an economy move." Fitzgerald, however, had a very different view of his firing. It was, he insisted, retaliation for his testimony the previous year to the House–Senate Subcommittee on Economy in Government, which was chaired by the outspoken scourge of wasteful military spending, Senator William Proxmire. In that testimony, the forty-three-year-old Fitzgerald had revealed massive cost overruns in the production of the Lockheed C-5A cargo plane. After his testimony, according to Fitzgerald, he was ostracized at work and gradually stripped of his previous duties.

Fitzgerald, however, had done more to embarrass the air force than just blow the whistle on the C-5A transport plane. During the summer of 1969, Fitzgerald had made the front page of the *New York Times* after a blistering memo he had written in December 1967 about waste and mismanagement in the Minuteman missile program found its way to Proxmire's subcommittee. Compounding the problem, Fitzgerald appeared before the subcommittee and revealed that his superior officer had forbidden him from discussing the memo, making the Pentagon appear not only to be inefficient and inept but secretive and corrupt. Proxmire predictably used the memo and Fitzgerald's admission to blast the Pentagon both for wasting taxpayer money and for having muzzled those brave enough to blow the whistle.

After Fitzgerald was fired, Proxmire strove to keep the public spotlight on the air force's actions by calling hearings to investigate the dismissal. First he gave Fitzgerald a chance to tell his version of events and then called in the secretary of the air force to explain the action. In December, the subject of Fitzgerald's dismissal was raised at President Richard Nixon's press conference, the reporter pressing Nixon to "do something about this, please." In January 1970, Fitzgerald filed a formal appeal with the Civil Service Commission, asking to be reinstated in his job. Fitzgerald was determined not to go quietly. Within a week of filing the appeal, it was announced that he had been hired by the Businessman's Education Fund to deliver speeches about Pentagon waste; he was also hired as a consultant to Proxmire's subcommittee. In Fitzgerald's first speech he called for slashing Pentagon spending by $20 billion, twice the amount that Proxmire had recently called for.

In January 1973, the Civil Service Commission held public hearings on Fitzgerald's dismissal. Testifying under oath, Air Force Secretary Robert Seamans invoked executive privilege, refusing to say whether the White House had been involved in the dismissal. The following day President Nixon told the press that he had indeed approved of the firing. This was not, Nixon said, "a case of someone down the line saying he should go. I made [the decision] and I stick by it." Nixon insisted that the White House had tried to find another job for Fitzgerald but had been unsuccessful in finding something "suitable." The next day, White House Press Secretary Ron Ziegler was asked the logical next question: why had the president decided to dismiss Fitzgerald, who was a civil servant not a political appointee? The White House quickly changed its tune, retracting Nixon's statement. The president's memory had failed him, Ziegler reported; in fact the decision to fire Fitzgerald had never been brought to the president's attention.

The veil of secrecy that the administration had placed over the firing was pulled back a little when a former Nixon aide, Clark Mollenhoff, appeared before the commission, bringing with him a sheaf of White House memos relating to Fitzgerald's firing. Those memos made it clear that Fitzgerald's case was discussed extensively by top White House aides. More damning was a memorandum written by Alexander Butterfield that came to light during the Watergate hearings. Dated January 20, 1970, Butterfield's memo to H. R. Haldeman noted that while "Fitzgerald is no doubt a top-notch cost expert . . . he must be given very low marks in loyalty; and after all, loyalty is the name of the game." Butterfield pointed out that in May 1969 Fitzgerald had "slipped off alone to a meeting of the

Democratic National Coalition" and told at least one person there that he intended to "blow the whistle" on the "shoddy purchasing practices" of the air force. Only "a basic no-goodnik," Butterfield wrote, "would take his official business grievances so far from normal channels." Butterfield's advice: "We should let him bleed, for a while at least. Any rush to pick him up and put him back on the Federal payroll would be tantamount to an admission of earlier wrong-doing on our part."

On September 19, 1973, the Commission issued its ruling: the air force had improperly disguised Fitzgerald's firing as an economy move when in fact he had been fired for "purely personal" reasons.[1] The commission ordered the air force to reinstate Fitzgerald in his old job or one of comparable responsibility and pay, and commanded that the air force pay Fitzgerald more than $100,000 in back pay. The air force reinstated Fitzgerald, though in a position that Fitzgerald maintained was not comparable to his old job. He returned to work but at the same time he filed suit for $3.5 million in damages. The suit named a number of top Pentagon officials as well as Alexander Butterfield.

The suit was initially tossed out because the District of Columbia's three-year statute of limitations had expired. The Court of Appeals, however, allowed the suit to go forward against Butterfield since his memo only came to light in the summer of 1973. The case then was remanded to the district court, at which point, in the summer of 1978, Fitzgerald amended his complaint by adding Richard Nixon as a defendant in the suit. Bolstering Fitzgerald's case was the release of a White House tape in which Nixon boasted—in an Oval Office conversation on January 30, 1973—that he had directed the air force to "get rid of that son of a bitch."

Nixon's lawyers insisted that the former president should be removed from the suit because a president could not be sued for his official actions. The district court rejected Nixon's claim of absolute immunity, as did the court of appeals. Nixon's last chance was the Supreme Court, which agreed to take the case in 1981. On June 24, 1982, more than twelve years after Fitzgerald's original firing, a narrowly divided Supreme Court announced its judgment.

* * * * * *

Justice Powell delivered the opinion of the Court. . . .

We hold that petitioner, as a former President of the United States, is entitled to absolute immunity from damages liability predicated on his official acts. We consider this immunity a functionally mandated incident of the President's unique office, rooted in the constitutional tradition of the separation of powers and supported by our history. Justice Story's analysis remains persuasive:

> There are . . . incidental powers belonging to the executive department
> which are necessarily implied from the nature of the functions which are
> confided to it. Among these must necessarily be included the power to per-
> form them. . . . The president cannot, therefore, be liable to arrest, imprison-
> ment, or detention, while he is in the discharge of the duties of his office,
> and, for this purpose, his person must be deemed, in civil cases at least, to
> possess an official inviolability.

The President occupies a unique position in the constitutional scheme.
Article II, § 1, of the Constitution provides that "the executive Power
shall be vested in a President of the United States. . . ." This grant of authority establishes the President as the chief constitutional officer of the
Executive Branch, entrusted with supervisory and policy responsibilities of utmost discretion and sensitivity. These include the enforcement
of federal law—it is the President who is charged constitutionally to
"take Care that the Laws be faithfully executed"; the conduct of foreign
affairs—a realm in which the Court has recognized that "it would be intolerable that courts, without the relevant information, should review
and perhaps nullify actions of the Executive taken on information properly held secret"; and management of the Executive Branch—a task for
which "imperative reasons require an unrestricted power [in the Presi-
dent] to remove the most important of his subordinates in their most important duties."

In arguing that the President is entitled only to qualified immunity, the
respondent [Fitzgerald] relies on cases in which we have recognized immunity of this scope for governors and cabinet officers. We find these
cases to be inapposite. The President's unique status under the Constitution distinguishes him from other executive officials.

Because of the singular importance of the President's duties, diversion
of his energies by concern with private lawsuits would raise unique risks
to the effective functioning of government. As is the case with prosecutors
and judges—for whom absolute immunity now is established—a President must concern himself with matters likely to "arouse the most intense
feelings." Yet, as our decisions have recognized, it is in precisely such
cases that there exists the greatest public interest in providing an official
"the maximum ability to deal fearlessly and impartially with" the duties
of his office. This concern is compelling where the officeholder must make
the most sensitive and far-reaching decisions entrusted to any official under our constitutional system. Nor can the sheer prominence of the President's office be ignored. In view of the visibility of his office and the effect of his actions on countless people, the President would be an easily
identifiable target for suits for civil damages. Cognizance of this personal
vulnerability frequently could distract a President from his public duties,

to the detriment of not only the President and his office but also the Nation that the Presidency was designed to serve.

Courts traditionally have recognized the President's constitutional responsibilities and status as factors counseling judicial deference and restraint. For example, while courts generally have looked to the common law to determine the scope of an official's evidentiary privilege, we have recognized that the Presidential privilege is "rooted in the separation of powers under the Constitution." It is settled law that the separation of powers doctrine does not bar every exercise of jurisdiction over the President of the United States. But our cases also have established that a court, before exercising jurisdiction, must balance the constitutional weight of the interest to be served against the dangers of intrusion on the authority and functions of the Executive Branch. When judicial action is needed to serve broad public interests—as when the Court acts not in derogation of the separation of powers, but to maintain their proper balance, or to vindicate the public interest in an ongoing criminal prosecution—the exercise of jurisdiction has been held warranted. In the case of this merely private suit for damages based on a President's official acts, we hold it is not.

In defining the scope of an official's absolute privilege, this Court has recognized that the sphere of protected action must be related closely to the immunity's justifying purposes. Frequently our decisions have held that an official's absolute immunity should extend only to acts in performance of particular functions of his office. But the Court also has refused to draw functional lines finer than history and reason would support. In view of the special nature of the President's constitutional office and functions, we think it appropriate to recognize absolute Presidential immunity from damages liability for acts within the "outer perimeter" of his official responsibility.

Under the Constitution and laws of the United States, the President has discretionary responsibilities in a broad variety of areas, many of them highly sensitive. In many cases, it would be difficult to determine which of the President's innumerable "functions" encompassed a particular action. In this case, for example, respondent argues that he was dismissed in retaliation for his testimony to Congress. . . . The Air Force, however, has claimed that the underlying reorganization was undertaken to promote efficiency. Assuming that petitioner Nixon ordered the reorganization in which respondent lost his job, an inquiry into the President's motives could not be avoided under the kind of "functional" theory asserted both by respondent and the dissent. Inquiries of this kind could be highly intrusive.

Here, respondent argues that petitioner Nixon would have acted outside the outer perimeter of his duties by ordering the discharge of an employee who was lawfully entitled to retain his job in the absence of "such cause as will promote the efficiency of the service." Because Congress has granted this legislative protection, respondent argues, no federal official could, within the outer perimeter of his duties of office, cause Fitzgerald to be dismissed without satisfying this standard in prescribed statutory proceedings.

This construction would subject the President to trial on virtually every allegation that an action was unlawful, or was taken for a forbidden purpose. Adoption of this construction thus would deprive absolute immunity of its intended effect. It clearly is within the President's constitutional and statutory authority to prescribe the manner in which the Secretary will conduct the business of the Air Force. Because this mandate of office must include the authority to prescribe reorganizations and reductions in force, we conclude that petitioner's alleged wrongful acts lay well within the outer perimeter of his authority.

A rule of absolute immunity for the President will not leave the Nation without sufficient protection against misconduct on the part of the Chief Executive. There remains the constitutional remedy of impeachment. In addition, there are formal and informal checks on Presidential action that do not apply with equal force to other executive officials. The President is subjected to constant scrutiny by the press. Vigilant oversight by Congress also may serve to deter Presidential abuses of office, as well as to make credible the threat of impeachment. Other incentives to avoid misconduct may include a desire to earn reelection, the need to maintain prestige as an element of Presidential influence, and a President's traditional concern for his historical stature.

The existence of alternative remedies and deterrents establishes that absolute immunity will not place the President "above the law." For the President, as for judges and prosecutors, absolute immunity merely precludes a particular private remedy for alleged misconduct in order to advance compelling public ends.

*   *   *   *   *   *

Justice White, with whom Justice Brennan, Justice Marshall, and Justice Blackmun join, dissenting.

The four dissenting Members of the Court in *Butz v. Economou* (1978) argued that all federal officials are entitled to absolute immunity from suit for any action they take in connection with their official duties.[2] That immunity would extend even to actions taken with express knowledge that the conduct was clearly contrary to the controlling statute or clearly violative of the Constitution. Fortunately, the majority of the Court rejected that approach: we held that, although public officials perform certain functions that entitle them to absolute immunity, the immunity attaches to particular functions—not to particular offices. Officials performing functions for which immunity is not absolute enjoy qualified immunity; they are liable in damages only if their conduct violated well-established law and if they should have realized that their conduct was illegal.

The Court now applies the dissenting view in *Butz* to the Office of the President: a President, acting within the outer boundaries of what Presidents normally do, may, without liability, deliberately cause serious injury to any number of citizens even though he knows his conduct violates a statute or tramples on the constitutional rights of those who are injured. Even if the President in this case ordered Fitzgerald fired by means of a trumped-up reduction in force, knowing that such a discharge was contrary to the civil service laws, he would be absolutely immune from suit. By the same token, if a President, without following the statutory procedures which he knows apply to himself as well as to other federal officials, orders his subordinates to wiretap or break into a home for the purpose of installing a listening device, and the officers comply with his request, the President would be absolutely immune from suit. He would be immune regardless of the damage he inflicts, regardless of how violative of the statute and of the Constitution he knew his conduct to be, and regardless of his purpose.

The Court intimates that its decision is grounded in the Constitution. If that is the case, Congress cannot provide a remedy against Presidential misconduct, and the criminal laws of the United States are wholly inapplicable to the President. I find this approach completely unacceptable. I do not agree that, if the Office of President is to operate effectively, the holder of that Office must be permitted, without fear of liability and regardless of the function he is performing, deliberately to inflict injury on others by conduct that he knows violates the law. . . .

The Court . . . makes no effort to distinguish categories of Presidential conduct that should be absolutely immune from other categories of conduct that should not qualify for that level of immunity. The Court instead concludes that, whatever the President does and however contrary to law he knows his conduct to be, he may, without fear of liability, injure federal employees or any other person within or without the Government.

Attaching absolute immunity to the Office of the President, rather than to particular activities that the President might perform, places the President above the law. It is a reversion to the old notion that the King can do no wrong. . . .

In declaring the President to be absolutely immune from suit for any deliberate and knowing violation of the Constitution or of a federal statute, the Court asserts that the immunity is "rooted in the constitutional tradition of the separation of powers and supported by our history." The decision thus has all the earmarks of a constitutional pronouncement—absolute immunity for the President's office is mandated by the Constitution. Although the Court appears to disclaim this, it is difficult to read the opinion coherently as standing for any narrower proposition: attempts to subject the President to liability either by Congress through a statutory action or by the courts . . . would violate the separation of powers. Such a generalized absolute immunity cannot be sustained when examined in the traditional manner and in light of the traditional judicial sources. . . .

The Court's response, until today . . . has been to apply the [immunity] argument to individual functions, not offices, and to evaluate the effect of liability on governmental decision making within that function in light of the substantive ends that are to be encouraged or discouraged. In this case, therefore, the Court should examine the functions implicated by the causes of action at issue here and the effect of potential liability on the performance of those functions.

The functional approach to the separation of powers doctrine and the Court's more recent immunity decisions converge on the following principle: the scope of immunity is determined by function, not office. The wholesale claim that the President is entitled to absolute immunity in all of his actions stands on no firmer ground than did the claim that all Presidential communications are entitled to an absolute privilege, which was rejected in favor of a functional analysis, by a unanimous Court in *United States v. Nixon* (1974). Therefore, whatever may be true of the necessity of such a broad immunity in certain areas of executive responsibility, the only question that must be answered here is whether the dismissal of employees falls within a constitutionally assigned executive function, the performance of which would be substantially impaired by the possibility of a private action for damages. I believe it does not. . . .

Because of the importance of this case, it is appropriate to examine the reasoning of the majority opinion. . . .

While the majority opinion recognizes that "it is settled law that the separation of powers doctrine does not bar every exercise of jurisdiction over the President of the United States," it bases its conclusion, at least in part, on a suggestion that there is a special jurisprudence of the Presidency.

But in *United States v. Nixon* (1974), we upheld the power of a Federal District Court to issue a subpoena duces tecum against the President. In other cases, we have enjoined executive officials from carrying out Presidential directives. See, e.g., *Youngstown Sheet & Tube Co. v. Sawyer* (1952). Not until this case has there ever been a suggestion that the mere formalism of the name's appearing on the complaint was more important in resolving separation of powers problems than the substantive character of the judicial intrusion upon executive functions. . . .

Focusing on the actual arguments the majority offers for its holding of absolute immunity for the President, one finds surprisingly little. As I read the relevant section of the Court's opinion, I find just three contentions from which the majority draws this conclusion. Each of them is little more than a makeweight; together, they hardly suffice to justify the wholesale disregard of our traditional approach to immunity questions.

First, the majority informs us that the President occupies a "unique position in the constitutional scheme," including responsibilities for the administration of justice, foreign affairs, and management of the Executive Branch. True as this may be, it says nothing about why a "unique" rule of immunity should apply to the President. . . .

Second, the majority contends that, because the President's "visibility" makes him particularly vulnerable to suits for civil damages, a rule of absolute immunity is required. The force of this argument is surely undercut by the majority's admission that "there is no historical record of numerous suits against the President." . . .

Finally, the Court suggests that potential liability "frequently could distract a President from his public duties." Unless one assumes that the President himself makes the countless high-level executive decisions required in the administration of government, this rule will not do much to insulate such decisions from the threat of liability. The logic of the proposition cannot be limited to the President; its extension, however, has been uniformly rejected by this Court. Furthermore, in no instance have we previously held legal accountability in itself to be an unjustifiable cost. The availability of the courts to vindicate constitutional and statutory wrongs has been perceived and protected as one of the virtues of our system of delegated and limited powers. . . . Our concern in fashioning absolute immunity rules has been that liability may pervert the decision making process in a particular function by undercutting the values we expect to guide those decisions. Except for the empty generality that the President should have "'the maximum ability to deal fearlessly and impartially with' the duties of his office," the majority nowhere suggests a particular, disadvantageous effect on a specific Presidential function. The caution that comes from requiring reasonable choices in areas that may intrude on individuals' legally protected rights has never before been counted as a cost.

The majority may be correct in its conclusion that "a rule of absolute immunity . . . will not leave the Nation without sufficient protection against misconduct on the part of the Chief Executive." Such a rule will, however, leave Mr. Fitzgerald without an adequate remedy for the harms that he may have suffered. More importantly, it will leave future plaintiffs without a remedy, regardless of the substantiality of their claims. The remedies in which the Court finds comfort were never designed to afford relief for individual harms. Rather, they were designed as political safety valves. Politics and history, however, are not the domain of the courts; the courts exist to assure each individual that he, as an individual, has enforceable rights that he may pursue to achieve a peaceful redress of his legitimate grievances

I find it ironic, as well as tragic, that the Court would so casually discard its own role of assuring "the right of every individual to claim the protection of the laws," in the name of protecting the principle of separation of powers. Accordingly, I dissent.

*   *   *   *   *   *

POSTSCRIPT

Although on the losing end of this historic case, Fitzgerald could point to some smaller victories. To begin with, in 1981, Nixon reached a settlement with Fitzgerald, paying him a $144,000 in damages, an agreement that only came to light after the Supreme Court had agreed to hear the case. Moreover, the Court—in a separate ruling issued at the same time as *Nixon v. Fitzgerald*—ruled that Fitzgerald could pursue his case against two Nixon aides, Butterfield and Bryce Harlow, since they were not protected by the same absolute immunity as the president. Most important, though, was a ruling by a federal judge in March 31, 1982—three months before the Supreme Court announced its decision—that the Pentagon had failed to restore Fitzgerald to a job of equivalent status, as they had been previously ordered to do by the Civil Service Commission. The air force was given thirty days to restore Fitzgerald to a job of genuinely comparable responsibility. And so, at last, Fitzgerald was allowed to resume his work of scrutinizing air force facilities and contractors.

Fitzgerald worked for the Pentagon for the next quarter century and continued to be a thorn in its side, frequently testifying before Congress about military cost overruns. In 2005, the seventy-nine-year-old Fitzgerald was back in court, complaining that the Bush administration had stripped him of the staff analysts he needed to do his job. But Fitzgerald's appeal fell on deaf ears this time. The following year, Fitzgerald retired, the ceremony held, fittingly, not in the Pentagon but in a Senate hearing room. The Defense Inspector General Thomas G. Gimble awarded Fitzgerald its Distinguished Civilian Service Medal. Presiding over the ceremony was Iowa senator Charles Grassley, before whom Fitzgerald had often testified about military waste. Only two reporters were on hand to hear Grassley's parting tribute to Fitzgerald: "To Ernie, saving the taxpayers' money was never just a goal—it was more than that. It was more like a calling. It was a matter of faith to him—keeping the faith with taxpayers."

NOTES

1. The commission did not, however, accept Fitzgerald's contention that he had been fired in retaliation for his 1968 testimony on the C-5A. Instead the commission concluded that the air force's action stemmed from a series of subsequent actions by Fitzgerald that had produced adverse publicity for the air force.

2. In *Butz v. Economou*, commodities trader Arthur Economou sued Nixon's Secretary of Agriculture Earl Butz and other government officials for attempting to revoke or suspend his trading license. In a 5–4 decision, the Court ruled that federal administrators were not protected by an absolute immunity against civil suits. Instead executive branch officials were generally entitled to a qualified or "good faith immunity" that protected them from suits so long as they acted without malice and without having knowingly committed an illegal act. Speaking for the majority, Justice Byron White insisted that administrators should not be given blanket immunity for their public actions if they knew or should have known that their action would deprive an individual of their statutory or constitutional rights. However, White also carved out an exception for agency officials who performed either "adjudicatory functions," such as an administrative law judge or a hearing examiner, or prosecutorial functions. In carrying out these functions, executive officials were entitled to absolute immunity because it was vital that they exercise their "independent judgment on the evidence before [them]," free from the threat of intimidation or harassment.

Executive Immunity

5

Clinton v. Jones (1997)

Shortly after her twenty-fifth birthday, Paula Rosalee Corbin began work as an office assistant at the Arkansas Industrial Development Commission (AIDC), a state agency. On May 8, 1991, AIDC hosted the third annual Governor's Quality Management Conference at the Excelsior Hotel in downtown Little Rock; the newly hired Corbin was assigned to work at the conference registration desk. Speaking at the conference was the state's forty-four-year-old governor, Bill Clinton. At about 2:30 in the afternoon, state trooper Danny Ferguson, who was part of Clinton's security detail, approached the registration desk and told Corbin that "the Governor would like to meet with you." Thinking it would be an honor to meet the governor of her state, Corbin accompanied the state trooper to the president's room, which was configured as a business suite: couch and chairs but no bed. Clinton shook Corbin's hand, invited her in, and closed the door; the state trooper remained stationed outside.

What happened next was revealed—or, more accurately, alleged—in a complaint filed by Paula Jones (she had since married) on May 6, 1994, just days before the statute of limitations would expire. According to Jones, "A few minutes of small talk ensued, which included asking . . . about her job." Clinton tossed in that the director of AIDC, Dave Harrington, was his "good friend." Clinton then pulled Corbin toward him "so that their bodies were in close proximity" and commented on her lovely curves and her flowing hair. He then placed "his hand on [her] leg

46

and started sliding it toward the hem of [her] culottes," whereupon he tried to kiss her on the neck. Corbin pulled away, exclaiming, "What are you doing?" and tried to distract the governor by talking about his wife. She then sat down at the end of a sofa near the door. Clinton then walked over to the couch "and as he sat down he lowered his trousers and underwear exposing his erect penis and asked Jones to 'kiss it.'" A "horrified" Jones leapt off the couch, spluttering that she was "not that kind of girl" and explaining that she had to go or she might "get in trouble for being away from the registration desk." Whereupon Clinton stood up and pulled up his pants, telling her he didn't want her to do anything she didn't want to do. He also said that if she did get into trouble for leaving the desk, just "have Dave call me immediately and I'll take care of it." His parting words, as she was leaving the room: "You are smart. Let's keep this between ourselves."

At first she did just that, though court records would show that she did tell several friends, co-workers, and family members about the alleged incident within a day or two of it happening. For a variety of reasons—ranging from fear that she might lose her job to concern that her fiancé and soon-to-be husband would blame her—Jones did not report the incident, despite being urged to do so by at least one co-worker who she told of the incident. Only after a story appeared in January 1994—in the fiercely anti-Clinton *American Spectator*—that falsely (according to Jones) intimated that Clinton and a woman identified only as "Paula" had engaged in oral sex at the Excelsior Hotel did she go public. At a press conference in February 1994 she set the record straight and asked for a presidential apology. When no apology was forthcoming, she filed a lawsuit asking for $700,000 in compensatory and punitive damages.

Clinton's advisors were hardly unaccustomed to dealing with tawdry allegations about their boss's sexual activities. Clinton's 1992 presidential campaign had almost been derailed by Gennifer Flowers' allegation of a twelve-year affair with Clinton. In the 1992 presidential campaign, Betsey Wright—who had served as Governor Clinton's chief of staff for seven years—headed up a rapid response team that was responsible for defending the candidate against what Wright famously termed "bimbo eruptions." The strategy generally entailed immediate denial followed by denigrating the credibility of the accuser. The White House followed those well-honed tactics as soon as Jones's allegations surfaced in February 1994: "It is not true," Communications Director Mark Gearen flatly declared. Clinton "was never alone in a hotel with her." As for the attacks on Jones, nobody did it better than Clinton's most quotable political strategist James Carville, who derided Jones as "trailer-park trash"—"Drag $100 bills through trailer parks," he wisecracked, and "there's no telling what you'll find." The Clinton administration also tried to turn public attention from the substance of Jones's allegations to the motives of the conservative Clinton-haters who helped her bring the suit against the president. As the president's lawyer Robert Bennett put it, Jones was "being used" by bitter partisans and her fabricated story was "really just another effort to rewrite the results of the election and . . . distract the President from his agenda." The Jones suit, Hillary Clinton explained, was further evidence of a "vast right-wing conspiracy" against her husband.

While pursuing a public strategy featuring firm denials coupled with ferocious counterattacks against the president's accusers, the administration also pursued a legal strategy based on a broad claim of temporary executive immunity. The president's lawyers argued that Jones should be free to refile her suit after Clinton had left the White House, but so long as he was the president of the United States he could not be sued. Federal District Judge Susan Webber Wright—a conservative Republican who had actually taken a class from Bill Clinton at the University of Arkansas law school in the early 1970s—agreed with the administration that the immunity question needed to be settled before proceeding with Jones's lawsuit. In December 1994, Wright rendered a verdict that made neither side happy. She rejected the president's sweeping immunity claims but agreed with the Clinton legal team that defending himself against Jones's lawsuit could adversely impact the president's ability to carry out his duties. In view of the ruling in *Fitzgerald*, Wright ruled that it was appropriate to stay the trial until after Clinton left office. However, Wright was also concerned to balance immunity against Jones's right to seek legal redress. So as to minimize the risk of witnesses dying or evidence being lost, Wright ruled that discovery and deposition of witnesses could proceed so that Jones would not be adversely affected.

The Court of Appeals for the Eighth Circuit, by a two-to-one vote (both of the judges who sided with Jones were conservative Republicans appointed to the bench by President Reagan; the one dissenter was a Nixon appointee), overturned Wright's ruling. Clinton now appealed to the Supreme Court, which quickly agreed to hear the case. The Court heard oral arguments on January 13, 1997, and announced its unanimous decision on May 27, 1997.

*   *   *   *   *   *

Justice Stevens delivered the opinion of the Court.

This case raises a constitutional and a prudential question concerning the Office of the President of the United States. Respondent, a private citizen, seeks to recover damages from the current occupant of that office based on actions allegedly taken before his term began. The President submits that in all but the most exceptional cases the Constitution requires federal courts to defer such litigation until his term ends and that, in any event, respect for the office warrants such a stay. Despite the force of the arguments supporting the President's submissions, we conclude that they must be rejected. . . .

Only three sitting Presidents have been defendants in civil litigation involving their actions prior to taking office. Complaints against Theodore Roosevelt and Harry Truman had been dismissed before they took office; the dismissals were affirmed after their respective inaugurations. Two companion cases arising out of an automobile accident were filed against John F. Kennedy in 1960 during the Presidential campaign. After taking office, he unsuccessfully argued that his status as Commander in Chief gave him a right to a stay under the Soldiers' and Sailors' Civil Relief Act of 1940. The motion for a stay was denied by the District Court, and the matter was settled out of court. Thus, none of those cases sheds any light on the constitutional issue before us.

The principal rationale for affording certain public servants immunity from suits for money damages arising out of their official acts is inapplicable to unofficial conduct. In cases involving prosecutors, legislators, and judges we have repeatedly explained that the immunity serves the public interest in enabling such officials to perform their designated functions effectively without fear that a particular decision may give rise to personal liability. . . .

That rationale provided the principal basis for our holding that a former President of the United States was "entitled to absolute immunity from damages liability predicated on his official acts." *Nixon v. Fitzgerald* (1981). Our central concern was to avoid rendering the President "unduly cautious in the discharge of his official duties."

This reasoning provides no support for an immunity for *unofficial* conduct. As we explained in *Fitzgerald*, "the sphere of protected action must be related closely to the immunity's justifying purposes." Because of the President's broad responsibilities, we recognized in that case an immunity from damages claims arising out of official acts extending to the "outer perimeter of his authority." But we have never suggested that the President, or any other official, has an immunity that extends beyond the scope of any action taken in an official capacity.

Moreover, when defining the scope of an immunity for acts clearly taken *within* an official capacity, we have applied a functional approach. "Frequently our decisions have held that an official's absolute immunity should extend only to acts in performance of particular functions of his office." Hence, for example, a judge's absolute immunity does not extend to actions performed in a purely administrative capacity. As our opinions have made clear, immunities are grounded in "the nature of the function performed, not the identity of the actor who performed it."

Petitioner's effort to construct an immunity from suit for unofficial acts grounded purely in the identity of his office is unsupported by precedent. . . .

Petitioner's strongest argument supporting his immunity claim is based on the text and structure of the Constitution. He does not contend that the occupant of the Office of the President is "above the law," in the sense that his conduct is entirely immune from judicial scrutiny. The President argues merely for a postponement of the judicial proceedings that will determine whether he violated any law. His argument is grounded in the character of the office that was created by Article II of the Constitution, and relies on separation of powers principles that have structured our constitutional arrangement since the founding.

As a starting premise, petitioner contends that he occupies a unique office with powers and responsibilities so vast and important that the public interest demands that he devote his undivided time and attention to his public duties. He submits that—given the nature of the office—the doctrine of separation of powers places limits on the authority of the Federal Judiciary to interfere with the Executive Branch that would be transgressed by allowing this action to proceed.

We have no dispute with the initial premise of the argument. Former presidents, from George Washington to George Bush, have consistently endorsed petitioner's characterization of the office. After serving his term, Lyndon Johnson observed: "Of all the 1,886 nights I was President, there were not many when I got to sleep before 1 or 2 A.M., and there were few mornings when I didn't wake up by 6 or 6:30." In 1967, the Twenty-fifth Amendment to the Constitution was adopted to ensure continuity in the performance of the powers and duties of the office; one of the sponsors of that Amendment stressed the importance of providing that "at all times" there be a President "who has complete control and will be able to perform" those duties. . . .

It does not follow, however, that separation of powers principles would be violated by allowing this action to proceed. The doctrine of separation of powers is concerned with the allocation of official power among the three coequal branches of our Government. The Framers "built into the tripartite Federal Government . . . a self executing safeguard against the encroachment or aggrandizement of one branch at the expense of the other."

Of course the lines between the powers of the three branches are not always neatly defined. But in this case there is no suggestion that the Federal Judiciary is being asked to perform any function that might in some way be described as "executive." Respondent is merely asking the courts to exercise their core Article III jurisdiction to decide cases and controversies. Whatever the outcome of this case, there is no possibility that the decision will curtail the scope of the official powers of the Executive Branch. The litigation of questions that relate entirely to the unofficial conduct of the individual who happens to be the President poses no perceptible risk of misallocation of either judicial power or executive power.

Rather than arguing that the decision of the case will produce either an aggrandizement of judicial power or a narrowing of executive power, petitioner contends that—as a by product of an otherwise traditional exercise of judicial power—burdens will be placed on the President that will hamper the performance of his official duties. We have recognized that "even when a branch does not arrogate power to itself . . . the separation of powers doctrine requires that a branch not impair another in the performance of its constitutional duties." As a factual matter, petitioner contends that this particular case—as well as the potential additional litigation that an affirmance of the Court of Appeals judgment might spawn—may impose an unacceptable burden on the President's time and energy, and thereby impair the effective performance of his office.

Petitioner's predictive judgment finds little support in either history or the relatively narrow compass of the issues raised in this particular case. As we have already noted, in the more than 200 year history of the Republic, only three sitting Presidents have been subjected to suits for their private actions. If the past is any indicator, it seems unlikely that a deluge of such litigation will ever engulf the Presidency. As for the case at hand, if properly managed by the District Court, it appears to us highly unlikely to occupy any substantial amount of petitioner's time. . . .

Of greater significance, petitioner errs by presuming that interactions between the Judicial Branch and the Executive, even quite burdensome interactions, necessarily rise to the level of constitutionally forbidden impairment of the Executive's ability to perform its constitutionally mandated functions. . . . The fact that a federal court's exercise of its traditional Article III jurisdiction may significantly burden the time and attention of the Chief Executive is not sufficient to establish a violation of the Constitution. Two long-settled propositions . . . support that conclusion.

First, we have long held that when the President takes official action, the Court has the authority to determine whether he has acted within the law. . . .

Second, it is also settled that the President is subject to judicial process in appropriate circumstances. Although Thomas Jefferson apparently thought otherwise, Chief Justice Marshall, when presiding in the treason trial of Aaron Burr, ruled that a subpoena *duces tecum* could be directed to the President. *United States v. Burr* (1807). We unequivocally and emphatically endorsed Marshall's position when we held that President Nixon was obligated to comply with a subpoena commanding him to produce certain tape recordings of his conversations with his aides. *United States v. Nixon* (1974). . . .

Sitting Presidents have responded to court orders to provide testimony and other information with sufficient frequency that such interactions between the Judicial and Executive Branches can scarcely be thought a novelty. President Monroe responded to written interrogatories, President Nixon . . . produced tapes in response to a subpoena *duces tecum*, President Ford complied with an order to give a deposition in a criminal trial, and President Clinton has twice given videotaped testimony in criminal proceedings. Moreover, sitting Presidents have also voluntarily complied with judicial requests for testimony. . . .

In sum, "It is settled law that the separation of powers doctrine does not bar every exercise of jurisdiction over the President of the United States." *Fitzgerald*. If the Judiciary may severely burden the Executive Branch by reviewing the legality of the President's official conduct, and if it may direct appropriate process to the President himself, it must follow that the federal courts have power to determine the legality of his unofficial conduct. The burden on the President's time and energy that is a mere by product of such review surely cannot be considered as onerous as the direct burden imposed by judicial review and the occasional invalidation of his official actions. We therefore hold that the doctrine of separation of powers does not require federal courts to stay all private actions against the President until he leaves office. . . .

We are persuaded that it was an abuse of discretion for the District Court to defer the trial until after the President leaves office. Such a lengthy and categorical stay takes no account whatever of the respondent's interest in bringing the case to trial. The complaint was filed within the statutory limitations period—albeit near the end of that period—and delaying trial would increase the danger of prejudice resulting from the loss of evidence, including the inability of witnesses to recall specific facts, or the possible death of a party.

The decision to postpone the trial was, furthermore, premature. The proponent of a stay bears the burden of establishing its need. . . . We think the District Court may have given undue weight to the concern that a trial might generate unrelated civil actions that could conceivably hamper the President in conducting the duties of his office. If and when that should occur, the court's discretion would permit it to manage those actions in such fashion (including deferral of trial) that interference with the President's duties would not occur. But no such impingement upon the President's conduct of his office was shown here.

We add a final comment on two matters that are discussed at length in the briefs: the risk that our decision will generate a large volume of politically motivated harassing and frivolous litigation, and the danger that national security concerns might prevent the President from explaining a legitimate need for a continuance.

We are not persuaded that either of these risks is serious. Most frivolous and vexatious litigation is terminated at the pleading stage or on summary judgment, with little if any personal involvement by the defendant. Moreover, the availability of sanctions provides a significant deterrent to litigation directed at the President in his unofficial capacity for purposes of political gain or harassment. History indicates that the likelihood that a significant number of such cases will be filed is remote. Although scheduling problems may arise, there is no reason to assume that the District Courts will be either unable to accommodate the President's needs or unfaithful to the tradition—especially in matters involving national security—of giving "the utmost deference to Presidential responsibilities." Several Presidents, including petitioner, have given testimony without jeopardizing the Nation's security. In short, we have confidence in the ability of our federal judges to deal with both of these concerns.

If Congress deems it appropriate to afford the President stronger protection, it may respond with appropriate legislation. . . .

The Federal District Court has jurisdiction to decide this case. Like every other citizen who properly invokes that jurisdiction, respondent has a right to an orderly disposition of her claims. Accordingly, the judgment of the Court of Appeals is affirmed.

* * * * * *

Justice Breyer, concurring in the judgment.

I agree with the majority that the Constitution does not automatically grant the President an immunity from civil lawsuits based upon his private conduct. Nor does the "doctrine of separation of powers . . . require federal courts to stay" virtually "all private actions against the President until he leaves office." Rather, as the Court of Appeals stated, the President cannot simply rest upon the claim that a private civil lawsuit for damages will "interfere with the constitutionally assigned duties of the Executive Branch . . . without detailing any specific responsibilities or explaining how or the degree to which they are affected by the suit." To obtain a postponement the President must "bea[r] the burden of establishing its need."

In my view, however, once the President sets forth and explains a conflict between judicial proceeding and public duties, the matter changes. At that point, the Constitution permits a judge to schedule a trial in an ordinary civil damages action (where postponement normally is possible without overwhelming damage to a plaintiff) only within the constraints of a constitutional principle—a principle that forbids a federal judge in such a case to interfere with the President's discharge of his public duties.

I have no doubt that the Constitution contains such a principle applicable to civil suits, based upon Article II's vesting of the entire "executive Power" in a single individual, implemented through the Constitution's structural separation of powers, and revealed both by history and case precedent.

I recognize that this case does not require us now to apply the principle specifically, thereby delineating its contours; nor need we now decide whether lower courts are to apply it directly or categorically through the use of presumptions or rules of administration. Yet I fear that to disregard it now may appear to deny it. I also fear that the majority's description of the relevant precedents de-emphasizes the extent to which they support a principle of the President's independent authority to control his own time and energy. . . .

The Constitution states that the "executive Power shall be vested in a President." This constitutional delegation means that a sitting President is unusually busy, that his activities have an unusually important impact upon the lives of others, and that his conduct embodies an authority bestowed by the entire American electorate. He (along with his constitutionally subordinate Vice President) is the only official for whom the entire Nation votes, and is the only elected officer to represent the entire Nation both domestically and abroad.

This constitutional delegation means still more. Article II makes a single President responsible for the actions of the Executive Branch in much the same way that the entire Congress is responsible for the actions of the Legislative Branch, or the entire Judiciary for those of the Judicial Branch. It thereby creates a constitutional equivalence between a single President, on the one hand, and many legislators, or judges, on the other.

The Founders created this equivalence by consciously deciding to vest Executive authority in one person rather than several. They did so in order to focus, rather than to spread, Executive responsibility, thereby facilitating accountability. They also sought to encourage energetic, vigorous, decisive, and speedy execution of the laws by placing in the hands of a single, constitutionally indispensable, individual the ultimate authority that, in respect to the other branches, the Constitution divides among many. . . .

For present purposes, this constitutional structure means that the President is not like Congress, for Congress can function as if it were whole, even when up to half of its members are absent. It means that the President is not like the Judiciary, for judges often can designate other judges, *e.g.*, from other judicial circuits, to sit even should an entire court be detained by personal litigation. It means that, unlike Congress, which is regularly out of session, the President never adjourns.

More importantly, these constitutional objectives explain why a President, though able to delegate duties to others, cannot delegate ultimate responsibility or the active obligation to supervise that goes with it. And the related constitutional equivalence between President, Congress, and the Judiciary, means that judicial scheduling orders in a private civil case must not only take reasonable account of, say, a particularly busy schedule, or a job on which others critically depend, or an underlying electoral mandate. They must also reflect the fact that interference with a President's ability to carry out his public responsibilities is constitutionally equivalent to interference with the ability of the entirety of Congress, or the Judicial Branch, to carry out their public obligations. . . .

Case law, particularly *Nixon v. Fitzgerald*, strongly supports the principle that judges hearing a private civil damages action against a sitting President may not issue orders that could significantly distract a President from his official duties. In *Fitzgerald*, the Court held that former President Nixon was absolutely immune from civil damage lawsuits based upon any conduct within the "outer perimeter" of his official responsibilities. The holding rested on six determinations that are relevant here.

First, the Court found that the Constitution assigns the President *singularly* important duties (thus warranting an "absolute," rather than a "qualified," immunity). Second, the Court held that "recognition of immunity" does not require a "specific textual basis" in the Constitution. Third, although physical constraint of the President was not at issue, the Court nevertheless considered Justice Story's constitutional analysis "persuasive." Fourth, the Court distinguished contrary precedent on the ground that it involved criminal, not civil, proceedings. Fifth, the Court's concerns encompassed the fact that "the sheer prominence of the President's office" could make him "an easily identifiable target for suits for civil damages." Sixth, and most important, the Court rested its conclusion in important part upon the fact that civil lawsuits "could distract a President from his public duties, to the detriment of not only the President and his office but also the Nation that the Presidency was designed to serve."

The majority argues that this critical, last-mentioned, feature of the case is dicta. In the majority's view, since the defendant was a *former* President, the lawsuit could not have *distracted* him from his official duties; hence the case must rest entirely upon an alternative concern, namely that a President's fear of civil lawsuits based upon his official duties could *distort* his official decision making. The majority, however, overlooks the fact that *Fitzgerald* set forth a single immunity (an absolute immunity) applicable *both* to sitting *and* former Presidents. Its reasoning focused upon both. Its key paragraph, explaining why the President enjoys an absolute immunity rather than a qualified immunity, contains seven sentences, four of which focus primarily upon time and energy *distraction* and three of which focus primarily upon official decision *distortion*. Indeed, that key paragraph begins by stating: "Because of the singular importance of the

President's duties, diversion of his energies by concern with private lawsuits would raise unique risks to the effective functioning of government." . . .

The majority points to the fact that private plaintiffs have brought civil damage lawsuits against a sitting President only three times in our Nation's history; and it relies upon the threat of sanctions to discourage, and "the court's discretion" to manage, such actions so that "interference with the President's duties would not occur." I am less sanguine. Since 1960, when the last such suit was filed, the number of civil lawsuits filed annually in Federal District Courts has increased from under 60,000 to about 240,000; the number of federal district judges has increased from 233 to about 650; the time and expense associated with both discovery and trial have increased; an increasingly complex economy has led to increasingly complex sets of statutes, rules and regulations, that often create potential liability, with or without fault. And this Court has now made clear that such lawsuits may proceed against a sitting President. The consequence, as the Court warned in *Fitzgerald*, is that a sitting President, given "the visibility of his office," could well become "an easily identifiable target for suits for civil damages." The threat of sanctions could well discourage much unneeded litigation, but some lawsuits (including highly intricate and complicated ones) could resist ready evaluation and disposition; and individual district court procedural rulings could pose a significant threat to the President's official functions.

I concede the possibility that district courts, supervised by the Courts of Appeals and perhaps this Court, might prove able to manage private civil damage actions against sitting Presidents without significantly interfering with the discharge of Presidential duties—at least if they manage those actions with the constitutional problem in mind. Nonetheless, predicting the future is difficult, and I am skeptical. Should the majority's optimism turn out to be misplaced, then, in my view, courts will have to develop administrative rules applicable to such cases (including postponement rules of the sort at issue in this case) in order to implement the basic constitutional directive. A Constitution that separates powers in order to prevent one branch of Government from significantly threatening the workings of another could not grant a single judge more than a very limited power to second guess a President's reasonable determination (announced in open court) of his scheduling needs, nor could it permit the issuance of a trial scheduling order that would significantly interfere with the President's discharge of his duties—in a private civil damage action the trial of which might be postponed without the plaintiff suffering enormous harm. . . . I agree with the majority's determination that a constitutional defense must await a more specific showing of need; I do not agree with what I believe to be an understatement of the "danger." And I believe that ordinary case-management principles are unlikely to prove sufficient to deal with private civil lawsuits for damages unless supplemented with a constitutionally based requirement that district courts schedule proceedings so as to avoid significant interference with the President's ongoing discharge of his official responsibilities. . . .

The District Court in this case determined that the Constitution required the postponement of trial during the sitting President's term. It may well be that the trial of this case cannot take place without significantly interfering with the President's ability to carry out his official duties. Yet, I agree with the majority that there is no automatic temporary immunity and that the President should have to provide the District Court with a reasoned explanation of why the immunity is needed; and I also agree that, in the absence of that explanation, the court's postponement of the trial date was premature. For those reasons, I concur in the result.

*   *   *   *   *   *

POSTSCRIPT

After the Supreme Court resolved the question of executive immunity, the case was remanded to the Federal District Judge Susan Webber Wright, who on April 1, 1998, dismissed the suit on the grounds that Jones had failed to establish that Clinton had sexually harassed her. If Jones's allegations were true, then Clinton's behavior was "certainly boorish and offensive." It did not, however, constitute sexual harassment. "It simply cannot be said," wrote Wright, that Clinton's alleged conduct toward Jones was "frequent, severe, or physically threatening." Clinton's acts, however deplorable, did "not constitute the kind of sustained and nontrivial conduct necessary for a claim of hostile work environment." Nor had Jones demonstrated that she had suffered "any tangible job detriment or adverse employment action" as a result of refusing Clinton's unwelcome advances.

Jones appealed to the Eighth Circuit where she received a sympathetic hearing from two of the three judges, the same two judges who had ruled in her favor in 1996. Several weeks later, on November 13, 1998, Clinton reached a settlement with Jones, paying her $850,000, but neither apologizing nor admitting wrongdoing. By then, however, the damage to Clinton's presidency had already been done. For in the course of the district court trial Clinton had been deposed, and the questioning went far beyond his interactions with Paula Jones. Using federal rules of evidence that allow prosecuting attorneys in cases of sexual misconduct to broadly probe a defendant's sexual history, Jones's attorneys asked Clinton whether he had ever had sexual relations with a young White House intern, Monica Lewinsky. Clinton said he had not, and with that deception began the descent into impeachment proceedings.

Justice John Paul Stevens had confidently predicted that the case was "highly unlikely to occupy any substantial amount of [Clinton's] time." Had the attorneys not asked about Lewinsky that prediction may very well have been borne out. But they did ask and Clinton had something very embarrassing to hide: oral sex with a White House intern. Between January 14, 1998, when he gave the intentionally misleading testimony in the Jones case, and February 12, 1999, when the United States Senate acquitted him of the two impeachment charges voted by the House—perjury and obstruction of justice—very substantial amounts of Clinton's time and attention were devoted to defending himself. Without the Supreme Court's decision in *Jones v. Clinton*, there might still have been a sex scandal but Clinton would not have been impeached because he would not have had the chance to lie under oath about his relations with Lewinsky. Whether that is a good or bad thing is up for debate.

6

Immigration and Naturalization Service v. Chadha (1983)

Intent on making the federal government more efficient, President Herbert Hoover pressed Congress for the power to reorganize the executive branch. Congress reluctantly agreed, but only after obtaining a concession from Hoover that if any of his reorganization plans failed to meet with congressional approval, then either the Senate or the House could nullify the president's actions by a simple majority vote. And so was born what became known as the "legislative veto."

At first Congress made only sporadic use of this new legislative device, but beginning in the early 1970s a Democratically controlled Congress increasingly relied on the legislative veto to rein in the "imperial presidency" of Richard Nixon. In the 1970s Congress not only used the veto more often but also applied it to a broader range of executive actions. Whereas the legislative veto was initially employed to negate a particular executive action, like reorganizing an executive agency or raising a tariff rate, Congress increasingly wielded the veto to provide legislative oversight of agency regulations. Before a regulation could go into effect, the agency was required to submit it to Congress, which then had a specified amount of time—generally sixty or ninety days—in which to veto the regulation. Depending on how the law was written, the veto might require a majority of both houses, one house, or just a committee.

Presidents have never looked favorably on the legislative veto. Hoover quickly became convinced he had made a mistake and vowed never to sign another bill that provided for a legislative veto of an executive action. Every subsequent president and attorney general has expressed misgivings about the constitutionality of the legislative veto. Sometimes those constitutional objections have prompted presidents to refuse to assent to a bill containing a legislative veto, but more often presidents have reluctantly signed the legislation, albeit frequently accompanied by a signing statement declaring the president's intent to disregard the legislative veto provision.

Congress's increased reliance on the legislative veto prompted executive branch officials to seek to challenge the constitutionality of the legislative veto in court. A golden opportunity to do just that came along in the case of Jagdish Rai Chadha. An East Indian who had been born and raised in Kenya, Chadha had come to the United States in 1966 on a student visa to study as an undergraduate at Bowling Green University in Ohio. After he finished his master's degree in political science at Bowling Green, his visa expired. The Kenyan government showed no interest in allowing Chadha to return to Kenya, insisting that he was a British subject—he traveled to the United States on a British passport and both his parents were British subjects—and therefore the responsibility of the British. Britain, however, had adopted a strict racial quota system that sharply limited the immigration of East African Asians—who had flooded into Britain from Kenya and Uganda in the 1960s in the face of repression and discrimination in those countries. The British told Chadha he would have to wait at least a year and probably much longer to become eligible to live and work in the United Kingdom. Nor could he work in the United States because no employer was willing to hire someone who was not a permanent resident. Unable to find work, Chadha went to an immigration office to renew his visa so that he would be able to work in the United States, at least until the UK was prepared to accept him. Instead the Immigration and Naturalization Service (INS), seeing that his visa had expired, immediately initiated deportation proceedings against him.

In June 1974, after several hearings, an immigration judge suspended the deportation ruling, finding that Chadha met the three requirements that are specified in Section 244(a)(1) of the Immigration and Nationality Act: he was a person of "good moral character," he had lived in the United States for seven years, and he would "suffer extreme hardship" if deported. After reviewing Chadha's case, the attorney general recommended to Congress that he be permitted to stay in the United States. Under the Immigration and Nationality Act—passed in 1952—Congress had until the close of the next legislative session to veto the attorney general's decision to suspend a deportation. On December 16, 1975, just three days before the deadline, the House of Representatives passed a resolution vetoing the grant of permanent residency to Chadha and five other aliens. The only explanation of the House action came from Pennsylvania Representative

Joshua Eilberg, the chairman of the Judiciary Subcommittee on Immigration, Citizenship, and International Law, who informed his House colleagues that his committee had concluded, after a review of 340 recommended suspended deportations, that six aliens, including Chadha, failed to "meet the statutory requirements, particularly as it relates to hardship." Without debate or even a recorded vote, the House approved Eilberg's resolution. On November 8, 1976, the same immigration judge who had originally suspended Chadha's deportation now ordered him to be deported.

Insisting that the legislative veto provision in the Immigration and Nationality Act was unconstitutional, Chadha appealed his deportation order to the Board of Immigration Appeals. The board dismissed his appeal, however, explaining that it lacked the power to declare an act of Congress to be unconstitutional. So Chadha took his case to the Court of Appeals. Eagerly joining his suit was the Carter administration, which hoped to use Chadha's case to deal a judicial body blow to the legislative veto. In December 1980, a three-judge panel unanimously agreed with Chadha and the Carter administration that the legislative veto provision was unconstitutional; the court's opinion was written by Anthony Kennedy, who in 1988 would take his seat on the Supreme Court.

Had the government not joined Chadha's case, it would have ended there, and Chadha would have been quietly granted permanent residency. But the government—now the Reagan administration—wanted the Supreme Court to rule on the matter. The Reagan administration, like the Carter administration, did not care particularly about whether Chadha was deported or not; instead what they cared about was ending the legislative veto. So the Immigration and Naturalization Service, which had sided with Chadha before the Appeals Court, now asked the Supreme Court to hear its appeal on the grounds that it was an aggrieved party since the Appeals Court had prevented it from complying with the House order to deport Chadha.

The Supreme Court consented to hear the case and oral arguments took place in February 1982. Court watchers eagerly anticipated the constitutionally momentous ruling sometime in the late spring or early summer of 1982, but the term came and went without any ruling. On the final day of the 1981–1982 term, the Court announced the case would be reargued on the opening day of the next session, December 7, 1982. Finally, on June 23, 1983, almost ten years from the date that Chadha's visa had expired, the Supreme Court rendered its long-awaited verdict.

*   *   *   *   *   *

Chief Justice Burger delivered the opinion of the Court.

[This case] presents a challenge to the constitutionality of the provision in § 244(c)(2) of the Immigration and Nationality Act, authorizing one

House of Congress, by resolution, to invalidate the decision of the Executive Branch, pursuant to authority delegated by Congress to the Attorney General of the United States, to allow a particular deportable alien to remain in the United States. . . .

We begin, of course, with the presumption that the challenged statute is valid. Its wisdom is not the concern of the courts; if a challenged action does not violate the Constitution, it must be sustained. . . .

By the same token, the fact that a given law or procedure is efficient, convenient, and useful in facilitating functions of government, standing alone, will not save it if it is contrary to the Constitution. Convenience and efficiency are not the primary objectives—or the hallmarks—of democratic government, and our inquiry is sharpened, rather than blunted, by the fact that congressional veto provisions are appearing with increasing frequency in statutes that delegate authority to executive and independent agencies:

> Since 1932, when the first veto provision was enacted into law, 295 congressional veto-type procedures have been inserted in 196 different statutes as follows: from 1932 to 1939, five statutes were affected; from 1940–49, nineteen statutes; between 1950–59, thirty-four statutes; and from 1960–69, forty-nine. From the year 1970 through 1975, at least one hundred sixty-three such provisions were included in eighty-nine laws. . . .

Justice White undertakes to make a case for the proposition that the one-House veto is a useful "political invention," and we need not challenge that assertion. We can even concede this utilitarian argument, although the long-range political wisdom of this "invention" is arguable. . . . But policy arguments supporting even useful "political inventions" are subject to the demands of the Constitution, which defines powers and, with respect to this subject, sets out just how those powers are to be exercised.

Explicit and unambiguous provisions of the Constitution prescribe and define the respective functions of the Congress and of the Executive in the legislative process. Since the precise terms of those familiar provisions are critical to the resolution of these cases, we set them out verbatim. Article I provides:

> All legislative Powers herein granted shall be vested in a Congress of the United States, which shall consist of a Senate *and* House of Representatives. Art. I, § 1. (Emphasis added.)

> Every Bill which shall have passed the House of Representatives *and* the Senate, *shall*, before it becomes a law, be presented to the President of the United States. . . . Art. I, § 7, cl. 2. (Emphasis added.)

Every Order, Resolution, or Vote to which the Concurrence of the Senate and House of Representatives may be necessary (except on a question of Adjournment) *shall* be presented to the President of the United States; and before the Same shall take Effect, *shall* be approved by him, or being disapproved by him, *shall* be repassed by two thirds of the Senate and House of Representatives, according to the Rules and Limitations prescribed in the Case of a Bill. Art. I, § 7, cl. 3. (Emphasis added.)

The records of the Constitutional Convention reveal that the requirement that all legislation be presented to the President before becoming law was uniformly accepted by the Framers. Presentment to the President and the Presidential veto were considered so imperative that the draftsmen took special pains to assure that these requirements could not be circumvented. During the final debate on Art. I, § 7, cl. 2, James Madison expressed concern that it might easily be evaded by the simple expedient of calling a proposed law a "resolution" or "vote," rather than a "bill." As a consequence, Art. I, § 7, cl. 3 was added.

The decision to provide the President with a limited and qualified power to nullify proposed legislation by veto was based on the profound conviction of the Framers that the powers conferred on Congress were the powers to be most carefully circumscribed. It is beyond doubt that lawmaking was a power to be shared by both Houses and the President. In The Federalist No. 73, Hamilton focused on the President's role in making laws:

If even no propensity had ever discovered itself in the legislative body to invade the rights of the Executive, the rules of just reasoning and theoretic propriety would of themselves teach us that the one ought not to be left to the mercy of the other, but ought to possess a constitutional and effectual power of self-defence.

The President's role in the lawmaking process also reflects the Framers' careful efforts to check whatever propensity a particular Congress might have to enact oppressive, improvident, or ill-considered measures. The President's veto role in the legislative process was described later during public debate on ratification:

It establishes a salutary check upon the legislative body, calculated to guard the community against the effects of faction, precipitancy, or of any impulse unfriendly to the public good, which may happen to influence a majority of that body. . . . The primary inducement to conferring the power in question upon the Executive is to enable him to defend himself; the secondary one is to increase the chances in favor of the community against the passing of bad laws, through haste, inadvertence, or design. Federalist No. 73.

The bicameral requirement of Art. I, § § 1, 7, was of scarcely less concern to the Framers than was the Presidential veto, and indeed the two concepts are interdependent. By providing that no law could take effect without the concurrence of the prescribed majority of the Members of both Houses, the Framers reemphasized their belief . . . that legislation should not be enacted unless it has been carefully and fully considered by the Nation's elected officials. In the Constitutional Convention debates on the need for a bicameral legislature, James Wilson, later to become a Justice of this Court, commented:

> Despotism comes on mankind in different shapes, sometimes in an Executive, sometimes in a military, one. Is there danger of a Legislative despotism? Theory & practice both proclaim it. If the Legislative authority be not restrained, there can be neither liberty nor stability; and it can only be restrained by dividing it within itself, into distinct and independent branches. In a single house there is no check but the inadequate one of the virtue & good sense of those who compose it.

We see therefore that the Framers were acutely conscious that the bicameral requirement and the Presentment Clauses would serve essential constitutional functions. The President's participation in the legislative process was to protect the Executive Branch from Congress and to protect the whole people from improvident laws. The division of the Congress into two distinctive bodies assures that the legislative power would be exercised only after opportunity for full study and debate in separate settings. The President's unilateral veto power, in turn, was limited by the power of two-thirds of both Houses of Congress to overrule a veto, thereby precluding final arbitrary action of one person. It emerges clearly that the prescription for legislative action in Art. I, §§ 1, 7, represents the Framers' decision that the legislative power of the Federal Government be exercised in accord with a single, finely wrought and exhaustively considered, procedure.

The Constitution sought to divide the delegated powers of the new Federal Government into three defined categories, Legislative, Executive, and Judicial, to assure, as nearly as possible, that each branch of government would confine itself to its assigned responsibility. The hydraulic pressure inherent within each of the separate Branches to exceed the outer limits of its power, even to accomplish desirable objectives, must be resisted.

Although not "hermetically" sealed from one another, the powers delegated to the three Branches are functionally identifiable. When any Branch acts, it is presumptively exercising the power the Constitution has delegated to it. When the Executive acts, he presumptively acts in an executive or administrative capacity as defined in Art. II. And when, as here, one House of Congress purports to act, it is presumptively acting within its assigned sphere.

Beginning with this presumption, we must nevertheless establish that the challenged action under § 244(c)(2) is of the kind to which the procedural requirements of Art. I, § 7, apply. Not every action taken by either House is subject to the bicameralism and presentment requirements of Art. I. Whether actions taken by either House are, in law and fact, an exercise of legislative power depends not on their form, but upon "whether they contain matter which is properly to be regarded as legislative in its character and effect."

Examination of the action taken here by one House pursuant to § 244(c)(2) reveals that it was essentially legislative in purpose and effect. In purporting to exercise power defined in Art. I, § 8, cl. 4, to "establish an uniform Rule of Naturalization," the House took action that had the purpose and effect of altering the legal rights, duties, and relations of persons, including the Attorney General, Executive Branch officials, and Chadha, all outside the Legislative Branch. . . .

The legislative character of the one-House veto in these cases is confirmed by the character of the congressional action it supplants. Neither the House of Representatives nor the Senate contends that, absent the veto provision in § 244(c)(2), either of them, or both of them acting together, could effectively require the Attorney General to deport an alien once the Attorney General, in the exercise of legislatively delegated authority, had determined the alien should remain in the United States. Without the challenged provision in § 244(c)(2), this could have been achieved, if at all, only by legislation requiring deportation. Similarly, a veto by one House of Congress . . . cannot be justified as an attempt at amending the standards set out in § 244(a)(1), or as a repeal of § 244 as applied to Chadha. Amendment and repeal of statutes, no less than enactment, must conform with Art. I

The nature of the decision implemented by the one-House veto in these cases further manifests its legislative character. After long experience with the clumsy, time-consuming private bill procedure, Congress made a deliberate choice to delegate to the Executive Branch, and specifically to the Attorney General, the authority to allow deportable aliens to remain in this country in certain specified circumstances. It is not disputed that this choice to delegate authority is precisely the kind of decision that can be implemented only in accordance with the procedures set out in Art. I. Disagreement with the Attorney General's decision on Chadha's deportation—that is, Congress' decision to deport Chadha—no less than Congress' original choice to delegate to the Attorney General the authority to make that decision, involves determinations of policy that Congress can implement in only one way; bicameral passage followed by presentment to the President. Congress must abide by its delegation of authority until that delegation is legislatively altered or revoked.

Finally, we see that when the Framers intended to authorize either House of Congress to act alone and outside of its prescribed bicameral legislative role, they narrowly and precisely defined the procedure for such action. There are four provisions in the Constitution, explicit and unambiguous, by which one House may act alone with the unreviewable force of law, not subject to the President's veto:

(a) The House of Representatives alone was given the power to initiate impeachments. Art. I, § 2, cl. 5;
(b) The Senate alone was given the power to conduct trials following impeachment on charges initiated by the House, and to convict following trial. Art. I, § 3, cl. 6;
(c) The Senate alone was given final unreviewable power to approve or to disapprove Presidential appointments. Art. II, § 2, cl. 2;
(d) The Senate alone was given unreviewable power to ratify treaties negotiated by the President. Art. II, § 2, cl. 2.

Clearly, when the Draftsmen sought to confer special powers on one House, independent of the other House, or of the President, they did so in explicit, unambiguous terms. These carefully defined exceptions from presentment and bicameralism underscore the difference between the legislative functions of Congress and other unilateral but important and binding one-House acts provided for in the Constitution. These exceptions are narrow, explicit, and separately justified; none of them authorize the action challenged here. On the contrary, they provide further support for the conclusion that congressional authority is not to be implied, and for the conclusion that the veto provided for in § 244(c)(2) is not authorized by the constitutional design of the powers of the Legislative Branch.

Since it is clear that the action by the House under § 244(c)(2) was not within any of the express constitutional exceptions authorizing one House to act alone, and equally clear that it was an exercise of legislative power, that action was subject to the standards prescribed in Art. I. . . . To accomplish what has been attempted by one House of Congress in this case requires action in conformity with the express procedures of the Constitution's prescription for legislative action: passage by a majority of both Houses and presentment to the President.

The veto authorized by § 244(c)(2) doubtless has been in many respects a convenient shortcut; the "sharing" with the Executive by Congress of its authority over aliens in this manner is, on its face, an appealing compromise. In purely practical terms, it is obviously easier for action to be taken by one House without submission to the President; but it is crystal clear from the records of the Convention, contemporaneous writings, and debates that the Framers ranked other values higher than efficiency. The records of the Convention and debates in the states preceding ratification underscore the common desire to define and limit the exercise of the newly created federal powers affecting the states and the people. There is unmistakable expression of a determination that legislation by the national Congress be a step-by-step, deliberate and deliberative process.

The choices we discern as having been made in the Constitutional Convention impose burdens on governmental processes that often seem clumsy, inefficient, even unworkable, but those hard choices were consciously made by men who had lived under a form of government that permitted arbitrary governmental acts to go unchecked. There is no support in the Constitution or decisions of this Court for the proposition that the cumbersomeness and delays often encountered in complying with explicit constitutional standards may be avoided, either by the Congress or by the President. With all the obvious flaws of delay, untidiness, and potential for abuse, we have not yet found a better way to preserve freedom than by making the exercise of power subject to the carefully crafted restraints spelled out in the Constitution.

We hold that the congressional veto provision in § 244(c)(2) is . . . unconstitutional. Accordingly, the judgment of the Court of Appeals is affirmed.

*   *   *   *   *   *

Justice White, dissenting.

Today the Court not only invalidates § 244(c)(2) of the Immigration and Nationality Act, but also sounds the death knell for nearly 200 other statutory provisions in which Congress has reserved a "legislative veto." For this reason, the Court's decision is of surpassing importance. . . .

The prominence of the legislative veto mechanism in our contemporary political system and its importance to Congress can hardly be overstated. It has become a central means by which Congress secures the accountability of executive and independent agencies. Without the legislative veto, Congress is faced with a Hobson's choice: either to refrain from delegating the necessary authority, leaving itself with a hopeless task of writing laws with the requisite specificity to cover endless special circumstances across the entire policy landscape, or, in the alternative, to abdicate its lawmaking function to the Executive Branch and independent agencies. To choose the former leaves major national problems unresolved; to opt for the latter risks unaccountable policymaking by those not elected to fill that role. Accordingly, over the past five decades, the legislative veto has been placed in nearly 200 statutes. The device is known in every field of governmental concern: reorganization, budgets, foreign affairs, war powers, and regulation of trade, safety, energy, the environment, and the economy. . . . Perhaps there are other means of accommodation and accountability, but the increasing reliance of Congress upon the legislative veto suggests that the alternatives to which Congress must now turn are not entirely satisfactory.

The history of the legislative veto also makes clear that it has not been a sword with which Congress has struck out to aggrandize itself at the expense of the other branches—the concerns of Madison and Hamilton. Rather, the veto has been a means of defense, a reservation of ultimate authority necessary if Congress is to fulfill its designated role under Art. I as the Nation's lawmaker. While the President has often objected to particular legislative vetoes, generally those left in the hands of congressional Committees, the Executive has more often agreed to legislative review as the price for a broad delegation of authority. To be sure, the President may have preferred unrestricted power, but that could be precisely why Congress thought it essential to retain a check on the exercise of delegated authority.

The apparent sweep of the Court's decision today is regrettable. The Court's Art. I analysis appears to invalidate all legislative vetoes, irrespective of form or subject. Because the legislative veto is commonly found as a check upon rulemaking by administrative agencies and upon broad-based policy decisions of the Executive Branch, it is particularly unfortunate that the Court reaches its decision in cases involving the exercise of a veto over deportation decisions regarding particular individuals. Courts should always be wary of striking statutes as unconstitutional; to strike an entire class of statutes based on consideration of a somewhat atypical and more readily indictable exemplar of the class is irresponsible. . . .

If the legislative veto were as plainly unconstitutional as the Court strives to suggest, its broad ruling today would be more comprehensible. But the constitutionality of the legislative veto is anything but clear-cut. The issue divides scholars, courts, Attorneys General, and the two other branches of the National Government. If the veto devices so flagrantly disregarded the requirements of Art. I as the Court today suggests, I find it incomprehensible that Congress, whose Members are bound by oath to uphold the Constitution, would have placed these mechanisms in nearly 200 separate laws over a period of 50 years.

The reality of the situation is that the constitutional question posed today is one of immense difficulty over which the Executive and Legislative Branches—as well as scholars and judges—have understandably disagreed. That disagreement stems from the silence of the Constitution on the precise question: the Constitution does not directly authorize or prohibit the legislative veto. Thus, our task should be to determine whether the legislative veto is consistent with the purposes of Art. I and the principles of separation of powers that are reflected in that Article and throughout the Constitution. We should not find the lack of a specific constitutional authorization for the legislative veto surprising, and I would not infer disapproval of the mechanism from its absence. From the summer of 1787 to the present, the Government of the United States has become an endeavor far beyond the contemplation of the Framers. Only within the last half century has the complexity and size of the Federal Government's responsibilities grown so greatly that the Congress must rely on the legislative veto as the most effective, if not the only, means to insure its role as the Nation's lawmaker. But the wisdom of the Framers was to anticipate that the Nation would grow and new problems of governance would require different solutions. Accordingly, our Federal Government was intentionally chartered with the flexibility to respond to contemporary needs without losing sight of fundamental democratic principles. . . .

In my view, neither Art. I of the Constitution nor the doctrine of separation of powers is violated by this mechanism by which our elected Representatives preserve their voice in the governance of the Nation.

The Court holds that the disapproval of a suspension of deportation by the resolution of one House of Congress is an exercise of legislative power without compliance with the prerequisites for lawmaking set forth in Art. I of the Constitution. Specifically, the Court maintains that the provisions of § 244(c)(2) are inconsistent with the requirement of bicameral approval, implicit in Art. I, § 1, and the requirement that all bills and resolutions that require the concurrence of both Houses be presented to the President, Art. I, § 7, cls. 2 and 3.

I do not dispute the Court's truismatic exposition of these Clauses.

It does not, however, answer the constitutional question before us. The power to exercise a legislative veto is not the power to write new law without bicameral approval or Presidential consideration. The veto must be authorized by statute, and may only negative what an Executive department or independent agency has proposed. On its face, the legislative veto no more allows one House of Congress to make law than does the Presidential veto confer such power upon the President.

When the Convention . . . turn[ed] its attention to the scope of Congress' lawmaking power, the Framers were expansive. The Necessary and Proper Clause, Art. I, § 8, cl. 18, vests Congress with the power "to make all Laws which shall be necessary and proper for carrying into Execution the foregoing Powers [the enumerated powers of § 8] and all other Powers vested by this Constitution in the Government of the United States, or in any Department or Officer thereof." It is long settled that Congress may "exercise its best judgment in the selection of measures, to carry into execution the constitutional powers of the government," and "avail itself of experience, to exercise its reason, and to accommodate its legislation to circumstances." *McCulloch v. Maryland* (1819).

The Court heeded this counsel in approving the modern administrative state. The Court's holding today that all legislative-type action must be enacted through the lawmaking process ignores that legislative authority is routinely delegated to the Executive Branch, to the independent regulatory agencies, and to private individuals and groups.

The rise of administrative bodies probably has been the most significant legal trend of the last century. . . . They have become a veritable fourth branch of the Government, which has deranged our three-branch legal theories. . . . This Court's decisions sanctioning such delegations make clear that Art. I does not require all action with the effect of legislation to be passed as a law. Theoretically, agencies and officials were asked only to "fill up the details," and the rule was that "Congress cannot delegate any part of its legislative power except under the limitation of a prescribed standard." In practice, however, restrictions on the scope of the power that could be delegated diminished and all but disappeared. In only two instances did the Court find an unconstitutional delegation: *Panama Refining Co. v. Ryan* (1935); *Schechter Poultry Corp. v. United States* (1935). In other cases, the "intelligible principle" through which agencies have attained enormous control over the economic affairs of the country was held to include such formulations as "just and reasonable," "public interest," "public convenience, interest, or necessity," and "unfair methods of competition."

The wisdom and the constitutionality of these broad delegations are matters that still have not been put to rest. But for present purposes, these cases establish that, by virtue of congressional delegation, legislative power can be exercised by independent agencies and Executive departments without the passage of new legislation. For some time, the sheer amount of law—the substantive rules that regulate private conduct and direct the operation of government—made by the agencies has far outnumbered the lawmaking engaged in by Congress through the traditional process. There is no question but that agency rulemaking is lawmaking in any functional or realistic sense of the term. The Administrative Procedure Act provides that a "rule" is an agency statement "designed to implement, interpret, or prescribe law or policy." When agencies are authorized to prescribe law through substantive rulemaking, the administrator's regulation is not only due deference, but is accorded "legislative effect." These regulations bind courts and officers of the Federal Government, may preempt state law, and grant rights to and impose obligations on the public. In sum, they have the force of law.

If Congress may delegate lawmaking power to independent and Executive agencies, it is most difficult to understand Art. I as prohibiting Congress from also reserving a check on legislative power for itself. Absent the veto, the agencies receiving delegations of legislative or quasi-legislative power may issue regulations having the force of law without bicameral approval and without the President's signature. It is thus not apparent why the reservation of a veto over the exercise of that legislative power must be subject to a more exacting test. In both cases, it is enough that the initial statutory authorizations comply with the Art. I requirements. . . .

I do not suggest that all legislative vetoes are necessarily consistent with separation of powers principles. A legislative check on an inherently executive function, for example, that of initiating prosecutions, poses an entirely different question. But the legislative veto device here—and in many other settings—is far from an instance of legislative tyranny over the Executive. It is a necessary check on the unavoidably expanding power of the agencies, both Executive and independent, as they engage in exercising authority delegated by Congress.

I regret that I am in disagreement with my colleagues on the fundamental questions that these cases present. But even more I regret the destructive scope of the Court's holding. It reflects a profoundly different conception of the Constitution than that held by the courts that sanctioned the modern administrative state. Today's decision strikes down in one fell swoop provisions in more laws enacted by Congress than the Court has cumulatively invalidated in its history. I fear it will now be more difficult to "insur[e] that the fundamental policy decisions in our society will be made not by an appointed official, but by the body immediately responsible to the people." I must dissent.

* * * * * *

POSTSCRIPT

In 1984, Chief Justice Warren Burger publicly proclaimed that *Chadha* was "certainly . . . one of the fifty most important" Supreme Court cases in the nation's history. Indeed it might be counted in the top ten, Burger revealed. Many disappointed members of Congress agreed, believing that the Court had dealt a lethal blow to the legislature's ability to oversee the executive branch. Certainly the Court's ruling had a profound effect on the life of Jagdish Rai Chadha, who was finally able to become a permanent resident of the United States. But how much did the ruling change the legislative process and the balance of power between the executive and the legislature?

According to Louis Fisher, the answer is: Not a lot. Even after the Court's ruling, Congress continued to insert legislative vetoes into bills and presidents continued to sign them. By Fisher's count, well over five hundred legislative vetoes have been signed into law since the Court's ruling a quarter century ago—not that Congress did not make adjustments in order to comply with *Chadha*. For instance, Congress amended the executive reorganization statute so that, rather than empowering one house of Congress to veto an executive reorganization plan, now a joint resolution of approval was required for a reorganization plan to take effect. Although the Court's ruling was widely seen as a rebuke of legislative encroachments on executive power, the revised reorganization plan actually made it easier rather than more difficult for Congress to thwart executive reorganization plans.

Most of the new legislative vetoes that have been passed since *Chadha* require executive agencies to obtain committee approval, frequently from appropriations committees. Presidents have periodically used signing statements to express their disapproval of these legislative veto provisions. In 1984, for instance, Ronald Reagan signed a housing appropriations bill that included seven provisions requiring agencies to gain committee approval before proceeding. In a signing statement, Reagan promised to implement the legislation "in a manner consistent with the *Chadha* decision"—executive agencies, in other words, would not be legally bound to obtain the committee's approval; notification would suffice. The House Appropriations Committee responded by threatening to remove not only the legislative veto provisions but also the agencies' administrative discretion. Faced with the prospect of being placed on an even tighter legislative leash, the affected agencies negotiated an informal agreement in which they pledged to honor the committee's vetoes.

Although presidents may rattle the sword, threatening to ignore legislative vetoes, executive agencies are generally compelled to find ways to reach an accommodation with the congressional committees that oversee their programs and control their purse. Open defiance of a legislative veto only invites Congress to draw the reins in tighter. What the Court's opinion failed to take adequately into account is that both the executive and the legislature benefited from the legislative veto: the executive gained flexibility and discretion that Congress would not otherwise have granted, and the legislature retained control over administrative discretion without having to pass additional laws. Perhaps it is not surprising then that the Court's pronouncement could not eradicate a practice that the other two branches found so useful.

7

Clinton v. City of New York (1998)

In December 1873, President Ulysses S. Grant submitted his annual message to Congress (what we call today the State of the Union Address), suggesting that Congress consider a constitutional amendment that would "authorize the Executive to approve of so much of any measure passing the two Houses of Congress as his judgment may dictate, without approving the whole, the disapproved portion or portions to be subject to the same rules as now." Empowered to approve some parts of a bill while negating others, the president would be able to "protect the public against the many abuses and waste of public moneys which creep into appropriation bills and other important measures." Armed with such power the president could ensure that the nation's budget would be balanced and its money well spent.

Congress paid no heed to Grant's recommendation. But presidents kept asking. Rutherford Hayes, Chester Arthur, and Grover Cleveland were among the presidents in the late nineteenth century who pleaded with Congress to grant them an item veto. In 1938, by which time all but nine states had endowed the governor with a line-item veto, President Franklin Roosevelt pressed Congress to give him the same sort of item veto power on appropriations bills that he had exercised while he was governor of New York. Roosevelt recognized that there was "a respectable difference of opinion" as to whether such a grant of power required a constitutional amendment, and he told members of Congress that he would leave to them the decision about whether to pursue a statutory or constitutional route. The House of Representatives obligingly passed a bill that granted FDR's wish, but the Senate refused to go along.

As the federal budget grew ever larger, the drumbeat for the item veto intensified. Congressional spending, critics maintained, was filled with waste. Appropriations bills were laden with the pet projects—what the critics derided as "pork"—of individual legislators: $250,000 for the National Cattle Congress in Waterloo, Iowa; $500,000 for the Teapot Museum in Sparta, North Carolina; $1 million for a Waterfree Urinal Conservation Initiative; $2 million to buy back the presidential yacht, the USS *Sequoia*; $50 million for an indoor rainforest in Coralville, Iowa. Armed only with the blunt instrument of the normal veto, the president was allegedly compelled to assent to spending that he and the public would otherwise reject. Give the president a precise scalpel and he could carefully carve away the wasteful spending, leaving only the meritorious and necessary portions of a lean budget. The item veto would make the appropriations process more accountable and more economical.

During the 1980s, support for the line-item veto increasingly became identified with the Republican Party. In 1984 Republicans endorsed the line-item veto in their party platform, and President Ronald Reagan pleaded for it in every State of the Union message of his second term. Frustrated at Congressional inaction, some conservative Republicans even flirted with the idea that the president had an inherent item veto authority, though President George Herbert Walker Bush eventually backed away from that radical notion. When the Republicans finally gained control of the House of Representatives in 1994, they promptly moved to fulfill their campaign promise—articulated in their "Contract with America"—to give the president a line-item veto in order "to restore fiscal responsibility to an out-of-control Congress." By a largely party-line vote of 232 to 177, the House approved the item veto, and the Senate followed suit, passing the legislation by a better than two-to-one margin. On April 9, 1996, Democratic President Bill Clinton, bucking his party, signed the bill into law, explaining that it "gives the president tools to cut wasteful spending, and, even more important, it empowers our citizens, for the exercise of this veto or even the possibility of its exercise will throw a spotlight of public scrutiny onto the darkest corners of the federal budget."

On January 2, 1997, the day after the law went into effect, six veteran legislators—four senators and two House members, all of whom were Democrats apart from the retiring Oregon senator Mark Hatfield—brought suit in federal court, arguing that the new statute violated the constitutionally prescribed lawmaking process. The district judge sided with the members of Congress, but the Supreme Court quickly reversed the ruling, holding that the members of Congress lacked standing to challenge the law since the president had not yet exercised the veto power and they had suffered no harm from the law.

The Court ruling freed President Clinton to exercise his newfound power, which he used to cancel eighty-two budgetary items in 1997. Among the canceled items was a section of the Balanced Budget Act that appropriated money for hospitals in New York City and a provision in the Taxpayer Relief Act that gave a tax break to potato farmers in Snake River, Idaho. New York City mayor Rudy Giuliani and representatives of the affected hospitals and hospital workers took the Clinton administration to court, as did representatives of the potato growers. Their cases were consolidated by a federal judge. Now that there were litigants who had suffered concrete harm, the Court was prepared to consider the case on its merits. On June 25, 1998, just two months after hearing oral arguments in the case, the Court announced its verdict.

*   *   *   *   *   *

Justice Stevens delivered the opinion of the Court.

The Line Item Veto Act gives the President the power to "cancel in whole" three types of provisions that have been signed into law: "(1) any dollar amount of discretionary budget authority; (2) any item of new direct spending; or (3) any limited tax benefit." It is undisputed that the New York case involves an "item of new direct spending" and that the Snake River case involves a "limited tax benefit" as those terms are defined in the Act. It is also undisputed that each of those provisions had been signed into law pursuant to Article I, Section 7, of the Constitution before it was canceled.

The Act requires the President to adhere to precise procedures whenever he exercises his cancellation authority. In identifying items for cancellation he must consider the legislative history, the purposes, and other relevant information about the items. He must determine, with respect to each cancellation, that it will "(i) reduce the Federal budget deficit; (ii) not impair any essential Government functions; and (iii) not harm the national interest." Moreover, he must transmit a special message to Congress notifying it of each cancellation within five calendar days (excluding Sundays) after the enactment of the canceled provision. It is undisputed that the President meticulously followed these procedures in these cases.

A cancellation takes effect upon receipt by Congress of the special message from the President. If, however, a "disapproval bill" pertaining to a special message is enacted into law, the cancellations set forth in that message become "null and void." The Act sets forth a detailed expedited procedure for the consideration of a "disapproval bill," but no such bill was passed for either of the cancellations involved in these cases.

A majority vote of both Houses is sufficient to enact a disapproval bill. The Act does not grant the President the authority to cancel a disapproval bill, but he does, of course, retain his constitutional authority to veto such a bill.

The effect of a cancellation is plainly stated in [the Line Item Veto Act], which defines the principal terms used in the Act. With respect to both an item of new direct spending and a limited tax benefit, the cancellation prevents the item "from having legal force or effect."

Thus, under the plain text of the statute, the two actions of the President that are challenged in these cases prevented one section of the Balanced Budget Act of 1997 and one section of the Taxpayer Relief Act of 1997 "from having legal force or effect." . . .

In both legal and practical effect, the President has amended two Acts of Congress by repealing a portion of each. . . . There is no provision in the Constitution that authorizes the President to enact, to amend, or to repeal statutes. Both Article I and Article II assign responsibilities to the President that directly relate to the lawmaking process, but neither addresses the issue presented by these cases. The President "shall from time to time give to the Congress Information on the State of the Union, and recommend to their Consideration such Measures as he shall judge necessary and expedient." Art. II, Section 3. Thus, he may initiate and influence legislative proposals. Moreover, after a bill has passed both Houses of Congress, but "before it become[s] a Law," it must be presented to the President. If he approves it, "he shall sign it, but if not he shall return it, with his Objections to that House in which it shall have originated, who shall enter the Objections at large on their Journal, and proceed to reconsider it." Art. I, Section 7. His "return" of a bill, which is usually described as a "veto," is subject to being overridden by a two-thirds vote in each House.

There are important differences between the President's "return" of a bill pursuant to Article I, Section 7, and the exercise of the President's cancellation authority pursuant to the Line Item Veto Act. The constitutional return takes place before the bill becomes law; the statutory cancellation occurs after the bill becomes law. The constitutional return is of the entire bill; the statutory cancellation is of only a part. Although the Constitution expressly authorizes the President to play a role in the process of enacting statutes, it is silent on the subject of unilateral Presidential action that either repeals or amends parts of duly enacted statutes.

There are powerful reasons for construing constitutional silence on this profoundly important issue as equivalent to an express prohibition. The procedures governing the enactment of statutes set forth in the text of Article I were the product of the great debates and compromises that produced the Constitution itself. Familiar historical materials provide abundant support for the conclusion that the power to enact statutes may only "be exercised in accord with a single, finely wrought and exhaustively considered, procedure." *INS v. Chadha.* Our first President understood the text of the Presentment Clause as requiring that he either "approve all the parts of a Bill, or reject it in toto." What has emerged in these cases from the President's exercise of his statutory cancellation powers, however, are truncated versions of two bills that passed both Houses of Congress. They are not the product of the "finely wrought" procedure that the Framers designed. . . .

The Item Veto Act authorizes the President himself to effect the repeal of laws, for his own policy reasons, without observing the procedures set out in Article I, Section 7. The fact that Congress intended such a result is of no moment. . . . Congress cannot alter the procedures set out in Article I, Section 7, without amending the Constitution.

Neither are we persuaded by the Government's contention that the President's authority to cancel new direct spending and tax benefit items is no greater than his traditional authority to decline to spend appropriated funds. The Government has reviewed in some detail the series of statutes in which Congress has given the Executive broad discretion over the expenditure of appropriated funds. For example, the First Congress appropriated "sum[s] not exceeding" specified amounts to be spent on various Government operations. In those statutes, as in later years, the President was given wide discretion with respect to both the amounts to be spent and how the money would be allocated among different functions. It is argued that the Line Item Veto Act merely confers comparable discretionary authority over the expenditure of appropriated funds. The critical difference between this statute and all of its predecessors, however, is that unlike any of them, this Act gives the President the unilateral power to change the text of duly enacted statutes. None of the Act's predecessors could even arguably have been construed to authorize such a change. . . .

Although they are implicit in what we have already written, the profound importance of these cases makes it appropriate to emphasize three points.

First, we express no opinion about the wisdom of the procedures authorized by the Line Item Veto Act. Many members of both major political parties who have served in the Legislative and the Executive Branches have long advocated the enactment of such procedures for the purpose of "ensur[ing] greater fiscal accountability in Washington." The text of the Act was itself the product of much debate and deliberation in both Houses of Congress and that precise text was signed into law by the President. We do not lightly conclude that their action was unauthorized by the Constitution. . . .

Second, although appellees challenge the validity of the Act on alternative grounds, the only issue we address concerns the "finely wrought" procedure commanded by the Constitution. We have been favored with extensive debate about the scope of Congress' power to delegate law-making authority, or its functional equivalent, to the President. The excellent briefs filed by the parties and their *amici curiae* have provided us with valuable historical information that illuminates the delegation issue but does not really bear on the narrow issue that is dispositive of these cases. Thus, because we conclude that the Act's cancellation provisions violate Article I, §7, of the Constitution, we find it unnecessary to consider the District Court's alternative holding that the Act "impermissibly disrupts the balance of powers among the three branches of government."

Third, our decision rests on the narrow ground that the procedures authorized by the Line Item Veto Act are not authorized by the Constitution. . . . If the Line Item Veto Act were valid, it would authorize the President to create a different law, one whose text was not voted on by either House of Congress or presented to the President for signature. Something that might be known as "Public Law 105-33 as modified by the President" may or may not be desirable, but it is surely not a document that may "become a law" pursuant to the procedures designed by the Framers of Article I, Section 7, of the Constitution.

If there is to be a new procedure in which the President will play a different role in determining the final text of what may "become a law," such change must come not by legislation but through the amendment procedures set forth in Article V of the Constitution.

*   *   *   *   *   *

Justice Breyer, dissenting.

The Line Item Veto Act does not violate any specific textual constitutional command, nor does it violate any implicit Separation of Powers principle. Consequently, I believe that the Act is constitutional.

I approach the constitutional question before us with three general considerations in mind. First, the Act represents a legislative effort to provide the President with the power to give effect to some, but not to all, of the expenditure and revenue-diminishing provisions contained in a single massive appropriations bill. And this objective is constitutionally proper.

When our Nation was founded, Congress could easily have provided the President with this kind of power. In that time period, our population was less than four million, federal employees numbered fewer than 5,000, annual federal budget outlays totaled approximately $4 million, and the entire operative text of Congress's first general appropriations law read as follows:

> Be it enacted . . . that there be appropriated for the service of the present year, to be paid out of the monies which arise, either from the requisitions heretofore

made upon the several states, or from the duties on import and tonnage, the following sums, viz. A sum not exceeding two hundred and sixteen thousand dollars for defraying the expenses of the civil list, under the late and present government; a sum not exceeding one hundred and thirty-seven thousand dollars for defraying the expenses of the department of war; a sum not exceeding one hundred and ninety thousand dollars for discharging the warrants issued by the late board of treasury, and remaining unsatisfied; and a sum not exceeding ninety-six thousand dollars for paying the pensions to invalids.

At that time, a Congress, wishing to give a President the power to select among appropriations, could simply have embodied each appropriation in a separate bill, each bill subject to a separate Presidential veto.

Today, however, our population is about 250 million, the Federal Government employs more than four million people, the annual federal budget is $1.5 trillion, and a typical budget appropriations bill may have a dozen titles, hundreds of sections, and spread across more than 500 pages of the Statutes at Large. Congress cannot divide such a bill into thousands, or tens of thousands, of separate appropriations bills, each one of which the President would have to sign, or to veto, separately. Thus, the question is whether the Constitution permits Congress to choose a particular novel means to achieve this same, constitutionally legitimate, end.

Second, the case in part requires us to focus upon the Constitution's generally phrased structural provisions, provisions that delegate all "legislative" power to Congress and vest all "executive" power in the President. The Court, when applying these provisions, has interpreted them generously in terms of the institutional arrangements that they permit.

Third, we need not here referee a dispute among the other two branches.

These three background circumstances mean that, when one measures the literal words of the Act against the Constitution's literal commands, the fact that the Act may closely resemble a different, literally unconstitutional, arrangement is beside the point. To drive exactly 65 miles per hour on an interstate highway closely resembles an act that violates the speed limit. But it does not violate that limit, for small differences matter when the question is one of literal violation of law. No more does this Act literally violate the Constitution's words. The background circumstances also mean that we are to interpret nonliteral Separation of Powers principles in light of the need for "workable government." *Youngstown Sheet and Tube Co.* (Jackson, J., concurring). If we apply those principles in light of that objective, as this Court has applied them in the past, the Act is constitutional. . . .

There are three relevant Separation of Powers questions here: (1) Has Congress given the President the wrong kind of power, i.e., "non-Executive" power? (2) Has Congress given the President the power to "encroach" upon Congress' own constitutionally reserved territory? (3) Has

Congress given the President too much power, violating the doctrine of "nondelegation?" These three limitations help assure "adequate control by the citizen's representatives in Congress." . . . And with respect to this Act, the answer to all these questions is "no."

Viewed conceptually, the power the Act conveys is the right kind of power. It is "executive"; . . . an exercise of that power "executes" the Act. Conceptually speaking, it closely resembles the kind of delegated authority—to spend or not to spend appropriations, to change or not to change tariff rates—that Congress has frequently granted the President, any differences being differences in degree, not kind. The fact that one could also characterize this kind of power as "legislative," say, if Congress itself (by amending the appropriations bill) prevented a provision from taking effect, is beside the point. This Court has frequently found that the exercise of a particular power, such as the power to make rules of broad applicability, can fall within the constitutional purview of more than one branch of Government. The Court does not "carry out the distinction between legislative and executive action with mathematical precision" or "divide the branches into watertight compartments," for, as others have said, the Constitution "blend[s]" as well as "separat[es]" powers in order to create a workable government. . . .

If there is a Separation of Powers violation, then, it must rest, not upon purely conceptual grounds, but upon some important conflict between the Act and a significant Separation of Powers objective.

The Act does not undermine what this Court has often described as the principal function of the Separation of Powers, which is to maintain the tripartite structure of the Federal Government—and thereby protect individual liberty—by providing a "safeguard against the encroachment or aggrandizement of one branch at the expense of the other." . . . One cannot say that the Act "encroaches" upon Congress' power, when Congress retained the power to insert, by simple majority, into any future appropriations bill, into any section of any such bill, or into any phrase of any section, a provision that says the Act will not apply. . . . Congress also retained the power to "disapprov[e]," and thereby reinstate, any of the President's cancellations. And it is Congress that drafts and enacts the appropriations statutes that are subject to the Act in the first place—and thereby defines the outer limits of the President's cancellation authority. . . .

Nor can one say that the Act's basic substantive objective is constitutionally improper, for the earliest Congresses could have . . . and often did, confer on the President this sort of discretionary authority over spending. And, if an individual Member of Congress, who say, favors aid to Country A but not to Country B, objects to the Act on the ground that the President may "rewrite" an appropriations law to do the opposite, one can respond, "But a majority of Congress voted that he have that power;

you may vote to exempt the relevant appropriations provision from the Act; and if you command a majority, your appropriation is safe." Where the burden of overcoming legislative inertia lies is within the power of Congress to determine by rule. Where is the encroachment?

Nor can one say the Act's grant of power "aggrandizes" the Presidential office. The grant is limited to the context of the budget. It is limited to the power to spend, or not to spend, particular appropriated items, and the power to permit, or not to permit, specific limited exemptions from generally applicable tax law from taking effect. These powers . . . resemble those the President has exercised in the past on other occasions. The delegation of those powers to the President may strengthen the Presidency, but any such change in Executive Branch authority seems minute when compared with the changes worked by delegations of other kinds of authority that the Court in the past has upheld. . . .

I recognize that the Act before us is novel. In a sense, it skirts a constitutional edge. But that edge has to do with means, not ends. The means chosen do not amount literally to the enactment, repeal, or amendment of a law. Nor, for that matter, do they amount literally to the "line item veto" that the Act's title announces. Those means do not violate any basic Separation of Powers principle. They do not improperly shift the constitutionally foreseen balance of power from Congress to the President. Nor, since they comply with Separation of Powers principles, do they threaten the liberties of individual citizens. They represent an experiment that may, or may not, help representative government work better. The Constitution, in my view, authorizes Congress and the President to try novel methods in this way. Consequently, with respect, I dissent.

*   *   *   *   *   *

Justice Scalia, dissenting.

The crux of the matter [is] whether Congress's authorizing the President to cancel an item of spending gives him a power that our history and traditions show must reside exclusively in the Legislative Branch. I may note, to begin with, that the Line Item Veto Act is not the first statute to authorize the President to "cancel" spending items. In *Bowsher v. Synar* (1986), we addressed the constitutionality of the Balanced Budget and Emergency Deficit Control Act of 1985, which required the President, if the federal budget deficit exceeded a certain amount, to issue a "sequestration" order mandating spending reductions specified by the Comptroller General. The effect of sequestration was that "amounts sequestered . . . shall be permanently cancelled." We held that the Act was unconstitutional, not because it impermissibly gave the Executive legislative power, but because it gave the Comptroller General, an officer of the Legislative Branch over whom Congress retained removal power, "the ultimate authority to determine the budget cuts to be made," "functions . . . plainly entailing execution of the law in constitutional terms." The President's discretion under the Line Item Veto Act is certainly broader than the Comptroller General's discretion was under the 1985 Act, but it is no broader than the discretion traditionally granted the President in his execution of spending laws.

Insofar as the degree of political, "law-making" power conferred upon the Executive is concerned, there is not a dime's worth of difference between Congress's authorizing the President to cancel a spending item, and Congress's authorizing money to be spent on a particular item at the President's discretion. And the latter has been done since the Founding of the Nation. From 1789–1791, the First Congress made lump-sum appropriations for the entire Government—"sum[s] not exceeding" specified amounts for broad purposes. From a very early date Congress also made permissive individual appropriations, leaving the decision whether to spend the money to the President's unfettered discretion. In 1803, it appropriated $50,000 for the President to build "not exceeding fifteen gun boats, to be armed, manned and fitted out, and employed for such purposes as in his opinion the public service may require.". . . Examples of appropriations committed to the discretion of the President abound in our history. During the Civil War, an Act appropriated over $76 million to be divided among various items "as the exigencies of the service may require." During the Great Depression, Congress appropriated $950 million "for such projects and/or purposes and under such rules and regulations as the President in his discretion may prescribe," and $4 billion for general classes of projects, the money to be spent "in the discretion and under the direction of the President." The constitutionality of such appropriations has never seriously been questioned. . . .

Certain Presidents have claimed Executive authority to withhold appropriated funds even absent an express conferral of discretion to do so. In 1876, for example, President Grant reported to Congress that he would not spend money appropriated for certain harbor and river improvements, because "under no circumstances [would he] allow expenditures upon works not clearly national," and in his view, the appropriations were for "works of purely private or local interest, in no sense national." President Franklin D. Roosevelt impounded funds appropriated for a flood control reservoir and levee in Oklahoma. President Truman ordered the impoundment of hundreds of millions of dollars that had been appropriated for military aircraft. President Nixon, the Mahatma Ghandi [*sic*] of all impounders, asserted at a press conference in 1973 that his "constitutional right" to impound appropriated funds was "absolutely clear." Our decision two years later in *Train v. City of New York* (1975), proved him wrong, but it implicitly confirmed that Congress may confer discretion upon the executive to withhold appropriated funds, even funds appropriated for a specific purpose. The statute at issue in *Train* authorized spending "not to exceed" specified sums for certain projects, and directed that such "sums authorized to be appropriated . . . shall be allotted" by the Administrator of the Environmental Protection Agency. Upon enactment of this statute, the President directed the Administrator to allot no more than a certain part of the amount authorized. This Court held, as a matter of statutory interpretation, that the statute did not grant the Executive discretion to withhold the funds, but required allotment of the full amount authorized.

The short of the matter is this: Had the Line Item Veto Act authorized the President to "decline to spend" any item of spending contained in the Balanced Budget Act of 1997, there is not the slightest doubt that authorization would have been constitutional. What the Line Item Veto Act does instead—authorizing the President to "cancel" an item of spending—is technically different. But the technical difference does not relate to the technicalities of the Presentment Clause, which have been fully complied with; and the doctrine of unconstitutional delegation, which is at issue here, is preeminently not a doctrine of technicalities. The title of the Line Item Veto Act, which was perhaps designed to simplify for public comprehension, or perhaps merely to comply with the terms of a campaign pledge, has succeeded in faking out the Supreme Court. The President's action it authorizes in fact is not a line-item veto and thus does not offend Article I, Section 7; and insofar as the substance of that action is concerned, it is no different from what Congress has permitted the President to do since the formation of the Union.

*   *   *   *   *   *

POSTSCRIPT

The Supreme Court's verdict invalidated the item veto but hardly brought an end to the calls to endow the president with such a power. In 2006, for instance, President George W. Bush used his State of the Union Address to call upon Congress to grant him a modified line-item veto. Such legislation, Bush argued, was necessary to enable him to "control unjustified and wasteful spending in the Federal budget." Bush insisted that his version of the item veto would pass constitutional muster because it provided "a fast-track procedure" that required Congress "to vote up or down on rescissions proposed by the President." If Congress voted to keep the spending item then it became law. In contrast, under the 1996 item veto Congress had to pass a "disapproval" bill to restore a canceled provision and that bill was subject to a presidential veto, which required the usual two-thirds vote in both houses to override.

On a largely party line vote (35 Democrats and 212 Republicans voted for the measure), the House of Representatives passed the Legislative Line Item Veto Act requested by the president. In the Senate, Bush found an unlikely ally in Senator John Kerry, the Democratic presidential nominee who Bush narrowly beat in 2004. Pointing to "pork barrel spending [that] has gone through the roof," Kerry urged his Senate colleagues to grant the president a line-item veto. Most of Kerry's Senate colleagues were not persuaded, however, and the bill was allowed to die.

Although the 2006 act failed, the line-item veto has enduring appeal that all but guarantees it will remain on the political agenda for the foreseeable future. In the 2008 presidential campaign, for instance, John McCain, a cosponsor of the 2006 act, bludgeoned his primary opponent Rudy Giuliani for having initiated the lawsuit that led the Court to strike down the line-item veto a decade earlier. "You can't be an economic conservative and in favor of fiscal discipline," McCain insisted, "if you oppose the line-item veto." A President McCain would almost certainly have renewed the call for a line-item veto; it remains to be seen whether President Barack Obama, who in accepting the Democratic nomination in August 2008 voted to "go through the federal budget, line by line, eliminating programs that no longer work," will ask Congress to trust him with that power.

II

WAR POWERS
AND DIPLOMACY

The "Sole Organ"
of Foreign Relations

8

United States v. Curtiss-Wright Export Corp. (1936)

In 1935, President Franklin Roosevelt and his New Deal policies were under attack from an aging, often hostile Supreme Court. Six justices were more than seventy years old, and FDR had not had the opportunity to appoint a single justice. All but two were Republican appointees, and one of the Democratic appointees was perhaps Roosevelt's most vitriolic critic, James Clark McReynolds, who was reported to have sworn that he would never quit the Court so "long as that crippled son-of-a-bitch is in the White House."

In January, the Court began its assault on the New Deal by invalidating a portion of the National Industrial Recovery Act (NIRA) of 1933 that had given the president the power to interdict trade. In an 8 to 1 vote, the Court ruled in *Panama Refining Company v. Ryan* that the legislation had failed to spell out precise criteria to govern executive actions and so the relevant section of the act involved an unconstitutional delegation of legislative power to the executive. In early May a divided Court struck down the Railroad Retirement Act of 1934, which had granted pensions to railway workers. Then on May 27, 1935, "black Monday," the Court announced three rulings, all by unanimous verdicts. First, in *Humphrey's Executor v. United States*, the Court held that the president could not remove a member of the Federal Trade Commission. Next the Court struck down the Frazier-Lemke Act, which afforded mortgage relief to struggling farmers. And, finally, and most significant for the fate of the New Deal, the

Court (in *Schechter Poultry Corp. v. United States*) gutted the heart of the NIRA, ruling that Congress had both exceeded its authority and unconstitutionally delegated power to the executive. The following year, the Court struck down three more legislative pieces of the New Deal: the Agricultural Adjustment Act, the Municipal Bankruptcy Act, and the Bituminous Coal Conservation Act, the latter of which was also decided on the grounds that Congress improperly delegated legislative power to the executive.

The Court's decisions in 1935 and 1936 propelled Roosevelt into a fury that would lead him, in February 1937, after his resounding reelection, to roll out his famed and ill-fated "court-packing" plan in which the number of Supreme Court justices would be expanded from nine to fifteen. As important, the Court's rulings, particularly those restricting Congress's power to delegate legislative power to the executive, invited aggrieved companies to challenge the legality of executive regulations and administrative rulings. One such company was Curtiss-Wright, which manufactured and sold airplanes. Initially, the company sold its planes domestically, but the Great Depression had led it to look abroad for buyers, particularly foreign governments engaged in military ventures. Among the company's best customers was the Bolivian government, which was engaged in a brutal war with Paraguay.

One hundred thousand people had died in the war and the League of Nations asked the United States to help end the fighting; Roosevelt responded by asking Congress to pass a joint resolution that would empower him to prohibit the sale of arms to Bolivia and Paraguay. Congress acted as the president had requested, and Roosevelt then ordered an embargo on the sale of weaponry to the two warring nations.[1] Curtiss-Wright, however, defied the order and tried to smuggle military equipment into the war-torn region. The company was caught and charged with violating the president's order. Curtiss-Wright's chief legal argument, relying on the Court's recent opinions in *Panama* and *Schechter*, was that the congressional resolution entailed an unconstitutional delegation of legislative power to the president. A federal district judge agreed with the company. The government appealed, insisting that the scope of allowable delegation was different in foreign policy than in domestic affairs. From the republic's earliest days, argued the government's lawyers, Congress had endowed the president with broad discretion to act in the international arena.

The Court agreed to hear the case and commenced oral arguments on November 19, 1936, just weeks after Roosevelt's resounding victory over his Republican opponent, Alf Landon. Just one month later, the Court issued its nearly unanimous verdict (the only dissenting justice was the crotchety McReynolds). The Court's opinion was penned by Justice

George Sutherland, one of the four justices—known popularly as the Four Horseman of the Apocalypse—who had consistently voted against New Deal legislation.

*   *   *   *   *   *

Mr. Justice Sutherland delivered the opinion of the Court.

The determination which we are called to make . . . is whether the Joint Resolution . . . is vulnerable to attack under the rule that forbids a delegation of the lawmaking power. In other words, assuming (but not deciding) that the challenged delegation, if it were confined to internal affairs, would be invalid, may it nevertheless be sustained on the ground that its exclusive aim is to afford a remedy for a hurtful condition within foreign territory?

It will contribute to the elucidation of the question if we first consider the differences between the powers of the federal government in respect of foreign or external affairs and those in respect of domestic or internal affairs. That there are differences between them, and that these differences are fundamental, may not be doubted.

The two classes of powers are different, both in respect of their origin and their nature. The broad statement that the federal government can exercise no powers except those specifically enumerated in the Constitution, and such implied powers as are necessary and proper to carry into effect the enumerated powers, is categorically true only in respect of our internal affairs. In that field, the primary purpose of the Constitution was to carve from the general mass of legislative powers *then possessed by the states* such portions as it was thought desirable to vest in the federal government, leaving those not included in the enumeration still in the states. That this doctrine applies only to powers that the states had is self-evident. And since the states severally never possessed international powers, such powers could not have been carved from the mass of state powers but obviously were transmitted to the United States from some other source. During the colonial period, those powers were possessed exclusively by, and were entirely under the control of, the Crown. By the Declaration of Independence, "the Representatives of the United States of America" declared the United (not the several) Colonies to be free and independent states, and, as such, to have "full Power to levy War, conclude Peace, contract Alliances, establish Commerce, and to do all other Acts and Things which Independent States may of right do."

As a result of the separation from Great Britain by the colonies, acting as a unit, the powers of external sovereignty passed from the Crown not to the colonies severally, but to the colonies in their collective and corporate capacity as the United States of America. Even before the Declaration, the colonies were a unit in foreign affairs, acting through a common agency—namely the Continental Congress, composed of delegates from the thirteen colonies. That agency exercised the powers of war and peace, raised an army, created a navy, and finally adopted the Declaration of Independence. Rulers come and go; governments end, and forms of government change; but sovereignty survives. A political society cannot endure without a supreme will somewhere. Sovereignty is never held in suspense. When, therefore, the external sovereignty of Great Britain in respect of the colonies ceased, it immediately passed to the Union. . . .

The Union existed before the Constitution, which was ordained and established, among other things, to form "a more perfect Union." Prior to that event, it is clear that the Union, declared by the Articles of Confederation to be "perpetual," was the sole possessor of external sovereignty, and in the Union it remained without change save insofar as the Constitution, in express terms, qualified its exercise. The Framers' Convention was called, and exerted its powers upon the irrefutable postulate that, though the states were several, their people, in respect of foreign affairs, were one. . . .

It results that the investment of the federal government with the powers of external sovereignty did not depend upon the affirmative grants of the Constitution. The powers to declare and wage war, to conclude peace, to make treaties, to maintain diplomatic relations with other sovereignties, if they had never been mentioned in the Constitution, would have vested in the federal government as necessary concomitants of nationality. . . . As a member of the family of nations, the right and power of the United States in that field are equal to the right and power of the other members of the international family. Otherwise, the United States is not completely sovereign. The power to acquire territory by discovery and occupation, the power to expel undesirable aliens, the power to make such international agreements as do not constitute treaties in the constitutional sense, none of which is expressly affirmed by the Constitution, nevertheless exist as inherently inseparable from the conception of nationality. . . .

Not only, as we have shown, is the federal power over external affairs in origin and essential character different from that over internal affairs, but participation in the exercise of the power is significantly limited. In this vast external realm, with its important, complicated, delicate and manifold problems, the President alone has the power to speak or listen as a representative of the nation. He makes treaties with the advice and consent of the Senate; but he alone negotiates. Into the field of negotiation the Senate cannot intrude; and Congress itself is powerless to invade it. As Marshall said in his great argument of March 7, 1800, in the House of Representatives, "The President is the sole organ of the nation in its external relations, and its sole representative with foreign nations." The Senate Committee on Foreign Relations at a very early day in our history (February 15, 1816), reported to the Senate, among other things, as follows:

The President is the constitutional representative of the United States with regard to foreign nations. He manages our concerns with foreign nations and must necessarily be most competent to determine when, how, and upon what subjects negotiation may be urged with the greatest prospect of success. For his conduct he is responsible to the Constitution. The committee considers this responsibility the surest pledge for the faithful discharge of his duty. They think the interference of the Senate in the direction of foreign negotiations [is] calculated to diminish that responsibility and thereby to impair the best security for the national safety. The nature of transactions with foreign nations moreover, requires caution and unity of design, and their success frequently depends on secrecy and dispatch.

It is important to bear in mind that we are here dealing not alone with an authority vested in the President by an exertion of legislative power, but with such an authority plus the very delicate, plenary and exclusive power of the President as the sole organ of the federal government in the field of international relations—a power which does not require as a basis for its exercise an act of Congress, but which, of course, like every other governmental power, must be exercised in subordination to the applicable provisions of the Constitution. It is quite apparent that if, in the maintenance of our international relations, embarrassment—perhaps serious embarrassment—is to be avoided and success for our aims achieved, congressional legislation which is to be made effective through negotiation and inquiry within the international field must often accord to the President a degree of discretion and freedom from statutory restriction which would not be admissible were domestic affairs alone involved. Moreover, he, not Congress, has the better opportunity of knowing the conditions that prevail in foreign countries, and especially is this true in time of war. He has his confidential sources of information. He has his agents in the form of diplomatic, consular and other officials. Secrecy in respect of information gathered by them may be highly necessary, and the premature disclosure of it productive of harmful results. Indeed, so clearly is this true that the first President refused to accede to a request to lay before the House of Representatives the instructions, correspondence and documents relating to the negotiation of the Jay Treaty—a refusal the wisdom of which was recognized by the House itself and has never since been doubted. In his reply to the request, President Washington said:

> The nature of foreign negotiations requires caution, and their success must often depend on secrecy; and even when brought to a conclusion a full disclosure of all the measures, demands, or eventual concessions which may have been proposed or contemplated would be extremely impolitic; for this might have a pernicious influence on future negotiations, or produce immediate inconveniences, perhaps danger and mischief, in relation to other powers. The necessity of such caution and secrecy was one cogent reason for vesting the

power of making treaties in the President, with the advice and consent of the
Senate, the principle on which that body was formed confining it to a small
number of members. To admit, then, a right in the House of Representatives
to demand and to have as a matter of course all the papers respecting a negotiation with a foreign power would be to establish a dangerous precedent.

The marked difference between foreign affairs and domestic affairs in
this respect is recognized by both houses of Congress in the very form of
their requisitions for information from the executive departments. In the
case of every department except the Department of State, the resolution
directs the official to furnish the information. In the case of the State Department, dealing with foreign affairs, the President is requested to furnish the information "if not incompatible with the public interest." A
statement that to furnish the information is not compatible with the public interest rarely, if ever, is questioned.

When the President is to be authorized by legislation to act in respect of
a matter intended to affect a situation in foreign territory, the legislator
properly bears in mind the important consideration that the form of the
President's action—or, indeed, whether he shall act at all—may well depend, among other things, upon the nature of the confidential information which he has or may thereafter receive, or upon the effect which his
action may have upon our foreign relations. This consideration, in connection with what we have already said on the subject discloses the un-
wisdom of requiring Congress in this field of governmental power to lay
down narrowly definite standards by which the President is to be governed. . . .

In the light of the foregoing observations, it is evident that this court
should not be in haste to apply a general rule that will have the effect of
condemning legislation like that under review as constituting an unlawful delegation of legislative power. The principles which justify such legislation find overwhelming support in the unbroken legislative practice
which has prevailed almost from the inception of the national government to the present day. . . .

Practically every volume of the United States Statutes contains one or
more acts or joint resolutions of Congress authorizing action by the President in respect of subjects affecting foreign relations, which either leave
the exercise of the power to his unrestricted judgment, or provide a standard far more general than that which has always been considered requisite with regard to domestic affairs. . . .

The result of holding that the joint resolution here under attack is void
and unenforceable as constituting an unlawful delegation of legislative
power would be to stamp this multitude of comparable acts and resolutions as likewise invalid. And while this court may not, and should not,

hesitate to declare acts of Congress, however many times repeated, to be unconstitutional if beyond all rational doubt it finds them to be so, an impressive array of legislation such as we have just set forth, enacted by nearly every Congress from the beginning of our national existence to the present day, must be given unusual weight in the process of reaching a correct determination of the problem. A legislative practice such as we have here, evidenced not by only occasional instances, but marked by the movement of a steady stream for a century and a half of time, goes a long way in the direction of proving the presence of unassailable ground for the constitutionality of the practice, to be found in the origin and history of the power involved, or in its nature, or in both combined. . . .

The uniform, long-continued and undisputed legislative practice just disclosed rests upon an admissible view of the Constitution which, even if the practice found far less support in principle than we think it does, we should not feel at liberty at this late day to disturb. . . .

It is enough to summarize by saying that, both upon principle and in accordance with precedent, we conclude there is sufficient warrant for the broad discretion vested in the President to determine whether the enforcement of the statute will have a beneficial effect upon the reestablishment of peace in the affected countries; whether he shall make proclamation to bring the resolution into operation; whether and when the resolution shall cease to operate and to make proclamation accordingly, and to prescribe limitations and exceptions to which the enforcement of the resolution shall be subject. . . .

*   *   *   *   *   *

POSTSCRIPT

The Court's emphatic ruling did not bring a halt to the legal wrangling, which ended only after the Curtiss-Wright Corporation agreed to plead guilty in February 1940. With the nations of Europe gearing up for war, the economic outlook for Curtiss-Wright looked bright—the company had sold $150 million in military aircraft and engines in 1938—and its executives wisely decided that getting off of the front page would be good for business. No executive went to jail for the illegal arms sales, though the company was fined more than $250,000.

The fate of the Curtiss-Wright Corporation is a forgotten footnote in one of the twentieth century's most sweeping and consequential judicial rulings. Ever since, executive branch officials have pointed to Sutherland's opinion in *Curtiss-Wright* to justify claims that the president, as the "sole organ of the federal government in the field of international relations," possesses an inherent power to act in the realm of foreign affairs even when congressional authorization is absent. In 1987, for instance, several members of the Reagan administration testified to Congress that the executive's clandestine efforts to sell arms to Iran and use the proceeds to fund insurgents in Nicaragua were justified by the landmark case of *Curtiss-Wright*. Those who oppose this expansive reading of inherent presidential power, including the congressional committee that issued the Iran-Contra Report, counter that policy-making powers in foreign affairs, as in the domestic arena, are properly shared by the president and Congress. The continuing debate vindicates Edward Corwin's famous observation that the Constitution is "an invitation to struggle for the privilege of directing American foreign policy." It is a political contest that the Supreme Court has generally been reluctant to referee.

NOTE

1. The resolution declared that "if the President finds that the prohibition of the sale of arms and munitions of war in the United States to those countries now engaged in armed conflict in the Chaco may contribute to the reestablishment of peace between those countries, and if after consultation with the governments of other American Republics and with their cooperation, as well as that of such other governments as he may deem necessary, he makes proclamation to that effect, it shall be unlawful to sell, except under such limitations and exceptions as the President prescribes, any arms or munitions of war in any place in the United States to the countries now engaged in that armed conflict, or to any person, company, or association acting in the interest of either country, until otherwise ordered by the President or by Congress."

Wartime and Emergency Powers
The Civil War

9

The Prize Cases (1863)

O n April 12, 1861, Confederate troops commenced the shelling of Fort Sumter in South Carolina. Federal troops inside the fort held out for two days before surrendering. The following day, five weeks after taking the oath of office, President Abraham Lincoln issued a proclamation directing the states to provide 75,000 troops "in order to suppress" the rebellion and "to cause the laws to be duly executed." He also directed Congress to convene a special legislative session, beginning on July 4, "to consider such measures, as in their wisdom, the public safety, and interest may seem to demand." Four days later Lincoln issued a second proclamation, setting up a blockade of southern ports. Any vessel leaving or entering a southern port could be seized and the ship and cargo treated as a prize of war.

A number of trading ships were promptly snared in the blockade's web. Understandably, owners of the seized ships and confiscated cargo were none too pleased, and several took their grievances to court. The owners of the captured ships argued that they were either ignorant of the blockade or had not been given sufficient notice of it. But the larger constitutional question that they raised was whether the United States could lawfully impose a blockade without a congressional action authorizing an act of war. To be sure, on July 13, 1861, Congress had enacted legislation "approving, legalizing, and making valid all acts, proclamations, and orders of the President . . . as if they had been issued and done under the previous express authority and direction of the Congress of the United States," but was this sufficient to make legal the blockade of the spring and early summer?

In calling out the militia and declaring the blockade, Lincoln had carefully avoided the language of war. He called out the militia because "combinations too powerful to be suppressed by the ordinary course of judicial proceedings" had made it impossible for him to execute the laws. The blockade had been made necessary, he explained, because of "a combination of persons engaged in [an] insurrection against the Government of the United States." Indeed Lincoln never acknowledged that the United States was engaged in a war against another government. The Southern states, in Lincoln's view, had never left the Union. The conflict was defined as a rebellion by individuals against the government, not a war between governments.

The naval blockade, however, belied the legal fiction to which Lincoln clung. It made no legal sense, as several of his cabinet members pointed out, for a government to blockade its own ports. Better, they advised, to close the ports since under international law a blockade signaled a state of war. When confronted with the contradiction by Thaddeus Stevens, the powerful chairman of the House Ways and Means Committee, Lincoln slyly played possum: "I don't know anything about the law of nations," he professed. The truth was that Lincoln fully understood the conceptual problem, but he believed that the blockade was a far more practical and effective means of strangling the Southern economy while avoiding conflict with European governments.

Although Congress had placed its stamp of approval on the blockade in July 1861, it remained unclear what the courts would do. Four different challenges to the government's actions made their way to the Supreme Court, which heard them all together in February 1863. The outcome was by no means certain. The court's eighty-six-year-old chief justice, Roger Taney, was the architect of the infamous *Dred Scott* ruling that not only denied blacks were citizens but denied Congress had the power to place restrictions on the spread of slavery. Five of the justices (John Catron, Samuel Nelson, Robert Cooper Grier, James Wayne, and Taney) who were still on the Court had sided against Dred Scott, and the court had since added a James Buchanan appointee (Nathan Clifford) who was widely regarded as proslavery and a Southern sympathizer. On the other hand, Lincoln had the benefit of having been able to appoint three of the Court's justices: Noah Swayne, Samuel Miller, and David Davis.

On March 10, 1863, a month after hearing oral arguments on the *Prize Cases*, the Court announced its decision. Writing for a 5–4 majority, which included the three Lincoln appointees, was Justice Grier, a Polk appointee who had been the lone Northern justice to side with the majority in *Dred Scott*.

*   *   *   *   *   *

Mr. Justice Grier delivered the opinion of the court.

Had the President a right to institute a blockade of ports in possession of persons in armed rebellion against the Government, on the principles of international law, as known and acknowledged among civilized States? . . .

That a blockade *de facto* actually existed, and was formally declared and notified by the President on the 27th and 30th of April, 1861, is an admitted fact in these cases. That the President, as the Executive Chief of the Government and Commander-in-chief of the Army and Navy, was the proper person to make such notification has not been, and cannot be disputed.

The right of prize and capture has its origin in the *"jus belli,"* and is governed and adjudged under the law of nations. To legitimate the capture of a neutral vessel or property on the high seas, a war must exist *de facto*, and the neutral must have knowledge or notice of the intention of one of the parties belligerent to use this mode of coercion against a port, city, or territory, in possession of the other.

Let us enquire whether, at the time this blockade was instituted, a state of war existed which would justify a resort to these means of subduing the hostile force. War has been well defined to be, "That state in which a nation prosecutes its right by force." The parties belligerent in a public war are independent nations. But it is not necessary, to constitute war, that both parties should be acknowledged as independent nations or sovereign States. A war may exist where one of the belligerents claims sovereign rights as against the other.

Insurrection against a government may or may not culminate in an organized rebellion, but a civil war always begins by insurrection against the lawful authority of the Government. A civil war is never solemnly declared; it becomes such by its accidents—the number, power, and organization of the persons who originate and carry it on. When the party in rebellion occupy and hold in a hostile manner a certain portion of territory, have declared their independence, have cast off their allegiance, have organized armies, have commenced hostilities against their former sovereign, the world acknowledges them as belligerents, and the contest a war. They claim to be in arms to establish their liberty and independence, in order to become a sovereign State, while the sovereign party treats them as insurgents and rebels who owe allegiance, and who should be punished with death for their treason.

The laws of war, as established among nations, have their foundation in reason, and all tend to mitigate the cruelties and misery produced by the scourge of war. Hence the parties to a civil war usually concede to each other belligerent rights. They exchange prisoners, and adopt the other courtesies and rules common to public or national wars.

As a civil war is never publicly proclaimed, *eo nomine*, against insurgents, its actual existence is a fact in our domestic history which the Court is bound to notice and to know.

The true test of its existence, as found in the writings of the sages of the common law, may be thus summarily stated: "When the regular course of justice is interrupted by revolt, rebellion, or insurrection, so that the Courts of Justice cannot be kept open, *civil war exists,* and hostilities may be prosecuted on the same footing as if those opposing the Government were foreign enemies invading the land."

By the Constitution, Congress alone has the power to declare a national or foreign war. It cannot declare war against a State, or any number of States, by virtue of any clause in the Constitution. The Constitution confers on the President the whole Executive power. He is bound to take care that the laws be faithfully executed. He is Commander-in-chief of the Army and Navy of the United States, and of the militia of the several States when called into the actual service of the United States. He has no power to initiate or declare a war either against a foreign nation or a domestic State. But, by the Acts of Congress of February 28th, 1795, and 3d of March, 1807, he is authorized to call out the militia and use the military and naval forces of the United States in case of invasion by foreign nations and to suppress insurrection against the government of a State or of the United States.

If a war be made by invasion of a foreign nation, the President is not only authorized but bound to resist force by force. He does not initiate the war, but is bound to accept the challenge without waiting for any special legislative authority. And whether the hostile party be a foreign invader or States organized in rebellion, it is nonetheless a war although the declaration of it be "unilateral." . . .

It is not the less a civil war, with belligerent parties in hostile array, because it may be called an "insurrection" by one side, and the insurgents be considered as rebels or traitors. It is not necessary that the independence of the revolted province or State be acknowledged in order to constitute it a party belligerent in a war according to the law of nations. Foreign nations acknowledge it as war by a declaration of neutrality. The condition of neutrality cannot exist unless there be two belligerent parties. . . .

The law of nations is also called the law of nature; it is founded on the common consent, as well as the common sense, of the world. It contains no such anomalous doctrine as that which this Court are now for the first time desired to pronounce, to-wit, that insurgents who have risen in rebellion against their sovereign, expelled her Courts, established a revolutionary government, organized armies, and commenced hostilities are not enemies because they are traitors, and a war levied on the Government by traitors, in order to dismember and destroy it, is not a war because it is an "insurrection."

Whether the President, in fulfilling his duties as Commander-in-chief in suppressing an insurrection, has met with such armed hostile resistance and a civil war of such alarming proportions as will compel him to accord to them the character of belligerents is a question to be decided by him, and this Court must be governed by the decisions and acts of the political department of the Government to which this power was entrusted. . . . The proclamation of blockade is itself official and conclusive evidence to the Court that a state of war existed which demanded and authorized a recourse to such a measure. . . .

Therefore, we are of the opinion that the President had a right, *jure belli,* to institute a blockade of ports in possession of the States in rebellion, which neutrals are bound to regard.

* * * * * *

Mr. Justice Nelson, dissenting.

In the case of a rebellion or resistance of a portion of the people of a country against the established government, there is no doubt . . . the government . . . may . . . recognize or declare the existence of a state of civil war, which will draw after it all the consequences and rights of war between the contending parties as in the case of a public war. . . . It is not to be denied, therefore, that if a civil war existed between that portion of the people in organized insurrection to overthrow this Government at the time this vessel and cargo were seized, and if she was guilty of a violation of the blockade, she would be lawful prize of war. But before this insurrection against the established Government can be dealt with on the footing of a civil war, within the meaning of the law of nations and the Constitution of the United States, and which will draw after it belligerent rights, it must be recognized or declared by the war-making power of the Government. No power short of this can change the legal status of the Government or the relations of its citizens from that of peace to a state of war, or bring into existence all those duties and obligations of neutral third parties growing out of a state of war. The war power of the Government must be exercised before this changed condition of the Government and people and of neutral third parties can be admitted. There is no difference in this respect between a civil or a public war. . . .

An idea seemed to be entertained that all that was necessary to constitute a war was organized hostility in the district of [the] country in a state of rebellion—that conflicts on land and on sea, the taking of towns and capture of fleets—in fine, the magnitude and dimensions of the resistance against the Government—constituted war with all the belligerent rights belonging to civil war. With a view to enforce this idea, we had, during the argument, an imposing historical detail of the several measures adopted by the Confederate States to enable them to resist the authority of the general Government, and of many bold and daring acts of resistance and of conflict. It was said that war was to be ascertained by looking at the armies and navies or public force of the contending parties, and the battles lost and won—that, in the language of one of the learned counsel, "Whenever the situation of opposing hostilities has assumed the proportions and pursued the methods of war, then peace is driven out, the ordinary authority and administration of law are suspended, and war in fact and by necessity is the status of the nation until peace is restored and the laws resumed their dominion."

Now, in one sense, no doubt this is war, and may be a war of the most extensive and threatening dimensions and effects, but it is a statement simply of its existence in a material sense, and has no relevancy or weight when the question is what constitutes war in a legal sense, in the sense of the law of nations, and of the Constitution of the United States. For it must be a war in this sense to attach to it all the consequences that belong to belligerent rights. Instead, therefore, of inquiring after armies and navies, and victories lost and won, or organized rebellion against the general Government, the inquiry should be into the law of nations and into the . . . fundamental laws of the Government. For we find there that to constitute a civil war in the sense in which we are speaking, before it can exist in contemplation of law, it must be recognized or declared by the sovereign power of the State, and which sovereign power by our Constitution is lodged in the Congress of the United States—civil war, therefore, under our system of government, can exist only by an act of Congress, which requires the assent of two of the great departments of the Government, the Executive and Legislative.

We have thus far been speaking of the war power under the Constitution of the United States, and as known and recognized by the law of nations. But we are asked, what would become of the peace and integrity of the Union in case of an insurrection at home or invasion from abroad if this power could not be exercised by the President in the recess of Congress, and until that body could be assembled?

The framers of the Constitution fully comprehended this question, and provided for the contingency. Indeed, it would have been surprising if they had not, as a rebellion had occurred in the State of Massachusetts while the Convention was in session, and which had become so general that it was quelled only by calling upon the military power of the State. The Constitution declares that Congress shall have power "to provide for calling forth the militia to execute the laws of the Union, suppress insurrections, and repel invasions." Another clause, "that the President shall be Commander-in-chief of the Army and Navy of the United States, and of the militia of the several States when called into the actual service of United States"; and, again, "He shall take care that the laws shall be faithfully executed."

Congress passed laws on this subject in 1792 and 1795. The [1795] Act provided that whenever the United States shall be invaded or be in imminent danger of invasion from a foreign nation, it shall be lawful for the President to call forth such number of the militia most convenient to the place of danger, and, in case of insurrection in any State against the Government thereof, it shall be lawful for the President, on the application of the Legislature of such State, if in session, or if not, of the Executive of the State, to call forth such number of militia of any other State or States as he may judge sufficient to suppress such insurrection.

The 2d section provides that when the laws of the United States shall be opposed, or the execution obstructed in any State by combinations too powerful to be suppressed by the course of judicial proceedings, it shall be lawful for the President to call forth the militia of such State, or of any other State or States as may be necessary to suppress such combinations; and by the Act [of] 1807 it is provided that, in case of insurrection or obstruction of the laws, either in the United States or of any State of Territory, where it is lawful for the President to call forth the militia for the purpose of suppressing such insurrection, and causing the laws to be executed, it shall be lawful to employ for the same purpose such part of the land and naval forces of the United States as shall be judged necessary.

It will be seen, therefore, that ample provision has been made under the Constitution and laws against any sudden and unexpected disturbance of the public peace from insurrection at home or invasion from abroad. The whole military and naval power of the country is put under the control of the President to meet the emergency. He may call out a force in proportion to its necessities, one regiment or fifty, one ship-of-war or any number at his discretion. If, like the insurrection in the State of Pennsylvania in 1793, the disturbance is confined to a small district of country, a few regiments of the militia may be sufficient to suppress it. If of the dimension of the present, when it first broke out, a much larger force would be required. But whatever its numbers, whether great or small, that may be required, ample provision is here made, and whether great or small, the nature of the power is the same. It is the exercise of a power under the municipal laws of the country and not under the law of nations, and, as we see, furnishes the most ample means of repelling attacks from abroad or suppressing disturbances at home until the assembling of Congress, who can, if it be deemed necessary, bring into operation the war power, and thus change the nature and character of the contest. Then, instead of being carried on under the municipal law of 1795, it would be under the law of nations, and the Acts of Congress as war measures with all the rights of war. . . .

In the breaking out of a rebellion against the established Government, the usage in all civilized countries, in its first stages, is to suppress it by confining the public forces and the operations of the Government against those in rebellion, and at the same time extending encouragement and support to the loyal people with a view to their cooperation in putting down the insurgents. This course is not only the dictate of wisdom, but of justice. This was the practice of England in Monmouth's rebellion in the reign of James the Second, and in the rebellions of 1715 and 1745, by the Pretender and his son, and also in the beginning of the rebellion of the Thirteen Colonies of 1776. It is a personal war against the individuals engaged in resisting the authority of the Government. . . .

So the war carried on by the President against the insurrectionary districts in the Southern States, as in the case of the King of Great Britain in the American Revolution, was a personal war against those in rebellion, and with encouragement and support of loyal citizens with a view to their cooperation and aid in suppressing the insurgents, with this difference, as the warmaking power belonged to the King, he might have recognized or declared the war at the beginning to be a civil war, which would draw after it all the rights of a belligerent, but in the case of the President, no such power existed; the war therefore, from necessity, was a personal war until Congress assembled and acted upon this state of things. . . .

Upon the whole, after the most careful consideration of this case . . . , I am compelled to the conclusion that no civil war existed between this Government and the States in insurrection till recognized by the Act of Congress 13th of July, 1861; that the President does not possess the power under the Constitution to declare war or recognize its existence within the meaning of the law of nations, which carries with it belligerent rights, and thus change the country and all its citizens from a state of peace to a state of war; that this power belongs exclusively to the Congress of the United States, and, consequently, that the President had no power to set on foot a blockade under the law of nations, and that the capture of the vessel and cargo in this case, and in all cases before us in which the capture occurred before the 13th of July, 1861 . . . are illegal and void, and that the decrees of condemnation should be reversed, and the vessel and cargo restored.

10

Ex parte Milligan (1866)

Lambdin Milligan was, in the language of the day, a "Copperhead," a Northern Democrat who sympathized with the Confederate cause and desired an immediate end to the war against the South. A prominent and politically ambitious Indiana attorney, Milligan vigorously assailed the Lincoln administration, the draft, and the war effort. He was also active in organizing a secret society, the Order of American Knights (one of the group's passwords was Nu-oh-lac, "Calhoun" spelled backwards), which sought, according to government agents who had infiltrated the group, to foment an armed uprising. The group's leaders were also accused of plotting to free Confederate prisoners from Union jails in Indiana, Ohio, and Illinois.

In October 1864, Milligan was arrested for conspiring against the government, giving aid and comfort to the military enemies of the United States, and inciting insurrection. Although martial law had never been declared in Indiana—unlike in Missouri and Kentucky—and the regular courts were functioning normally, the government chose to try Milligan and his confederates before a military tribunal rather than prosecute him in a regular court of law. A little over two weeks after his arrest, Milligan was found guilty and sentenced to death.

Fortunately for Milligan, the date of execution was set for May 19, 1865, six weeks after Robert E. Lee surrender's at Appomattox. With the long and bloody war finally over, many pleaded for the government to show mercy to Milligan and his co-conspirators. Indiana governor Oliver Morton, a staunch Republican and the object of some of Milligan's bitterest wartime attacks, pressed the new president, Andrew Johnson, to commute Milligan's sentence. Johnson, who had serious misgivings about the use of military tribunals, agreed to commute Milligan's sentence to life imprisonment with hard labor.

Although a life of hard labor was a marked improvement over death by hanging, Milligan challenged his conviction in the courts on the grounds that military tribunals had no authority to try and sentence him in a state where civilian courts were in working order. His crimes, if crimes they were, must be tried in civilian courts. The Supreme Court agreed to hear the case and in March 1866 listened to oral arguments on the case for six days. Milligan's chances were certainly not harmed by the all-star legal team that had been assembled to argue his case, including David Dudley Field, a prominent New York lawyer and the older brother of Supreme Court justice Stephen Field; Jeremiah Black, who had served as chief justice of the Pennsylvania supreme court as well as attorney general and secretary of state in the Buchanan administration (and had missed by one vote securing a seat on the U.S. Supreme Court); and James Garfield, then a young and talented House Republican who would later become its floor leader and, in 1880, president of the United States.

Despite the legal talent at Milligan's disposal, he appeared to face an uphill struggle in getting his conviction thrown out. Five of the justices on the Court, including Chief Justice Salmon Chase, had been put there by President Lincoln, whose wartime actions were now being called into question. Only two years earlier, in February 1864, the Court had refused to review the judgment of a military commission that had found one of the nation's most prominent Copperheads, Ohio's Clement L. Vallandigham, guilty of "declaring disloyal sentiments and opinions with the object of weakening the power of the Government in its efforts to suppress an unlawful rebellion." The Court let stand a circuit judge's ruling that Vallandigham's military trial and sentence were a legitimate exercise of the president's war powers. But those opinions were issued, as was the Court's decision in the *Prize Cases*, when the outcome of the war was still in doubt. By the time the Court heard Milligan's appeal, the war had been finished for nearly a year. And what a difference that year made.

On April 3, 1866, the chief justice announced the Court's decision. The military commission did not have jurisdiction to try Milligan, and so he should be released from the military prison. A week later Milligan was freed. Nine months later the Court explained why in an opinion penned by David Davis, Lincoln's close friend and campaign manager in the 1860 election.

*   *   *   *   *   *

Mr. Justice Davis delivered the opinion of the court.

The importance of the main question . . . cannot be overstated; for it involves the very framework of the government and the fundamental principles of American liberty.

During the late wicked Rebellion, the temper of the times did not allow that calmness in deliberation and discussion so necessary to a correct conclusion of a purely judicial question. Then, considerations of safety were mingled with the exercise of power; and feelings and interests prevailed which are happily terminated. Now that the public safety is assured, this question, as well as all others, can be discussed and decided without passion or the admixture of any element not required to form a legal judgment. We approach the investigation of this case, fully sensible of the magnitude of the inquiry and the necessity of full and cautious deliberation. . . .

The controlling question in the case is this: . . . had the military commission . . . jurisdiction, legally, to try and sentence him? Milligan, not a resident of one of the rebellious states, or a prisoner of war, but a citizen of Indiana for twenty years past, and never in the military or naval service, is, while at his home, arrested by the military power of the United States, imprisoned, and, on certain criminal charges preferred against him, tried, convicted, and sentenced to be hanged by a military commission, organized under the direction of the military commander of the military district of Indiana. Had this tribunal the legal power and authority to try and punish this man?

No graver question was ever considered by this court, nor one which more nearly concerns the rights of the whole people; for it is the birthright of every American citizen when charged with crime, to be tried and punished according to law. . . . By the protection of the law human rights are secured; withdraw that protection, and they are at the mercy of wicked rulers, or the clamor of an excited people. . . .

The Constitution of the United States is a law for rulers and people, equally in war and in peace, and covers with the shield of its protection all classes of men, at all times, and under all circumstances. No doctrine, involving more pernicious consequences, was ever invented by the wit of man than that any of its provisions can be suspended during any of the great exigencies of government. Such a doctrine leads directly to anarchy or despotism, but the theory of necessity on which it is based is false; for the government, within the Constitution, has all the powers granted to it, which are necessary to preserve its existence; as has been happily proved by the result of the great effort to throw off its just authority.

Have any of the rights guaranteed by the Constitution been violated in the case of Milligan? And if so, what are they?

Every trial involves the exercise of judicial power; and from what source did the military commission that tried him derive their authority? Certainly no part of the judicial power of the country was conferred on them; because the Constitution expressly vests it "in one supreme court and such inferior courts as the Congress may from time to time ordain and establish," and it is not pretended that the commission was a court ordained and established by Congress. They cannot justify on the mandate of the President; because he is controlled by law, and has his appropriate sphere of duty, which is to execute, not to make, the laws. . . .

But it is said that the jurisdiction is complete under the "laws and usages of war." It can serve no useful purpose to inquire what those laws and usages are, whence they originated, where found, and on whom they operate; they can never be applied to citizens in states which have upheld the authority of the government, and where the courts are open and their process unobstructed. This court has judicial knowledge that in Indiana the Federal authority was always unopposed, and its courts always open to hear criminal accusations and redress grievances; and no usage of war could sanction a military trial there for any offence whatever of a citizen in civil life, in nowise connected with the military service. Congress could grant no such power; and to the honor of our national legislature be it said, it has never been provoked by the state of the country even to attempt its exercise. One of the plainest constitutional provisions was, therefore, infringed when Milligan was tried by a court not ordained and established by Congress, and not composed of judges appointed during good behavior.

Why was he not delivered to the Circuit Court of Indiana to be proceeded against according to law? No reason of necessity could be urged against it; because Congress had declared penalties against the offences charged, provided for their punishment, and directed that court to hear and determine them. And soon after this military tribunal was ended, the Circuit Court met, peacefully transacted its business, and adjourned. It needed no bayonets to protect it, and required no military aid to execute its judgments. It was held in a state, eminently distinguished for patriotism, by judges commissioned during the Rebellion, who were provided with juries, upright, intelligent, and selected by a marshal appointed by the President. The government had no right to conclude that Milligan, if guilty, would not receive in that court merited punishment; for its records disclose that it was constantly engaged in the trial of similar offences, and was never interrupted in its administration of criminal justice. . . .

Another guarantee of freedom was broken when Milligan was denied a trial by jury. The great minds of the country have differed on the correct interpretation to be given to various provisions of the Federal Constitution; and judicial decision has been often invoked to settle their true meaning; but until recently no one ever doubted that the right of trial by jury was fortified in the organic law against the power of attack. It is now assailed; but if ideas can be expressed in words, and language has any meaning, this right—one of the most valuable in a free country—is preserved to every one accused of crime who is not attached to the army, or navy, or militia in actual service. . . .

It is claimed that martial law covers with its broad mantle the proceedings of this military commission. The proposition is this: that in a time of war the commander of an armed force (if in his opinion the exigencies of the country demand it, and of which he is to judge) has the power, within the lines of his military district, to suspend all civil rights and their remedies, and subject citizens as well as soldiers to the rule of his will; and in the exercise of his lawful authority cannot be restrained, except by his superior officer or the President of the United States.

If this position is sound to the extent claimed, then when war exists, foreign or domestic, and the country is subdivided into military departments for mere convenience, the commander of one of them can, if he chooses, within his limits, on the plea of necessity, with the approval of the Executive, substitute military force for and to the exclusion of the laws, and punish all persons, as he thinks right and proper, without fixed or certain rules.

The statement of this proposition shows its importance; for, if true, republican government is a failure, and there is an end of liberty regulated by law. Martial law, established on such a basis, destroys every guarantee of the Constitution, and effectually renders the "military independent of and superior to the civil power"—the attempt to do which by the King of Great Britain was deemed by our fathers such an offence, that they assigned it to the world as one of the causes which impelled them to declare their independence. Civil liberty and this kind of martial law cannot endure together; the antagonism is irreconcilable; and, in the conflict, one or the other must perish.

This nation, as experience has proved, cannot always remain at peace, and has no right to expect that it will always have wise and humane rulers, sincerely attached to the principles of the Constitution. Wicked men, ambitious of power, with hatred of liberty and contempt of law, may fill the place once occupied by Washington and Lincoln; and if this right is conceded, and the calamities of war again befall us, the dangers to human liberty are frightful to contemplate. If our fathers had failed to provide for just such a contingency, they would have been false to the trust reposed in them. They knew—the history of the world told them—the nation they were founding, be its existence short or long, would be involved in war; how often or how long continued, human foresight could not tell; and that unlimited power, wherever lodged at such a time, was especially hazardous to freemen. For this, and other equally weighty reasons, they secured the inheritance they had fought to maintain, by incorporating in a written constitution the safeguards which time had proved were essential to its preservation. Not one of these safeguards can the President, or Congress, or the Judiciary disturb, except the one concerning the writ of habeas corpus.[1]

It is essential to the safety of every government that, in a great crisis, like the one we have just passed through, there should be a power somewhere of suspending the writ of habeas corpus. In every war, there are men of previously good character, wicked enough to counsel their fellow-citizens to resist the measures deemed necessary by a good government to sustain its just authority and overthrow its enemies; and their influence may lead to dangerous combinations. In the emergency of the times, an immediate public investigation according to law may not be possible; and yet, the peril to the country may be too imminent to suffer such persons to go at large. Unquestionably, there is then an exigency which demands that the government, if it should see fit in the exercise of a proper discretion to make arrests, should not be required to produce the persons arrested in answer to a writ of habeas corpus. The Constitution goes no further. It does not say after a writ of habeas corpus is denied a citizen, that he shall be tried otherwise than by the course of the common law; if it had intended this result, it was easy by the use of direct words to have accomplished it. The illustrious men who framed that instrument were guarding the foundations of civil liberty against the abuses of unlimited power; they were full of wisdom, and the lessons of history informed them that a trial by an established court, assisted by an impartial jury, was the only sure way of protecting the citizen against oppression and wrong. Knowing this, they limited the suspension to one great right, and left the rest to remain forever inviolable. But, it is insisted that the safety of the country in time of war demands that this broad claim for martial law shall be sustained. If this were true, it could be well said that a country, preserved at the sacrifice of all the cardinal principles of liberty, is not worth the cost of preservation.[2] Happily, it is not so. . . .

There are occasions when martial rule can be properly applied. If, in foreign invasion or civil war, the courts are actually closed, and it is impossible to administer criminal justice according to law, then, on the theatre of active military operations, where war really prevails, there is a necessity to furnish a substitute for the civil authority, thus overthrown, to preserve the safety of the army and society; and as no power is left but the military, it is allowed to govern by martial rule until the laws can have their free course. As necessity creates the rule, so it limits its duration; for, if this government is continued after the courts are reinstated, it is a gross usurpation of power. Martial rule can never exist where the courts are open, and in the proper and unobstructed exercise of their jurisdiction. . . .

*   *   *   *   *   *

POSTSCRIPT

All nine justices agreed that Milligan should be freed. But Chief Justice Salmon Chase wrote a separate opinion—signed by three other justices, including two Lincoln appointees, Noah Swayne and Samuel Miller— that rejected the broad scope of the Court's opinion. In particular, Chase disagreed with the Court that Congress lacked the power to authorize military commissions even if civil courts were operational. What made the military commissions unconstitutional was not that the civil courts were open in Indiana—a military district at the time Milligan was arrested—but that Congress had not authorized the commissions. Congress must have the power to authorize military commissions in a military district, Chase argued, because while the courts "might be open and undisturbed in the execution of their functions" they might still be "wholly incompetent to avert threatened danger, or to punish, with adequate promptitude and certainty, the guilty conspirators."

For Chase and other Republicans concerned with the postwar reconstruction of the South this was a distinction of massive importance. For even where ordinary courts were open in Southern military districts they could not always be trusted to render justice. Chase feared that President Andrew Johnson, who was at loggerheads with Congressional Republicans over reconstruction in the South, would use the *Milligan* ruling to close down the extensive system of military commissions that were employed across the South. That was why Thaddeus Stevens assailed the Court's decision in *Milligan* as "far more dangerous" to the cause of the black man than even the infamous *Dred Scott* decision, in which the Court ruled that the federal government could not prohibit slavery in the territories, that slaves were private property and could not sue in courts, and that blacks could not be considered citizens of the United States. Johnson did indeed invoke *Milligan* to justify canceling military trials in the South, just as Chase and Stevens had feared, but the president lacked the political support and acumen to achieve his objectives. The agreement he reached with the army stipulated that military trials should not be used "where justice can be attained through the medium of civil authority," language that was far closer to Chase's careful concurring opinion than to Davis's sweeping declaration that military tribunals were always unconstitutional when civil courts were open for business.

In March 1867, three months after the Court issued its opinion in *Milligan*, Congress enacted the first Reconstruction Act. Brushing aside the Court's "thunderously quotable" words, Congress authorized military commanders in Southern states to use military commissions rather than local civil courts if they deemed a military trial was necessary in order to protect persons and property, suppress an insurrection, or punish criminals. During 1867 and 1868, almost three hundred military trials were held in military districts across the South.[3] Even during the first year of the Grant administration military commissions continued to be held in the states of Texas and Mississippi, neither of which was readmitted to the Union until early in 1870.

It is one of the great historical ironies that a case that was widely seen in the 1860s as an obstacle to securing civil rights for African Americans is commonly hailed today as a monument to civil liberties, "one of the bulwarks of American liberty," in the words of the distinguished legal historian Charles Warren. And it is equally ironic that a case that is so often cited as an example of brave judicial resistance to executive power in wartime was seen by contemporaries as a politically motivated, conservative assault upon congressional power.

NOTES

1. Article 1, section 9 of the Constitution provides that "The Privilege of the Writ of Habeas Corpus shall not be suspended, unless when in Cases of Rebellion or Invasion the public Safety may require it."

2. Cf. Lincoln's justification of the suspension of habeas corpus in his message to Congress on July 4, 1861: "are all the laws, but one, to go unexecuted, and the government itself go to pieces, lest that one be violated. Even in such a case, would not the official oath be broken, if the government should be overthrown, when it was believed that disregarding the single law, would tend to preserve it."

3. In 1867, Justice David Davis explained that he never expected the Supreme Court's ruling to bring an immediate halt to military trials in the South because the Court recognized that the government possessed the power to hold military tribunals "in insurrectionary States." Although a military district at the time of Milligan's arrest and trial, Indiana was a loyal Union state, whereas the Southern states had seceded and, apart from Tennessee, had not yet been readmitted to the Union.

Wartime and Emergency Powers
World War II

11

Ex parte Quirin (1942)

Over the phone came a strong German accent. Identifying himself only as "Mr. Pastorious," the caller informed the FBI's New York office that he had just arrived from Germany via U-boat and that he was coming to the nation's capital to provide FBI director J. Edgar Hoover with information vital to America's national security. The mysterious caller was George John Dasch, who a little more than twenty-four hours earlier had been deposited—along with three confederates—near the tip of Long Island by a German submarine. His mission was to engage in industrial sabotage, particularly focused on the aluminum factories that Americans needed to produce airplanes.

The FBI thought the caller was likely a crank and took no action. Five days later, on June 19, 1942, Dasch arrived in Washington, D.C., and, true to his word, contacted the FBI, asking to speak with Hoover. After being shunted from one receptionist to another, Dasch finally got to speak with an agent—Duane Traynor—who took him seriously. For the next five days Dasch poured out to Traynor his life story of failed jobs and confused allegiances as well as the precise details of the daring sabotage plot—code named Operation Pastorious—that had been hatched at the highest levels of the Nazi regime. Using the information that Dasch provided, the FBI was able to quickly corral not only the three men who had landed on Long Island with Dasch but also another four men who had landed in Florida as part of the same espionage plot.

The FBI treated Dasch very well, at first. After each day of interrogation he was allowed to go back to his room at the Mayflower Hotel. Once the FBI had extracted the information they needed from Dasch they arrested him, but agents promised to seek a presidential pardon for him if he would plead guilty in a civil court and keep silent about his role as an informant. Dasch initially decided to go along with this plan, but then got cold feet. He did not believe he was guilty, and he wanted the world to know his story and the sentencing judge to take into account the role he had played in apprehending the saboteurs. According to Dasch, his plan had been to use the Nazi sabotage plot to return to the United States—where he had lived for most of the past two decades and where his wife still lived—and then to betray his co-conspirators to help to undermine the Nazi regime, which he regarded as evil.

FBI agents had initially planned to try the saboteurs in civil court. But those higher up in the chain of command were beginning to have second thoughts about this course, especially now that Dasch wanted to tell his story. Hoover had been quick to publicize the arrests of the German spies, and the press had dutifully run stories in praise of the efficiency and brilliance of the FBI in tracking the agents down. But if Dasch told his story in open court, the FBI's performance would lose some of its luster; the FBI had after all been slow to believe Dasch and without his help might not have apprehended the spies at all. Hoover was not anxious to have that happen. Nor was the Roosevelt administration eager to publicize how simple it had been for two German submarines to enter American waters undetected. The administration feared that it could create panic among the population. Roosevelt also did not want the Germans to know how the Americans had been so quick to unravel the plan and arrest the men. Moreover, administration officials worried that the civil courts would not be able to serve up the sort of harsh penalties they sought: the maximum sentence for sabotage was thirty years. Finally, the government was concerned that it might not be able to make a sabotage charge stick in a civil court since the men never got close to carrying out the sabotage they intended. In that case the government might be stuck with pursuing lesser charges. A military tribunal, in contrast, would enable the government to move quickly and secretly and to seek the death penalty—a punishment that FDR told his attorney general was "almost obligatory" in this case.

One week after the last of the eight saboteurs had been arrested, Roosevelt issued a proclamation titled "Denying Certain Enemies Access to the Courts of the United States." The proclamation contended that "all enemies who have entered upon the territory of the United States as part of an invasion or predatory incursion, or who have entered in order to commit sabotage, espionage, or other hostile or warlike acts, should be promptly tried in accordance with the laws of war." The proclamation denied such individuals any access to the regular court system "except under such regulations as the Attorney General, with the approval of the Secretary of War, may from time to prescribe." But Roosevelt had no intention of allowing the Nazi saboteurs to have their case heard in the regular courts, telling his attorney general flatly: "I won't give them up. . . . I won't hand them over to any United States marshall armed with a writ of habeas corpus."

On the same day he issued the proclamation (July 2), FDR established the military tribunal and appointed its members as well as the prosecuting and defending attorneys. Six days later, on July 8, the trial commenced. Before the trial had even begun, the defense attorneys questioned the constitutionality of the proceedings. One of the attorneys, Kenneth Royall, managed to persuade the Supreme Court to hear oral arguments on the case; perhaps it helped that the defense team included the son of the chief justice of the Supreme Court, Harlan Stone. More likely, Stone and his brethren on the Court instinctively recoiled against the executive's sweeping claim that the judiciary could play no role in the process unless the executive permitted it. On July 29 and 30, with the military tribunal still in progress, the Court heard nine hours of oral argument. The government's position was that the decision as to how to deal with the saboteurs was the president's alone. "The President's power over enemies who enter this country in time of war, as armed invaders intending to commit hostile acts, must be absolute." The defense team countered that *Ex parte Milligan* had established the principle that the president could not establish a military tribunal where the civil courts were "open and functioning regularly."

On July 31, the chief justice announced the Court's verdict: the military tribunal had jurisdiction to try the case. None of the eight men, including the two who were American citizens, could file petitions for writs of habeas corpus. The Court, however, did not explain why they had reached this judgment; instead they promised a full opinion would be forthcoming in the near future. The following day the military tribunal concluded its proceeding, deliberated on the evidence, and decided that each of the conspirators was guilty and should be put to death. Roosevelt commuted Dasch's sentence—and the sentence of Ernest Burger, who had helped Dasch—to life imprisonment; the other six men were executed on August 8, less than two months after they had landed in the United States.

Drafting the opinion proved more difficult than the quick verdict might have suggested. Several members of the Court, including Stone, had doubts about those aspects of Roosevelt's order that seemed to be in conflict with or to depart from the legislatively enacted Articles of War. For instance, FDR's order required a two-thirds vote to convict, whereas the Articles of War required a unanimous vote to sentence an individual to death. The Articles of War also set out a review structure that ensured the trial court's decision would be reviewed by another military review board, but FDR had directed that the case come directly to him for review. The justices, however, found themselves in the uncomfortable position now of finding reasons to justify the position they had already staked out; six men after all were already dead as a result of their decision. Although Stone had initially agreed to hear the appeal as a way to assert the Court's relevance, he feared now that he had inadvertently hitched the Court to "an executive juggernaut." Pushing aside their doubts and second thoughts, the Supreme Court released its unanimous opinion on October 29, 1942.

*   *   *   *   *   *

Mr. Chief Justice Stone delivered the opinion of the Court.

It is conceded that, ever since petitioners' arrest, the state and federal courts in Florida, New York, and the District of Columbia, and in the states in which each of the petitioners was arrested or detained, have been open and functioning normally. . . .

Petitioners' main contention is that the President is without any statutory or constitutional authority to order the petitioners to be tried by military tribunal for offenses with which they are charged; that, in consequence, they are entitled to be tried in the civil courts with the safeguards, including trial by jury, which the Fifth and Sixth Amendments guarantee to all persons charged in such courts with criminal offenses. . . .

The Government . . . insists that petitioners must be denied access to the courts, both because they are enemy aliens or have entered our territory as enemy belligerents, and because the President's Proclamation undertakes . . . to deny such access to the class of persons defined by the Proclamation, which aptly describes the character and conduct of petitioners. . . .

We are not here concerned with any question of the guilt or innocence of petitioners. Constitutional safeguards for the protection of all who are charged with offenses are not to be disregarded in order to inflict merited punishment on some who are guilty. But the detention and trial of petitioners—ordered by the President in the declared exercise of his powers as Commander in Chief of the Army in time of war and of grave public danger—are not to be set aside by the courts without the clear conviction that they are in conflict with the Constitution or laws of Congress constitutionally enacted.

Congress and the President, like the courts, possess no power not derived from the Constitution. But one of the objects of the Constitution, as declared by its preamble, is to "provide for the common defence." . . .

The Constitution . . . invests the President, as Commander in Chief, with the power to wage war which Congress has declared, and to carry into effect all laws passed by Congress for the conduct of war and for the government and regulation of the Armed Forces, and all laws defining and punishing offenses against the law of nations, including those which pertain to the conduct of war.

By the Articles of War, Congress has provided rules for the government of the Army. It has provided for the trial and punishment, by courts martial, of violations of the Articles by members of the armed forces and by specified classes of persons associated or serving with the Army. But the Articles also recognize the "military commission" appointed by military command as an appropriate tribunal for the trial and punishment of offenses against the law of war not ordinarily tried by court martial. Articles 38 and 46 authorize the President, with certain limitations, to prescribe the procedure for military commissions. Articles 81 and 82 authorize trial, either by court martial or military commission, of those charged with relieving, harboring or corresponding with the enemy and those charged with spying. And Article 15 declares that "the provisions of these articles conferring jurisdiction upon courts martial shall not be construed as depriving military commissions . . . or other military tribunals of concurrent jurisdiction in respect of offenders or offenses that, by statute or by the law of war may be triable by such military commissions . . . or other military tribunals." Article 2 includes among those persons subject to military law the personnel of our own military establishment. But this, as Article 12 provides, does not exclude from that class "any other person who by the law of war is subject to trial by military tribunals" and who, under Article 12, may be tried by court martial or under Article 15 by military commission. . . .

An important incident to the conduct of war is the adoption of measures by the military command not only to repel and defeat the enemy, but to seize and subject to disciplinary measures those enemies who, in their attempt to thwart or impede our military effort, have violated the law of war. It is unnecessary for present purposes to determine to what extent the President as Commander in Chief has constitutional power to create military commissions without the support of Congressional legislation. For here, Congress has authorized trial of offenses against the law of war before such commissions. We are concerned only with the question whether it is within the constitutional power of the National Government to place petitioners upon trial before a military commission for the offenses with which they are charged. We must therefore first inquire whether any of the acts charged is an offense against the law of war cognizable before a military tribunal, and, if so, whether the Constitution prohibits the trial. . . .

By universal agreement and practice, the law of war draws a distinction between the armed forces and the peaceful populations of belligerent nations, and also between those who are lawful and unlawful combatants. Lawful combatants are subject to capture and detention as prisoners of war by opposing military forces. Unlawful combatants are likewise subject to capture and detention, but, in addition, they are subject to trial and punishment by military tribunals for acts that render their belligerency unlawful. The spy who secretly and without uniform passes the military lines of a belligerent in time of war, seeking to gather military information and communicate it to the enemy, or an enemy combatant who without uniform comes secretly through the lines for the purpose of waging war by destruction of life or property, are familiar examples of belligerents who are generally deemed not to be entitled to the status of prisoners of war, but to be offenders against the law of war subject to trial and punishment by military tribunals. . . .

Our Government, by . . . defining lawful belligerents entitled to be treated as prisoners of war, has recognized that there is a class of unlawful belligerents not entitled to that privilege, including those who, though combatants, do not wear "fixed and distinctive emblems." And, by Article 15 of the Articles of War, Congress has made provision for their trial and punishment by military commission, according to "the law of war."

By a long course of practical administrative construction by its military authorities, our Government has likewise recognized that those who, during time of war, pass surreptitiously from enemy territory into our own, discarding their uniforms upon entry, for the commission of hostile acts involving destruction of life or property, have the status of unlawful combatants punishable as such by military commission. This precept of the law of war has been so recognized in practice both here and abroad, and has so generally been accepted as valid by authorities on international law that we think it must be regarded as a rule or principle of the law of war recognized by this Government by its enactment of the Fifteenth Article of War. . . .

Entry upon our territory in time of war by enemy belligerents, including those acting under the direction of the armed forces of the enemy, for the purpose of destroying property used or useful in prosecuting the war, is a hostile and warlike act. It subjects those who participate in it without uniform to the punishment prescribed by the law of war for unlawful belligerents. It is without significance that petitioners were not alleged to have borne conventional weapons or that their proposed hostile acts did not necessarily contemplate collision with the Armed Forces of the United States. . . . Modern warfare is directed at the destruction of enemy war supplies and the implements of their production and transportation, quite as much as at the armed forces. . . . The law of war cannot rightly treat those agents of enemy armies who enter our territory, armed with explosives intended for the destruction of war industries and supplies, as any the less belligerent enemies than are agents similarly entering for the purpose of destroying fortified places or our Armed Forces. By passing our boundaries for such purposes without uniform or other emblem signifying their belligerent status, or by discarding that means of identification after entry, such enemies become unlawful belligerents subject to trial and punishment.

Citizenship in the United States of an enemy belligerent does not relieve him from the consequences of a belligerency which is unlawful because in violation of the law of war. Citizens who associate themselves with the military arm of the enemy government, and, with its aid, guidance and direction, enter this country bent on hostile acts, are enemy belligerents within the meaning of the Hague Convention and the law of war. . . .

Nor are petitioners any the less belligerents if, as they argue, they have not actually committed or attempted to commit any act of depredation or entered the theatre or zone of active military operations. The argument leaves out of account the nature of the offense which the Government charges and which the Act of Congress, by incorporating the law of war, punishes. It is that each petitioner, in circumstances which gave him the status of an enemy belligerent, passed our military and naval lines and defenses or went behind those lines, in civilian dress and with hostile purpose. The offense was complete when, with that purpose, they entered— or, having so entered, they remained upon—our territory in time of war without uniform or other appropriate means of identification. For that reason, even when committed by a citizen, the offense is distinct from the crime of treason defined in Article III, § 3 of the Constitution, since the absence of uniform essential to one is irrelevant to the other.

But petitioners insist that, even if the offenses with which they are charged are offenses against the law of war, their trial is subject to the requirement of the Fifth Amendment that no person shall be held to answer for a capital or otherwise infamous crime unless on a presentment or indictment of a grand jury, and that such trials . . . must be by jury in a civil court. . . .

We cannot say that Congress, in preparing the Fifth and Sixth Amendments, intended to extend trial by jury to the cases of alien or citizen offenders against the law of war otherwise triable by military commission, while withholding it from members of our own armed forces charged with infractions of the Articles of War punishable by death. It is equally inadmissible to construe the Amendments—whose primary purpose was to continue unimpaired presentment by grand jury and trial by petit jury in all those cases in which they had been customary—as either abolishing all trials by military tribunals, save those of the personnel of our own armed forces, or, what in effect comes to the same thing, as imposing on all such tribunals the necessity of proceeding against unlawful enemy belligerents only on presentment and trial by jury. We conclude that the Fifth and Sixth Amendments did not restrict whatever authority was conferred by the Constitution to try offenses against the law of war by military commission, and that petitioners, charged with such an offense not required to be tried by jury at common law, were lawfully placed on trial by the Commission without a jury.

Petitioners . . . stress the pronouncement of this Court in the *Milligan* case that the law of war "can never be applied to citizens in states which have upheld the authority of the government, and where the courts are open, and their process unobstructed." Elsewhere in its opinion, the Court was at pains to point out that Milligan, a citizen twenty years resident in Indiana, who had never been a resident of any of the states in rebellion, was not an enemy belligerent either entitled to the status of a prisoner of war or subject to the penalties imposed upon unlawful belligerents. We construe the Court's statement as to the inapplicability of the law of war to Milligan's case as having particular reference to the facts before it. From them, the Court concluded that Milligan, not being a part of or associated with the armed forces of the enemy, was a non-belligerent, not subject to the law of war save as—in circumstances found not there to be present, and not involved here—martial law might be constitutionally established.

The Court's opinion is inapplicable to the case presented by the present record. We have no occasion now to define with meticulous care the ultimate boundaries of the jurisdiction of military tribunals to try persons according to the law of war. It is enough that petitioners here, upon the conceded facts, were plainly within those boundaries, and were held in good faith for trial by military commission, charged with being enemies who, with the purpose of destroying war materials and utilities, entered, or after entry remained in, our territory without uniform—an offense against the law of war. We hold only that those particular acts constitute an offense against the law of war that the Constitution authorizes to be tried by military commission.

*   *   *   *   *   *

POSTSCRIPT

At the close of the war, an effort was made to secure a pardon for both Dasch and Burger. Traynor, the FBI agent to whom Dasch had first told his story, wrote to Hoover, pleading that the Bureau had "a moral obligation to Dasch" for his role in helping the FBI to round up the saboteurs. The FBI director, however, had no interest in seeking a pardon for Dasch, who he regarded as a communist sympathizer and "a mental case." Hoover's opinion of Dasch was shared by others who knew him. A prison psychiatrist diagnosed Dasch as "an obsessive, compulsive, neurotic personality type," and the warden at the federal prison where Dasch was housed characterized him as "a communist troublemaker" and an unstable person who antagonized his fellow prisoners by "belittling their intelligence" and boasting continually about his exploits. So unpopular was Dasch that his fellow prisoners used him as a negotiating ploy in a standoff with prison authorities, threatening to push him from a roof if officials would not comply with their demands. Even his co-conspirator Burger—who the prison warden regarded as a cooperative, honest, and reliable—came to distrust and in fact despise Dasch.

Although Dasch won few friends with his erratic behavior, in April 1948 President Harry Truman offered clemency to Dasch and Burger on condition that they return to Germany. Truman was apparently persuaded by Attorney General Tom Clark's argument that as the Cold War heated up, the United States had a powerful interest in sending a clear message that foreign agents could expect to be rewarded if they turned sides and helped the United States. But it was far from a happy ending for Dasch and Burger. Many Germans regarded the two men as cowards and traitors who had betrayed six of their fellow countrymen to the gallows in order to save their own necks. Finding and keeping work was difficult for the two men, though evidently not for some of the committed Nazis who had trained Dasch and Burger to commit acts of sabotage; in December 1948, a nearly destitute Burger encountered one of his former Nazi sabotage teachers gainfully employed with the U.S. Army as a liaison with the German railroads.

After Dasch arrived in Germany he immediately violated the terms of his release by entering the Soviet zone. His aim, he insisted, was to collect affidavits from people who could attest to his anti-Nazi sympathies. He apparently hoped that such testimonies might persuade American government officials to recognize that he really had set out on the espionage mission with the purpose of undermining Nazism and to let him return home to the United States where his wife still lived. Perhaps too he hoped that the Soviets might show more appreciation than the Americans for what he had risked. The Soviets, however, suspected that this strange man was an American agent and expelled him. And the Americans, largely because of Hoover's intransigence, never allowed Dasch to return to the United States, despite his many pleas and petitions to countless government officials.[1]

NOTE

1. In 1958, the State Department had drawn up a memo recommending that Dasch finally be granted a visa. Hoover wrote across the memo: "This is outrageous. . . . Make as strong a case against Dasch as possible." Ironically Hoover developed very cordial relations with Burger, who reported regularly to the FBI chief about the activities of other former Nazis. Burger even sent Christmas cards to Hoover on occasion.

Wartime and Emergency Powers
World War II

12

Korematsu v. United States (1944)

Fred Korematsu was twenty-three years old when he was seized by police on a street corner in San Leandro, California, on May 30, 1942. He was not drinking or dealing drugs or fighting or otherwise making a nuisance of himself. But in the spring of 1942 being free had become a crime for Japanese Americans who lived on the West Coast, courtesy of Executive Order 9066. Issued by President Franklin Roosevelt on February 19, the order authorized the secretary of war to designate parts of the country as military areas from which "any or all persons" could be excluded. Under cover of this order, the military forcibly removed 110,000 Japanese resident aliens and Japanese Americans from their homes and relocated them to internment camps in the interior of the country.

Instead of turning himself in to the military authorities, as the military order required, Korematsu tried to avoid detection. Hoping not to be separated from his Italian American girlfriend, he changed his name and even had plastic surgery to make himself look less Asian. But Korematsu's amateurish attempts to disguise his identity were as ineffective in shielding him from the exclusion order as was the fact that he was an American citizen, born and raised in the United States.

With the help of the American Civil Liberties Union, Korematsu challenged the constitutionality of the exclusion order, and in October 1944 his case made its way to the Supreme Court. This was not the first time the Court had been asked to consider the constitutionality of FDR's order. The previous year, the Court had listened to arguments in the case of *Hirabayashi v. United States*. Unlike Korematsu, who attempted to evade the government's order, Gordon Hirabayashi had marched into an FBI office in downtown Seattle and announced he could not, in good conscience, obey the exclusion order or the military's nighttime curfew that had been imposed on Japanese Americans. Hirabayashi was immediately arrested and charged with violating the curfew and the exclusion order.

In *Hirabayashi*, the Court had carefully sidestepped the question of the constitutionality of the exclusion order, preferring to focus on the curfew instead. Writing for a unanimous Court, Chief Justice Harlan Stone opined that the curfew restriction was well within the government's authority. "At a time of threatened Japanese attack upon this country," wrote Stone, it was "reasonable" for the government to secure the nation's defenses by imposing a curfew upon Japanese Americans. There was, in short, a "rational basis" for singling out Americans of Japanese descent even if those citizens had "no particular association with Japan." As to the question of whether Roosevelt had exceeded his authority by acting without prior congressional authorization, Stone pointed out that Congress had afterward ratified the president's order by an act of Congress. Therefore, there was no need for the Court to consider the question of "whether the President, acting alone, could lawfully have made the curfew order in question."

If the Court had hoped it could avoid deciding on the constitutionality of the president's more sweeping and draconian exclusion order, it was sorely disappointed. Since the government still had not closed the internment camps, Korematsu's challenge to the government's action would have to be met. On December 18, 1944—the day after the War Department finally announced that it would close the internment camps and that Japanese Americans could once again be "permitted the same freedom of movement throughout the United States as other loyal citizens and law-abiding aliens"—the Court issued its ruling. Once again the Court sided with the government but, unlike in *Hirabayashi*, it did not speak with one voice. Three justices, Robert Jackson, Owen Roberts, and most passionately, Frank Murphy, wrote dissenting opinions.

*   *   *   *   *   *

Mr. Justice Black delivered the opinion of the Court.

All legal restrictions which curtail the civil rights of a single racial group are immediately suspect. That is not to say that all such restrictions are unconstitutional. It is to say that courts must subject them to the most rigid scrutiny. Pressing public necessity may sometimes justify the existence of such restrictions; racial antagonism never can. . . .

In *Hirabayashi v. United States* (1942), we sustained a conviction obtained for violation of the curfew order. The Hirabayashi conviction and this one . . . rest on the same 1942 Congressional Act and the same basic executive and military orders, all of which orders were aimed at the twin dangers of espionage and sabotage. . . . We upheld the curfew order as an exercise of the power of the government to take steps necessary to prevent espionage and sabotage in an area threatened by Japanese attack.

In the light of the principles we announced in the *Hirabayashi* case, we are unable to conclude that it was beyond the war power of Congress and the Executive to exclude those of Japanese ancestry from the West Coast war area at the time they did. True, exclusion from the area in which one's home is located is a far greater deprivation than constant confinement to the home from 8 P.M. to 6 A.M. Nothing short of apprehension by the proper military authorities of the gravest imminent danger to the public safety can constitutionally justify either. But exclusion from a threatened area, no less than curfew, has a definite and close relationship to the prevention of espionage and sabotage. The military authorities, charged with the primary responsibility of defending our shores, concluded that curfew provided inadequate protection and ordered exclusion. They did so, as pointed out in our *Hirabayashi* opinion, in accordance with Congressional authority to the military to say who should, and who should not, remain in the threatened areas. . . .

Here, as in the *Hirabayashi* case, "we cannot reject as unfounded the judgment of the military authorities and of Congress that there were disloyal members of that population, whose number and strength could not be precisely and quickly ascertained. We cannot say that the war-making branches of the Government did not have ground for believing that, in a critical hour, such persons could not readily be isolated and separately dealt with, and constituted a menace to the national defense and safety which demanded that prompt and adequate measures be taken to guard against it."

Like curfew, exclusion of those of Japanese origin was deemed necessary because of the presence of an unascertained number of disloyal members of the group, most of whom we have no doubt were loyal to this country. It was because we could not reject the finding of the military authorities that it was impossible to bring about an immediate segregation of the disloyal from the loyal that we sustained the validity of the curfew order as applying to the whole group. In the instant case, temporary exclusion of the entire group was rested by the military on the same ground. The judgment that exclusion of the whole group was, for the same reason, a military imperative answers the contention that the exclusion was in the nature of group punishment based on antagonism to those of Japanese origin. That there were members of the group who retained loyalties to Japan has been confirmed by investigations made subsequent to the exclusion. Approximately five thousand American citizens of Japanese ancestry refused to swear unqualified allegiance to the United States and to renounce allegiance to the Japanese Emperor, and several thousand evacuees requested repatriation to Japan.

We uphold the exclusion order as of the time it was made and when the petitioner violated it. In doing so, we are not unmindful of the hardships imposed by it upon a large group of American citizens. But hardships are part of war, and war is an aggregation of hardships. All citizens alike, both in and out of uniform, feel the impact of war in greater or lesser measure. Citizenship has its responsibilities, as well as its privileges, and, in time of war, the burden is always heavier. Compulsory exclusion of large groups of citizens from their homes, except under circumstances of direst emergency and peril, is inconsistent with our basic governmental institutions. But when, under conditions of modern warfare, our shores are threatened by hostile forces, the power to protect must be commensurate with the threatened danger. . . .

It is said that we are dealing here with the case of imprisonment of a citizen in a concentration camp solely because of his ancestry, without evidence or inquiry concerning his loyalty and good disposition towards the United States. Our task would be simple, our duty clear, were this a case involving the imprisonment of a loyal citizen in a concentration camp because of racial prejudice. Regardless of the true nature of the assembly and relocation centers—and we deem it unjustifiable to call them concentration camps, with all the ugly connotations that term implies—we are dealing specifically with nothing but an exclusion order. To cast this case into outlines of racial prejudice, without reference to the real military dangers which were presented, merely confuses the issue. Korematsu was not excluded from the Military Area because of hostility to him or his race. He was excluded because we are at war with the Japanese Empire, because the properly constituted military authorities feared an invasion of our West Coast and felt constrained to take proper security measures, because they decided that the military urgency of the situation demanded that all citizens of Japanese ancestry be segregated from the West Coast temporarily, and, finally, because Congress, reposing its confidence in this time of war in our military leaders—as inevitably it must—determined that they should have the power to do just this. There was evidence of disloyalty on the part of some, the military authorities considered that the need for action was great, and time was short. We cannot—by availing ourselves of the calm perspective of hindsight—now say that, at that time, these actions were unjustified.

*   *   *   *   *   *

Mr. Justice Frankfurter, concurring.

I join in the opinion of the Court, but should like to add a few words of my own.

The provisions of the Constitution which confer on the Congress and the President powers to enable this country to wage war are as much part of the Constitution as provisions looking to a nation at peace. And we have had recent occasion to quote approvingly the statement of former Chief Justice Hughes that the war power of the Government is "the power to wage war successfully" (*Hirabayashi v. United States*). Therefore, the validity of action under the war power must be judged wholly in the context of war. That action is not to be stigmatized as lawless because like action in times of peace would be lawless. . . . To recognize that military orders are "reasonably expedient military precautions" in time of war, and yet to deny them constitutional legitimacy, makes of the Constitution an instrument for dialectic subtleties not reasonably to be attributed to the hard-headed Framers, of whom a majority had had actual participation in war. If a military order such as that under review does not transcend the means appropriate for conducting war, such action by the military is as constitutional as would be any authorized action by the Interstate Commerce Commission within the limits of the constitutional power to regulate commerce. And, being an exercise of the war power explicitly granted by the Constitution for safeguarding the national life by prosecuting war effectively, I find nothing in the Constitution which denies to Congress the power to enforce such a valid military order by making its violation an offense triable in the civil courts. To find that the Constitution does not forbid the military measures now complained of does not carry with it approval of that which Congress and the Executive did. That is their business, not ours.

*   *   *   *   *   *

Mr. Justice Murphy, dissenting.

This exclusion of "all persons of Japanese ancestry, both alien and non-alien," from the Pacific Coast area on a plea of military necessity in the absence of martial law ought not to be approved. Such exclusion goes over "the very brink of constitutional power," and falls into the ugly abyss of racism.

In dealing with matters relating to the prosecution and progress of a war, we must accord great respect and consideration to the judgments of the military authorities who are on the scene and who have full knowledge of the military facts. The scope of their discretion must, as a matter of necessity and common sense, be wide. And their judgments ought not to be overruled lightly by those whose training and duties ill-equip them to deal intelligently with matters so vital to the physical security of the nation.

At the same time, however, it is essential that there be definite limits to military discretion, especially where martial law has not been declared.

Individuals must not be left impoverished of their constitutional rights on a plea of military necessity that has neither substance nor support. Thus, like other claims conflicting with the asserted constitutional rights of the individual, the military claim must subject itself to the judicial process of having its reasonableness determined and its conflicts with other interests reconciled.

The judicial test of whether the Government, on a plea of military necessity, can validly deprive an individual of any of his constitutional rights is whether the deprivation is reasonably related to a public danger that is so "immediate, imminent, and impending" as not to admit of delay and not to permit the intervention of ordinary constitutional processes to alleviate the danger. Civilian Exclusion Order No. 34, banishing from a prescribed area of the Pacific Coast "all persons of Japanese ancestry, both alien and non-alien," clearly does not meet that test. Being an obvious racial discrimination, the order deprives all those within its scope of the equal protection of the laws as guaranteed by the Fifth Amendment. It further deprives these individuals of their constitutional rights to live and work where they will, to establish a home where they choose and to move about freely. In excommunicating them without benefit of hearings, this order also deprives them of all their constitutional rights to procedural due process. Yet no reasonable relation to an "immediate, imminent, and impending" public danger is evident to support this racial restriction, which is one of the most sweeping and complete deprivations of constitutional rights in the history of this nation in the absence of martial law.

It must be conceded that the military and naval situation in the spring of 1942 was such as to generate a very real fear of invasion of the Pacific Coast, accompanied by fears of sabotage and espionage in that area. The military command was therefore justified in adopting all reasonable means necessary to combat these dangers. In adjudging the military action taken in light of the then apparent dangers, we must not erect too high or too meticulous standards; it is necessary only that the action have some reasonable relation to the removal of the dangers of invasion, sabotage and espionage. But the exclusion, either temporarily or permanently, of all persons with Japanese blood in their veins has no such reasonable relation. And that relation is lacking because the exclusion order necessarily must rely for its reasonableness upon the assumption that all persons of Japanese ancestry may have a dangerous tendency to commit sabotage and espionage and to aid our Japanese enemy in other ways. It is difficult to believe that reason, logic, or experience could be marshalled in support of such an assumption.

That this forced exclusion was the result in good measure of this erroneous assumption of racial guilt, rather than bona fide military necessity, is evidenced by the Commanding General's Final Report on the evacuation from the Pacific Coast area. In it, he refers to all individuals of Japanese descent as "subversive," as belonging to "an enemy race" whose "racial strains are undiluted," and as constituting "over 112,000 potential enemies . . . at large today" along the Pacific Coast. In support of this blanket condemnation of all persons of Japanese descent, however, no reliable evidence is cited to show that such individuals were generally disloyal, or had generally so conducted themselves in this area as to constitute a special menace to defense installations or war industries, or had otherwise, by their behavior, furnished reasonable ground for their exclusion as a group.

Justification for the exclusion is sought, instead, mainly upon questionable racial and sociological grounds not ordinarily within the realm of expert military judgment, supplemented by certain semi-military conclusions drawn from an unwarranted use of circumstantial evidence. Individuals of Japanese ancestry are condemned because they are said to be "a large, unassimilated, tightly knit racial group, bound to an enemy nation by strong ties of race, culture, custom and religion." They are claimed to be given to "emperor worshipping ceremonies," and to "dual citizenship." Japanese language schools and allegedly pro-Japanese organizations are cited as evidence of possible group disloyalty, together with facts as to certain persons being educated and residing at length in Japan. It is intimated that many of these individuals deliberately resided "adjacent to strategic points," thus enabling them "to carry into execution a tremendous program of sabotage on a mass scale should any considerable number of them have been inclined to do so." The need for protective custody is also asserted. The report refers, without identity, to "numerous incidents of violence," as well as to other admittedly unverified or cumulative incidents. From this, plus certain other events not shown to have been connected with the Japanese Americans, it is concluded that the "situation was fraught with danger to the Japanese population itself," and that the general public "was ready to take matters into its own hands." Finally, it is intimated, though not directly charged or proved, that persons of Japanese ancestry were responsible for three minor isolated shellings and bombings of the Pacific Coast area, as well as for unidentified radio transmissions and night signaling.

The main reasons relied upon by those responsible for the forced evacuation, therefore, do not prove a reasonable relation between the group characteristics of Japanese Americans and the dangers of invasion, sabotage and espionage. The reasons appear, instead, to be largely an accumulation of much of the misinformation, half-truths and insinuations that for years have been directed against Japanese Americans by people with racial and economic prejudices—the same people who have been among the foremost advocates of the evacuation. A military judgment based upon such racial and sociological considerations is not entitled to the great weight ordinarily given the judgments based upon strictly military considerations. Especially is this so when every charge relative to race, religion, culture, geographical location, and legal and economic status has been substantially discredited by independent studies made by experts in these matters.

The military necessity that is essential to the validity of the evacuation order thus resolves itself into a few intimations that certain individuals actively aided the enemy, from which it is inferred that the entire group of Japanese Americans could not be trusted to be or remain loyal to the United States. No one denies, of course, that there were some disloyal persons of Japanese descent on the Pacific Coast who did all in their power to aid their ancestral land. Similar disloyal activities have been engaged in by many persons of German, Italian and even more pioneer stock in our country. But to infer that examples of individual disloyalty prove group disloyalty and justify discriminatory action against the entire group is to deny that, under our system of law, individual guilt is the sole basis for deprivation of rights. Moreover, this inference, which is at the very heart of the evacuation orders, has been used in support of the abhorrent and despicable treatment of minority groups by the dictatorial tyrannies that this nation is now pledged to destroy. To give constitutional sanction to that inference in this case, however well intentioned may have been the military command on the Pacific Coast, is to adopt one of the cruelest of the rationales used by our enemies to destroy the dignity of the individual and to encourage and open the door to discriminatory actions against other minority groups in the passions of tomorrow.

No adequate reason is given for the failure to treat these Japanese Americans on an individual basis by holding investigations and hearings to separate the loyal from the disloyal, as was done in the case of persons of German and Italian ancestry. It is asserted merely that the loyalties of this group "were unknown and time was of the essence." Yet nearly four months elapsed after Pearl Harbor before the first exclusion order was issued; nearly eight months went by until the last order was issued, and the last of these "subversive" persons was not actually removed until almost eleven months had elapsed. Leisure and deliberation seem to have been more of the essence than speed. And the fact that conditions were not such as to warrant a declaration of martial law adds strength to the belief that the factors of time and military necessity were not as urgent as they have been represented to be.

Moreover, there was no adequate proof that the Federal Bureau of Investigation and the military and naval intelligence services did not have the espionage and sabotage situation well in hand during this long period. Nor is there any denial of the fact that not one person of Japanese ancestry was accused or convicted of espionage or sabotage after Pearl Harbor while they were still free, a fact which is some evidence of the loyalty of the vast majority of these individuals and of the effectiveness of the established methods of combating these evils. It seems incredible that, under these circumstances, it would have been impossible to hold loyalty hearings for the mere 112,000 persons involved—or at least for the 70,000 American citizens—especially when a large part of this number represented children and elderly men and women. Any inconvenience that may have accompanied an attempt to conform to procedural due process cannot be said to justify violations of constitutional rights of individuals.

I dissent, therefore, from this legalization of racism. Racial discrimination in any form and in any degree has no justifiable part whatever in our democratic way of life. It is unattractive in any setting, but it is utterly revolting among a free people who have embraced the principles set forth in the Constitution of the United States. All residents of this nation are kin in some way by blood or culture to a foreign land. Yet they are primarily and necessarily a part of the new and distinct civilization of the United States. They must, accordingly, be treated at all times as the heirs of the American experiment, and as entitled to all the rights and freedoms guaranteed by the Constitution.

*   *   *   *   *   *

Mr. Justice Jackson, dissenting.

Korematsu was born on our soil, of parents born in Japan. The Constitution makes him a citizen of the United States by nativity, and a citizen of California by residence. No claim is made that he is not loyal to this country. There is no suggestion that, apart from the matter involved here, he is not law abiding and well disposed. Korematsu, however, has been convicted of an act not commonly a crime. It consists merely of being present in the state whereof he is a citizen, near the place where he was born, and where all his life he has lived.

Even more unusual is the series of military orders that made this conduct a crime. They forbid such a one to remain, and they also forbid him to leave. They were so drawn that the only way Korematsu could avoid violation was to give himself up to the military authority. This meant submission to custody, examination, and transportation out of the territory, to be followed by indeterminate confinement in detention camps.

A citizen's presence in the locality, however, was made a crime only if his parents were of Japanese birth. Had Korematsu been one of four—the others being, say, a German alien enemy, an Italian alien enemy, and a citizen of American-born ancestors, convicted of treason but out on parole— only Korematsu's presence would have violated the order. The difference between their innocence and his crime would result, not from anything he did, said, or thought, different than they, but only in that he was born of different racial stock.

Now, if any fundamental assumption underlies our system, it is that guilt is personal and not inheritable. Even if all of one's antecedents had been convicted of treason, the Constitution forbids its penalties to be visited upon him, for it provides that "no attainder of treason shall work corruption of blood, or forfeiture except during the life of the person attainted." But here is an attempt to make an otherwise innocent act a crime merely because this prisoner is the son of parents as to whom he had no choice, and belongs to a race from which there is no way to resign. If Congress, in peacetime legislation, should enact such a criminal law, I should suppose this Court would refuse to enforce it.

But the "law" which this prisoner is convicted of disregarding is not found in an act of Congress, but in a military order. Neither the Act of Congress nor the Executive Order of the President, nor both together, would afford a basis for this conviction. It rests on the orders of General DeWitt. And it is said that, if the military commander had reasonable military grounds for promulgating the orders, they are constitutional, and become law, and the Court is required to enforce them. There are several reasons why I cannot subscribe to this doctrine.

It would be impracticable and dangerous idealism to expect or insist that each specific military command in an area of probable operations will conform to conventional tests of constitutionality. When an area is so beset that it must be put under military control at all, the paramount consideration is that its measures be successful, rather than legal. The armed services must protect a society, not merely its Constitution. The very essence of the military job is to marshal physical force, to remove every obstacle to its effectiveness, to give it every strategic advantage. Defense measures will not, and often should not, be held within the limits that bind civil authority in peace. No court can require such a commander in such circumstances to act as a reasonable man; he may be unreasonably cautious and exacting. Perhaps he should be. But a commander, in temporarily focusing the life of a community on defense, is carrying out a military program; he is not making law in the sense the courts know the term. He issues orders, and they may have a certain authority as military commands, although they may be very bad as constitutional law.

But if we cannot confine military expedients by the Constitution, neither would I distort the Constitution to approve all that the military may deem expedient. That is what the Court appears to be doing, whether consciously or not. I cannot say, from any evidence before me, that the orders of General DeWitt were not reasonably expedient military precautions, nor could I say that they were. But even if they were permissible military procedures, I deny that it follows that they are constitutional. If, as the Court holds, it does follow, then we may as well say that any military order will be constitutional, and have done with it.

The limitation under which courts always will labor in examining the necessity for a military order are illustrated by this case. How does the Court know that these orders have a reasonable basis in necessity? No evidence whatever on that subject has been taken by this or any other court. There is sharp controversy as to the credibility of the DeWitt report. So the Court, having no real evidence before it, has no choice but to accept General DeWitt's own unsworn, self-serving statement, untested by any cross-examination, that what he did was reasonable. And thus it will always be when courts try to look into the reasonableness of a military order.

In the very nature of things, military decisions are not susceptible of intelligent judicial appraisal. They do not pretend to rest on evidence, but are made on information that often would not be admissible and on assumptions that could not be proved. Information in support of an order could not be disclosed to courts without danger that it would reach the enemy. Neither can courts act on communications made in confidence. Hence, courts can never have any real alternative to accepting the mere declaration of the authority that issued the order that it was reasonably necessary from a military viewpoint.

Much is said of the danger to liberty from the Army program for deporting and detaining these citizens of Japanese extraction. But a judicial construction of the due process clause that will sustain this order is a far more subtle blow to liberty than the promulgation of the order itself. A military order, however unconstitutional, is not apt to last longer than the military emergency. Even during that period, a succeeding commander may revoke it all. But once a judicial opinion rationalizes such an order to show that it conforms to the Constitution, or rather rationalizes the Constitution to show that the Constitution sanctions such an order, the Court for all time has validated the principle of racial discrimination in criminal procedure and of transplanting American citizens. The principle then lies about like a loaded weapon, ready for the hand of any authority that can bring forward a plausible claim of an urgent need. Every repetition imbeds that principle more deeply in our law and thinking and expands it to new purposes. All who observe the work of courts are familiar with what Judge Cardozo described as "the tendency of a principle to expand itself to the limit of its logic." A military commander may overstep the bounds of constitutionality, and it is an incident. But if we review and approve, that passing incident becomes the doctrine of the Constitution. There it has a generative power of its own, and all that it creates will be in its own image. Nothing better illustrates this danger than does the Court's opinion in this case.

It argues that we are bound to uphold the conviction of Korematsu because we upheld one in *Hirabayashi v. United States*, when we sustained these orders insofar as they applied a curfew requirement to a citizen of Japanese ancestry. I think we should learn something from that experience.

In that case, we were urged to consider only the curfew feature, that being all that technically was involved, because it was the only count necessary to sustain Hirabayashi's conviction and sentence. We yielded, and the Chief Justice guarded the opinion as carefully as language will do. He said: "Our investigation here does not go beyond the inquiry whether, in the light of all the relevant circumstances preceding and attending their promulgation, the challenged orders and statute *afforded a reasonable basis for the action taken in imposing the curfew.*" "We decide only the issue as we have defined it—we decide only that the *curfew order,* as applied, and at the time it was applied, was within the boundaries of the war power." And again: "It is unnecessary to consider whether or to what extent *such findings would support orders differing from the curfew order.*" However, in spite of our limiting words, we did validate a discrimination on the basis of ancestry for mild and temporary deprivation of liberty. Now the principle of racial discrimination is pushed from support of mild measures to very harsh ones, and from temporary deprivations to indeterminate ones. And the precedent that it is said requires us to do so is *Hirabayashi.* The Court is now saying that, in *Hirabayashi,* we did decide the very things we there said we were not deciding. Because we said that these citizens could be made to stay in their homes during the hours of dark, it is said we must require them to leave home entirely, and if that, we are told they may also be taken into custody for deportation, and, if that, it is argued, they may also be held for some undetermined time in detention camps. How far the principle of this case would be extended before plausible reasons would play out, I do not know.

I should hold that a civil court cannot be made to enforce an order which violates constitutional limitations even if it is a reasonable exercise of military authority. The courts can exercise only the judicial power, can apply only law, and must abide by the Constitution, or they cease to be civil courts and become instruments of military policy.

Of course, the existence of a military power resting on force, so vagrant, so centralized, so necessarily heedless of the individual, is an inherent threat to liberty. But I would not lead people to rely on this Court for a review that seems to me wholly delusive. The military reasonableness of these orders can only be determined by military superiors. If the people ever let command of the war power fall into irresponsible and unscrupulous hands, the courts wield no power equal to its restraint. The chief restraint upon those who command the physical forces of the country, in the future as in the past, must be their responsibility to the political judgments of their contemporaries and to the moral judgments of history.

My duties as a justice, as I see them, do not require me to make a military judgment as to whether General DeWitt's evacuation and detention program was a reasonable military necessity. I do not suggest that the courts should have attempted to interfere with the Army in carrying out its task. But I do not think they may be asked to execute a military expedient that has no place in law under the Constitution. I would reverse the judgment and discharge the prisoner.

*   *   *   *   *   *

POSTSCRIPT

In 1945, Fred Korematsu along with over 100,000 other interned Japanese and Japanese Americans were allowed to return to their homes. Korematsu went back to San Leandro, California, where he married, had two children, and tried to resume a normal life as an American citizen in the post–World War II world. Finding a good job was difficult, however, since his violation of the exclusion act meant that he had a criminal record. Like so many who spent time in the internment camps, he did not like to talk about the camps or even his case. But inside he burned with indignation about the wrong that had been done him. In 1981, that indignation became harnessed to legal action, thanks to the detective work of Peter Irons, a young legal historian at the University of California, San Diego.

In the process of researching internment cases, Irons found incontrovertible evidence that Solicitor General Charles Fahy, the man who argued the government's case before the Supreme Court, suppressed military intelligence and FBI reports that found that the nation faced no security risk from Japanese Americans; those who were deemed a threat had already been rounded up by the government. Irons showed the relevant documents to Korematsu, and together they determined to ask the courts to overturn his nearly forty-year-old conviction. They were successful; in November 1983 a federal judge in San Francisco sided with Korematsu and erased his conviction (in 1986 a federal judge in Seattle would do the same for Gordon Hirabayashi). The federal government did not appeal the judge's ruling, and in 1988 Congress enacted legislation that formally apologized to all Japanese Americans for their internment and provided $20,000 for every living Japanese American interned during the war. A decade later, in 1998, at the age of seventy-nine, Korematsu was given the President Medal of Freedom in recognition of his long fight against injustice.

Wartime and Emergency Powers
The Korean War and the Cold War

13

Youngstown Sheet & Tube Co. v. Sawyer (1952)

O nly five years after the end of World War II, the United States found itself back at war again after Communist North Korea invaded South Korea on June 25, 1950. Unlike in World War II, however, Congress never declared the United States to be at war with North Korea. Instead the United States was taken into war by President Harry S Truman, who declared the war in Korea to be a "police action" authorized by a United Nations Security Council resolution.

By whatever name, the military conflict in Korea required mobilization of resources on the home front if the United States was to prevail. Here Congress cooperated fully. Not only did Congress finance the troop buildup, but in September 1950 it passed the Defense Production Act (DPA), which gave the president broad powers to require firms to accept government contracts and make the fulfillment of those government orders a priority if they were deemed necessary to national defense. The act, in short, empowered the executive to ensure that the government had the equipment and supplies it needed to fight in Korea. In addition, the act authorized the president to enact wage and price controls.

The administration's war mobilization efforts, however, were being undercut by rapidly rising wages and prices. Making matters worse, the Chinese entered the war in November with devastating military and psychological effects, which prompted the government to accelerate military production still further. To help meet the growing crisis,

Truman declared a national emergency and the following day, on December 16, established the Office of Defense Mobilization (ODM), which he charged with coordinating production controls and overseeing economic stabilization measures. In January 1951, over the strong objections of organized labor, a nationwide freeze on wages and prices was announced.

The freeze on wages and prices helped to bring inflation under control but public discontent was rampant. The war quickly became intensely unpopular and many chafed under governmental controls. Under intense pressure from industry, Congress passed an amendment to the DPA in the summer of 1951 that allowed companies to secure price increases if they could show their costs had increased over the past year. Workers were unhappy with the freeze on wages, believing that businesses were taking advantage of the war to drive up profits and decrease wages. By the end of 1951 only 23 percent of Americans approved of Truman's job performance, according to a Gallup poll.

Among those least satisfied with their contracts were steelworkers. The steel companies, however, were in no mood to negotiate, insisting that the government first offer assurances that they would be allowed to raise prices. After several efforts to reach an accommodation between the two sides failed, the United Steelworkers announced that they would go on strike on April 9. Under existing law (the Taft-Hartley Act, which was passed in 1947 over Truman's veto), Truman had the power to order the steelworkers to return to work for eighty days while federal mediators helped to negotiate a mutually acceptable contract, but using the Republicans' favorite union-busting legislation was an unappealing political option for a Democratic president. And in any event Truman had little reason to think that sixty days would enable the two sides to achieve what they had failed to do over the previous six months.

Facing the prospect that steel factories would shut down and "immediately jeopardize and imperil our national defense," Truman ordered his secretary of commerce to take control of the steel mills until an agreement could be reached between workers and management. The steelworkers would become government employees. Announcing his nationalization order just two hours before the strike was to take effect, Truman justified his extraordinary actions by appealing to the national emergency that he had proclaimed in December 1950 and to his constitutional powers as president of the United States and commander in chief.

The steel companies immediately took the president to court, arguing that the president's action was illegal. A district judge agreed with the steel industry, prompting the steelworkers to begin their strike. The government then appealed to the D.C. Circuit Court, which stayed the lower judge's decision so that the government could make its case to the

Supreme Court. On May 12 the Supreme Court heard oral arguments and on June 2 announced their opinion.

Although Truman knew that his order nationalizing the steel industry placed him on constitutional thin ice, he expected to prevail. Even if the Court did not accept the more expansive understanding of presidential power that was being peddled by the government's lawyers, most observers expected the Court to find narrower grounds on which to uphold the government's position. After all, all nine of the Supreme Court justices had been appointed by either Roosevelt or Truman. Five of the justices (Hugo Black, Stanley Reed, Felix Frankfurter, William Douglas, and Robert Jackson) had been on the Court when it unanimously upheld the government's wartime actions in *Ex parte Quirin* and *Hirabayashi*; and only one of the three dissenters in *Korematsu* was still on the court (Jackson). The other four were Truman appointees, and three of them were staunch Democrats (Chief Justice Fred Vinson, Sherman Minton, and Tom Clark), and two of those (Vinson and Minton) had extremely close friendships with Truman that went back to their days together in the legislature. Moreover, Vinson had privately encouraged Truman to seize the steel mills, assuring him that such an action had a solid legal grounding.

But Truman was to be disappointed. Only two justices (Minton and Reed) signed onto the chief justice's long and angry dissent. Vinson's dissent reflected more than just his personal loyalty to Truman, however. It also stemmed from his own background in the executive branch. Prior to becoming chief justice, Vinson served as Truman's secretary of the treasury, and before that, during the closing years of World War II, he had been director of the Office of Economic Stabilization and director of War Mobilization and Reconversion, doing much the same sort of work that the ODM had been tasked with carrying out.

The six justices who voted to repudiate Truman's action did not speak with a single voice. Indeed each of the six wrote separate opinions and only three endorsed the reasoning put forth in the opinion of the Court written by Justice Black. Vinson might have regarded his robed brethren as naive, but there was executive experience on the majority's side as well. Jackson had been Roosevelt's attorney general before being elevated to the bench, and Clark had not only served as Truman's attorney general for four years but had also coordinated the relocation of Japanese Americans at the beginning of World War II. Truman never forgave Clark for his betrayal, telling one interviewer that appointing that "dumb son of a bitch" was his "biggest mistake" as president. The most enduring legacy of the case, however, lies not in Clark's disloyalty to his former boss or Black's sweeping repudiation of presidential authority, but rather Jackson's more nuanced view that the scope of presidential power depended in large part on congressional action: presidential power, Jackson explained, was greatest where it was supported by Congress, "at its lowest ebb" when Congress opposed the presidential action, and somewhere in the middle when Congress was silent.

* * * * * *

Mr. Justice Black delivered the opinion of the Court.

We are asked to decide whether the President was acting within his constitutional power when he issued an order directing the Secretary of Commerce to take possession of and operate most of the Nation's steel mills. The mill owners argue that the President's order amounts to law-making, a legislative function that the Constitution has expressly confided to the Congress, and not to the President. The Government's position is that the order was made on findings of the President that his action was necessary to avert a national catastrophe which would inevitably result from a stoppage of steel production, and that, in meeting this grave emergency, the President was acting within the aggregate of his constitutional powers as the Nation's Chief Executive and the Commander in Chief of the Armed Forces of the United States. . . .

The President's power, if any, to issue the order must stem either from an act of Congress or from the Constitution itself. There is no statute that expressly authorizes the President to take possession of property as he did here. Nor is there any act of Congress to which our attention has been directed from which such a power can fairly be implied. . . .

Moreover, the use of the seizure technique to solve labor disputes in order to prevent work stoppages was not only unauthorized by any congressional enactment; prior to this controversy, Congress had refused to adopt that method of settling labor disputes. When the Taft-Hartley Act was under consideration in 1947, Congress rejected an amendment which would have authorized such governmental seizures in cases of emergency. . . .

It is clear that, if the President had authority to issue the order he did, it must be found in some provision of the Constitution. And it is not claimed that express constitutional language grants this power to the President. The contention is that presidential power should be implied from the aggregate of his powers under the Constitution. Particular reliance is placed on provisions in Article II which say that "The executive Power shall be vested in a President . . ."; that "he shall take Care that the Laws be faithfully executed", and that he "shall be Commander in Chief of the Army and Navy of the United States."

The order cannot properly be sustained as an exercise of the President's military power as Commander in Chief of the Armed Forces. The Government attempts to do so by citing a number of cases upholding broad powers in military commanders engaged in day-to-day fighting in a theater of war. Such cases need not concern us here. Even though "theater of war" be an expanding concept, we cannot with faithfulness to our constitutional system hold that the Commander in Chief of the Armed Forces has the ultimate power as such to take possession of private property in order to keep labor disputes from stopping production. This is a job for the Nation's lawmakers, not for its military authorities.

Nor can the seizure order be sustained because of the several constitutional provisions that grant executive power to the President. In the framework of our Constitution, the President's power to see that the laws are faithfully executed refutes the idea that he is to be a lawmaker. The Constitution limits his functions in the lawmaking process to the recommending of laws he thinks wise and the vetoing of laws he thinks bad. And the Constitution is neither silent nor equivocal about who shall make laws which the President is to execute. The first section of the first article says that "All legislative Powers herein granted shall be vested in a Congress of the United States. . . ." After granting many powers to the Congress, Article I goes on to provide that Congress may "make all Laws which shall be necessary and proper for carrying into Execution the foregoing Powers, and all other Powers vested by this Constitution in the Government of the United States, or in any Department or Officer thereof."

The President's order does not direct that a congressional policy be executed in a manner prescribed by Congress—it directs that a presidential policy be executed in a manner prescribed by the President. The preamble of the order itself, like that of many statutes, sets out reasons why the President believes certain policies should be adopted, proclaims these policies as rules of conduct to be followed, and again, like a statute, authorizes a government official to promulgate additional rules and regulations consistent with the policy proclaimed and needed to carry that policy into execution. The power of Congress to adopt such public policies as those proclaimed by the order is beyond question. It can authorize the taking of private property for public use. It can make laws regulating the relationships between employers and employees, prescribing rules designed to settle labor disputes, and fixing wages and working conditions in certain fields of our economy. The Constitution does not subject this lawmaking power of Congress to presidential or military supervision or control.

It is said that other Presidents, without congressional authority, have taken possession of private business enterprises in order to settle labor disputes. But even if this be true, Congress has not thereby lost its exclusive constitutional authority to make laws necessary and proper to carry out the powers vested by the Constitution "in the Government of the United States, or any Department or Officer thereof."

The Founders of this Nation entrusted the lawmaking power to the Congress alone in both good and bad times. It would do no good to recall the historical events, the fears of power, and the hopes for freedom that lay behind their choice. Such a review would but confirm our holding that this seizure order cannot stand.

*   *   *   *   *   *

Mr. Justice Jackson, concurring in the judgment and opinion of the Court.

That comprehensive and undefined presidential powers hold both practical advantages and grave dangers for the country will impress anyone who has served as legal adviser to a President in time of transition and public anxiety. While an interval of detached reflection may temper teachings of that experience, they probably are a more realistic influence on my views than the conventional materials of judicial decision that seem unduly to accentuate doctrine and legal fiction. But, as we approach the question of presidential power, we half overcome mental hazards by recognizing them. The opinions of judges, no less than executives and publicists, often suffer the infirmity of confusing the issue of a power's validity with the cause it is invoked to promote, of confounding the permanent executive office with its temporary occupant. The tendency is strong to emphasize transient results upon policies—such as wages or stabilization—and lose sight of enduring consequences upon the balanced power structure of our Republic.

A judge, like an executive adviser, may be surprised at the poverty of really useful and unambiguous authority applicable to concrete problems of executive power as they actually present themselves. Just what our forefathers did envision, or would have envisioned had they foreseen modern conditions, must be divined from materials almost as enigmatic as the dreams Joseph was called upon to interpret for Pharaoh. A century and a half of partisan debate and scholarly speculation yields no net result, but only supplies more or less apt quotations from respected sources on each side of any question. They largely cancel each other. And court decisions are indecisive because of the judicial practice of dealing with the largest questions in the most narrow way.

The actual art of governing under our Constitution does not, and cannot, conform to judicial definitions of the power of any of its branches based on isolated clauses, or even single Articles torn from context. While the Constitution diffuses power the better to secure liberty, it also contemplates that practice will integrate the dispersed powers into a workable government. It enjoins upon its branches separateness but interdependence, autonomy but reciprocity. Presidential powers are not fixed but fluctuate depending upon their disjunction or conjunction with those of Congress. We may well begin by a somewhat over-simplified grouping of practical situations in which a President may doubt, or others may challenge, his powers, and by distinguishing roughly the legal consequences of this factor of relativity.

1. When the President acts pursuant to an express or implied authorization of Congress, his authority is at its maximum, for it includes all that he possesses in his own right plus all that Congress can delegate. In these circumstances, and in these only, may he be said (for what it may be worth) to personify the federal sovereignty. If his act is held unconstitutional under these circumstances, it usually means that the Federal Government, as an undivided whole, lacks power. A seizure executed by the President pursuant to an Act of Congress would be supported by the strongest of presumptions and the widest latitude of judicial interpretation, and the burden of persuasion would rest heavily upon any who might attack it.

2. When the President acts in absence of either a congressional grant or denial of authority, he can only rely upon his own independent powers, but there is a zone of twilight in which he and Congress may have concurrent authority, or in which its distribution is uncertain. Therefore, congressional inertia, indifference or quiescence may sometimes, at least, as a practical matter, enable, if not invite, measures on independent presidential responsibility. In this area, any actual test of power is likely to depend on the imperatives of events and contemporary imponderables, rather than on abstract theories of law.

3. When the President takes measures incompatible with the expressed or implied will of Congress, his power is at its lowest ebb, for then he can rely only upon his own constitutional powers minus any constitutional powers of Congress over the matter. Courts can sustain exclusive presidential control in such a case only by disabling the Congress from acting upon the subject. Presidential claim to a power at once so conclusive and preclusive must be scrutinized with caution, for what is at stake is the equilibrium established by our constitutional system.

Into which of these classifications does this executive seizure of the steel industry fit? It is eliminated from the first by admission, for it is conceded that no congressional authorization exists for this seizure. That takes away also the support of the many precedents and declarations which were made in relation, and must be confined, to this category.

Can it then be defended under flexible tests available to the second category? It seems clearly eliminated from that class, because Congress has not left seizure of private property an open field, but has covered it by three statutory policies inconsistent with this seizure. In cases where the purpose is to supply needs of the Government itself, two courses are provided: one, seizure of a plant which fails to comply with obligatory orders placed by the Government, another, condemnation of facilities, including temporary use under the power of eminent domain. The third is applicable where it is the general economy of the country that is to be protected, rather than exclusive governmental interests. None of these were invoked.

In choosing a different and inconsistent way of his own, the President cannot claim that it is necessitated or invited by failure of Congress to legislate upon the occasions, grounds and methods for seizure of industrial properties.

This leaves the current seizure to be justified only by the severe tests under the third grouping, where it can be supported only by any remainder of executive power after subtraction of such powers as Congress may have over the subject. In short, we can sustain the President only by holding that seizure of such strike-bound industries is within his domain and beyond control by Congress. Thus, this Court's first review of such seizures occurs under circumstances which leave presidential power most vulnerable to attack and in the least favorable of possible constitutional postures. . . .

The Solicitor General seeks the power of seizure in three clauses of the Executive Article, the first reading, "The executive Power shall be vested in a President of the United States of America." Lest I be thought to exaggerate, I quote the interpretation that his brief puts upon it: "In our view, this clause constitutes a grant of all the executive powers of which the Government is capable." If that be true, it is difficult to see why the forefathers bothered to add several specific items, including some trifling ones.

The example of such unlimited executive power that must have most impressed the forefathers was the prerogative exercised by George III, and the description of its evils in the Declaration of Independence leads me to doubt that they were creating their new Executive in his image. Continental European examples were no more appealing. And, if we seek instruction from our own times, we can match it only from the executive powers in those governments we disparagingly describe as totalitarian. I cannot accept the view that this clause is a grant in bulk of all conceivable executive power, but regard it as an allocation to the presidential office of the generic powers thereafter stated.

The clause on which the Government next relies is that "The President shall be Commander in Chief of the Army and Navy of the United States. . . ." These cryptic words have given rise to some of the most persistent controversies in our constitutional history. Of course, they imply something more than an empty title. But just what authority goes with the name has plagued presidential advisers who would not waive or narrow it by nonassertion, yet cannot say where it begins or ends. It undoubtedly puts the Nation's armed forces under presidential command. Hence, this loose appellation is sometimes advanced as support for any presidential action, internal or external, involving use of force, the idea being that it vests power to do anything, anywhere, that can be done with an army or navy.

That seems to be the logic of an argument tendered at our bar—that the President having, on his own responsibility, sent American troops abroad derives from that act "affirmative power" to seize the means of producing a supply of steel for them. To quote, "Perhaps the most forceful illustration of the scope of Presidential power in this connection is the fact that American troops in Korea, whose safety and effectiveness are so directly involved here, were sent to the field by an exercise of the President's constitutional powers." Thus, it is said, he has invested himself with "war powers."

I cannot foresee all that it might entail if the Court should indorse this argument. Nothing in our Constitution is plainer than that declaration of a war is entrusted only to Congress. Of course, a state of war may, in fact, exist without a formal declaration. But no doctrine that the Court could promulgate would seem to me more sinister and alarming than that a President whose conduct of foreign affairs is so largely uncontrolled, and often even is unknown, can vastly enlarge his mastery over the internal affairs of the country by his own commitment of the Nation's armed forces to some foreign venture. . . .

There are indications that the Constitution did not contemplate that the title Commander in Chief *of the Army and Navy* will constitute him also Commander in Chief of the country, its industries and its inhabitants. He has no monopoly of "war powers," whatever they are. While Congress cannot deprive the President of the command of the army and navy, only Congress can provide him an army or navy to command. It is also empowered to make rules for the "Government and Regulation of land and naval Forces," by which it may, to some unknown extent, impinge upon even command functions.

We should not use this occasion to circumscribe, much less to contract, the lawful role of the President as Commander in Chief. I should indulge the widest latitude of interpretation to sustain his exclusive function to command the instruments of national force, at least when turned against the outside world for the security of our society. But, when it is turned inward not because of rebellion, but because of a lawful economic struggle between industry and labor, it should have no such indulgence. His command power is not such an absolute as might be implied from that office in a militaristic system, but is subject to limitations consistent with a constitutional Republic whose law and policymaking branch is a representative Congress. The purpose of lodging dual titles in one man was to insure that the civilian would control the military, not to enable the military to subordinate the presidential office. No penance would ever expiate the sin against free government of holding that a President can escape control of executive powers by law through assuming his military role. What the power of command may include I do not try to envision, but I think it is not a military prerogative, without support of law, to seize persons or property because they are important or even essential for the military and naval establishment.

The third clause in which the Solicitor General finds seizure powers is that "he shall take Care that the Laws be faithfully executed. . . ." That authority must be matched against words of the Fifth Amendment that "No person shall be . . . deprived of life, liberty or property, without due process of law. . . ." One gives a governmental authority that reaches so far as there is law, the other gives a private right that authority shall go no farther. These signify about all there is of the principle that ours is a government of laws, not of men, and that we submit ourselves to rulers only if under rules.

The Solicitor General lastly grounds support of the seizure upon nebulous, inherent powers never expressly granted, but said to have accrued to the office from the customs and claims of preceding administrations. The plea is for a resulting power to deal with a crisis or an emergency according to the necessities of the case, the unarticulated assumption being that necessity knows no law.

Loose and irresponsible use of adjectives colors all nonlegal and much legal discussion of presidential powers. "Inherent" powers, "implied" powers, "incidental" powers, "plenary" powers, "war" powers and "emergency" powers are used, often interchangeably and without fixed or ascertainable meanings.

The vagueness and generality of the clauses that set forth presidential powers afford a plausible basis for pressures within and without an administration for presidential action beyond that supported by those whose responsibility it is to defend his actions in court. The claim of inherent and unrestricted presidential powers has long been a persuasive dialectical weapon in political controversy. While it is not surprising that counsel should grasp support from such unadjudicated claims of power, a judge cannot accept self-serving press statements of the attorney for one of the interested parties as authority in answering a constitutional question, even if the advocate was himself. But prudence has counseled that actual reliance on such nebulous claims stop short of provoking a judicial test. . . .

The appeal, however, that we declare the existence of inherent powers *ex necessitate* to meet an emergency asks us to do what many think would be wise, although it is something the forefathers omitted. They knew what emergencies were, knew the pressures they engender for authoritative action, knew, too, how they afford a ready pretext for usurpation. We may also suspect that they suspected that emergency powers would tend to kindle emergencies. Aside from suspension of the privilege of the writ of habeas corpus in time of rebellion or invasion, when the public safety may require it, they made no express provision for exercise of extraordinary authority because of a crisis. I do not think we rightfully may so amend their work, and, if we could, I am not convinced it would be wise to do so, although many modern nations have forthrightly recognized that war and economic crises may upset the normal balance between liberty and authority. . . .

In the practical working of our Government, we already have evolved a technique within the framework of the Constitution by which normal executive powers may be considerably expanded to meet an emergency. Congress may and has granted extraordinary authorities which lie dormant in normal times but may be called into play by the Executive in war or upon proclamation of a national emergency. In 1939, upon congressional request, the Attorney General listed ninety-nine such separate statutory grants by Congress of emergency or wartime executive powers. They were invoked from time to time as need appeared. Under this procedure, we retain Government by law—special, temporary law, perhaps, but law nonetheless. The public may know the extent and limitations of the powers that can be asserted, and persons affected may be informed from the statute of their rights and duties.

In view of the ease, expedition and safety with which Congress can grant and has granted large emergency powers, certainly ample to embrace this crisis, I am quite unimpressed with the argument that we should affirm possession of them without statute. Such power either has no beginning or it has no end. If it exists, it need submit to no legal restraint. I am not alarmed that it would plunge us straightway into dictatorship, but it is at least a step in that wrong direction.

As to whether there is imperative necessity for such powers, it is relevant to note the gap that exists between the President's paper powers and his real powers. The Constitution does not disclose the measure of the actual controls wielded by the modern presidential office. That instrument must be understood as an Eighteenth-Century sketch of a government hoped for, not as a blueprint of the Government that is. Vast accretions of federal power, eroded from that reserved by the States, have magnified the scope of presidential activity. Subtle shifts take place in the centers of real power that do not show on the face of the Constitution.

Executive power has the advantage of concentration in a single head in whose choice the whole Nation has a part, making him the focus of public hopes and expectations. In drama, magnitude and finality, his decisions so far overshadow any others that, almost alone, he fills the public eye and ear. No other personality in public life can begin to compete with him in access to the public mind through modern methods of communications. By his prestige as head of state and his influence upon public opinion, he exerts a leverage upon those who are supposed to check and balance his power which often cancels their effectiveness.

Moreover, rise of the party system has made a significant extraconstitutional supplement to real executive power. No appraisal of his necessities is realistic which overlooks that he heads a political system, as well as a legal system. Party loyalties and interests, sometimes more binding than law, extend his effective control into branches of government other than his own, and he often may win, as a political leader, what he cannot command under the Constitution. Indeed, Woodrow Wilson, commenting on the President as leader both of his party and of the Nation, observed, "If he rightly interpret the national thought and boldly insist upon it, he is irresistible. . . . His office is anything he has the sagacity and force to make it." I cannot be brought to believe that this country will suffer if the Court refuses further to aggrandize the presidential office, already so potent and so relatively immune from judicial review, at the expense of Congress.

But I have no illusion that any decision by this Court can keep power in the hands of Congress if it is not wise and timely in meeting its problems. A crisis that challenges the President equally, or perhaps primarily, challenges Congress. If not good law, there was worldly wisdom in the maxim attributed to Napoleon that "The tools belong to the man who can use them." We may say that power to legislate for emergencies belongs in the hands of Congress, but only Congress itself can prevent power from slipping through its fingers.

The essence of our free Government is "leave to live by no man's leave, underneath the law"—to be governed by those impersonal forces which we call law. Our Government is fashioned to fulfill this concept so far as humanly possible. The Executive, except for recommendation and veto, has no legislative power. The executive action we have here originates in the individual will of the President, and represents an exercise of authority without law. No one, perhaps not even the President, knows the limits of the power he may seek to exert in this instance, and the parties affected cannot learn the limit of their rights. We do not know today what powers over labor or property would be claimed to flow from Government possession if we should legalize it, what rights to compensation would be claimed or recognized, or on what contingency it would end. With all its defects, delays and inconveniences, men have discovered no technique for long preserving free government except that the Executive be under the law, and that the law be made by parliamentary deliberations.

Such institutions may be destined to pass away. But it is the duty of the Court to be last, not first, to give them up.

*   *   *   *   *   *

Mr. Chief Justice Vinson, with whom Mr. Justice Reed and Mr. Justice Minton join, dissenting.

Some members of the Court are of the view that the President is without power to act in time of crisis in the absence of express statutory authorization. Other members of the Court affirm on the basis of their reading of certain statutes. Because we cannot agree that affirmance is proper on any ground, and because of the transcending importance of the questions presented not only in this critical litigation, but also to the powers of the President and of future Presidents to act in time of crisis, we are compelled to register this dissent.

In passing upon the question of Presidential powers in this case, we must first consider the context in which those powers were exercised.

Those who suggest that this is a case involving extraordinary powers should be mindful that these are extraordinary times. A world not yet recovered from the devastation of World War II has been forced to face the threat of another and more terrifying global conflict. . . .

For almost two full years, our armed forces have been fighting in Korea, suffering casualties of over 108,000 men. . . . Congressional support of the action in Korea has been manifested by provisions for increased military manpower and equipment and for economic stabilization. . . . Congress, recognizing the "grim fact . . . that the United States is now engaged in a struggle for survival" and that "it is imperative that we now take those necessary steps to make our strength equal to the peril of the hour," granted authority to draft men into the armed forces. As a result, we now have over 3,500,000 men in our armed forces.

Appropriations for the Department of Defense, which had averaged less than $13 billion per year for the three years before attack in Korea, were increased by Congress to $48 billion for fiscal year 1951 and to $60 billion for fiscal year 1952. . . . The bulk of the increase is for military equipment and supplies—guns, tanks, ships, planes and ammunition—all of which require steel. Other defense programs requiring great quantities of steel include the large scale expansion of facilities for the Atomic Energy Commission and the expansion of the Nation's productive capacity affirmatively encouraged by Congress.

Congress recognized the impact of these defense programs upon the economy. Following the attack in Korea, the President asked for authority to requisition property and to allocate and fix priorities for scarce goods. In the Defense Production Act of 1950, Congress granted the powers requested and, in addition, granted power to stabilize prices and wages and to provide for settlement of labor disputes arising in the defense program. The Defense Production Act was extended in 1951, a Senate Committee noting that, in the dislocation caused by the programs for purchase of military equipment "lies the seed of an economic disaster that might well destroy the military might we are straining to build." Significantly, the Committee examined the problem "in terms of just one commodity, steel," and found "a graphic picture of the over-all inflationary danger growing out of reduced civilian supplies and rising incomes." Even before Korea, steel production at levels above theoretical 100% capacity was not capable of supplying civilian needs alone. Since Korea, the tremendous military demand for steel has far exceeded the increases in productive capacity. This Committee emphasized that the shortage of steel, even with the mills operating at full capacity, coupled with increased civilian purchasing power, presented grave danger of disastrous inflation.

The President has the duty to execute the foregoing legislative programs. Their successful execution depends upon continued production of steel and stabilized prices for steel. Accordingly, when the collective bargaining agreements between the Nation's steel producers and their employees, represented by the United Steel Workers, were due to expire on December 31, 1951, and a strike shutting down the entire basic steel industry was threatened, the President acted to avert a complete shutdown of steel production. . . .

One is not here called upon even to consider the possibility of executive seizure of a farm, a corner grocery store or even a single industrial plant. Such considerations arise only when one ignores the central fact of this case—that the Nation's entire basic steel production would have shut down completely if there had been no Government seizure. Even ignoring for the moment whatever confidential information the President may possess as "the Nation's organ for foreign affairs," the uncontroverted affidavits in this record amply support the finding that "a work stoppage would immediately jeopardize and imperil our national defense." . . .

Accordingly, if the President has any power under the Constitution to meet a critical situation in the absence of express statutory authorization, there is no basis whatever for criticizing the exercise of such power in this case.

The steel mills were seized for a public use. The power of eminent domain, invoked in this case, is an essential attribute of sovereignty, and has long been recognized as a power of the Federal Government. . . . Admitting that the Government could seize the mills, plaintiffs claim that the implied power of eminent domain can be exercised only under an Act of Congress; under no circumstances, they say, can that power be exercised by the President unless he can point to an express provision in enabling legislation. . . .

Under this view, the President is left powerless at the very moment when the need for action may be most pressing and when no one, other than he, is immediately capable of action. Under this view, he is left powerless because a power not expressly given to Congress is nevertheless found to rest exclusively with Congress . . .

The Presidency was deliberately fashioned as an office of power and independence. Of course, the Framers created no autocrat capable of arrogating any power unto himself at any time. But neither did they create an automaton impotent to exercise the powers of Government at a time when the survival of the Republic itself may be at stake. . . .

A review of executive action demonstrates that our Presidents have on many occasions exhibited the leadership contemplated by the Framers when they made the President Commander in Chief, and imposed upon him the trust to "take Care that the Laws be faithfully executed." With or without explicit statutory authorization, Presidents have at such times dealt with national emergencies by acting promptly and resolutely to enforce legislative programs, at least to save those programs until Congress could act. Congress and the courts have responded to such executive initiative with consistent approval.

Our first President displayed at once the leadership contemplated by the Framers. When the national revenue laws were openly flouted in some sections of Pennsylvania, President Washington, without waiting for a call from the state government, summoned the militia and took decisive steps to secure the faithful execution of the laws. When international disputes engendered by the French Revolution threatened to involve this country in war, and while congressional policy remained uncertain, Washington issued his Proclamation of Neutrality. Hamilton, whose defense of the Proclamation has endured the test of time, invoked the argument that the Executive has the duty to do that which will preserve peace until Congress acts and, in addition, pointed to the need for keeping the Nation informed of the requirements of existing laws and treaties as part of the faithful execution of the laws. . . .

Jefferson's initiative in the Louisiana Purchase, the Monroe Doctrine, and Jackson's removal of Government deposits from the Bank of the United States further serve to demonstrate by deed what the Framers described by word when they vested the whole of the executive power in the President.

Without declaration of war, President Lincoln took energetic action with the outbreak of the War Between the States. He summoned troops and paid them out of the Treasury without appropriation therefore. He proclaimed a naval blockade of the Confederacy and seized ships violating that blockade. Congress, far from denying the validity of these acts, gave them express approval. The most striking action of President Lincoln was the Emancipation Proclamation, issued in aid of the successful prosecution of the War Between the States, but wholly without statutory authority.

In an action furnishing a most apt precedent for this case, President Lincoln, without statutory authority, directed the seizure of rail and telegraph lines leading to Washington. Many months later, Congress recognized and confirmed the power of the President to seize railroads and telegraph lines and provided criminal penalties for interference with Government operation. This Act did not confer on the President any additional powers of seizure. Congress plainly rejected the view that the President's acts had been without legal sanction until ratified by the legislature. Sponsors of the bill declared that its purpose was only to confirm the power which the President already possessed. Opponents insisted a statute authorizing seizure was unnecessary, and might even be construed as limiting existing Presidential powers. . . .

This is but a cursory summary of executive leadership. But it amply demonstrates that Presidents have taken prompt action to enforce the laws and protect the country whether or not Congress happened to provide in advance for the particular method of execution. At the minimum, the executive actions reviewed herein sustain the action of the President in this case. And many of the cited examples of Presidential practice go far beyond the extent of power necessary to sustain the President's order to seize the steel mills. The fact that temporary executive seizures of industrial plants to meet an emergency have not been directly tested in this Court furnishes not the slightest suggestion that such actions have been illegal. Rather, the fact that Congress and the courts have consistently recognized and given their support to such executive action indicates that such a power of seizure has been accepted throughout our history.

History bears out the genius of the Founding Fathers, who created a Government subject to law but not left subject to inertia when vigor and initiative are required . . . .

Focusing now on the situation confronting the President on the night of April 8, 1952, we cannot but conclude that the President was performing his duty under the Constitution to "take Care that the Laws be faithfully executed"—a duty described by President Benjamin Harrison as "the central idea of the office."

The President reported to Congress the morning after the seizure that he acted because a work stoppage in steel production would immediately imperil the safety of the Nation by preventing execution of the legislative programs for procurement of military equipment. And, while a shutdown could be averted by granting the price concessions requested by plaintiffs, granting such concessions would disrupt the price stabilization program also enacted by Congress. Rather than fail to execute either legislative program, the President acted to execute both.

Much of the argument in this case has been directed at straw men. We do not now have before us the case of a President acting solely on the basis of his own notions of the public welfare. Nor is there any question of unlimited executive power in this case. The President himself closed the door to any such claim when he sent his Message to Congress stating his purpose to abide by any action of Congress, whether approving or disapproving his seizure action. Here, the President immediately made sure that Congress was fully informed of the temporary action he had taken only to preserve the legislative programs from destruction until Congress could act.

The absence of a specific statute authorizing seizure of the steel mills as a mode of executing the laws—both the military procurement program and the anti-inflation program—has not until today been thought to prevent the President from executing the laws. Unlike an administrative commission confined to the enforcement of the statute under which it was created, or the head of a department when administering a particular statute, the President is a constitutional officer charged with taking care that a "mass of legislation" be executed. Flexibility as to mode of execution to meet critical situations is a matter of practical necessity. . . .

There is no statute prohibiting seizure as a method of enforcing legislative programs. Congress has in no wise indicated that its legislation is not to be executed by the taking of private property (subject, of course, to the payment of just compensation) if its legislation cannot otherwise be executed. . . .

Whatever the extent of Presidential power on more tranquil occasions, and whatever the right of the President to execute legislative programs as he sees fit without reporting the mode of execution to Congress, the single Presidential purpose disclosed on this record is to faithfully execute the laws by acting in an emergency to maintain the status quo, thereby preventing collapse of the legislative programs until Congress could act. The President's action served the same purposes as a judicial stay entered to maintain the status quo in order to preserve the jurisdiction of a court. In his Message to Congress immediately following the seizure, the President explained the necessity of his action in executing the military procurement and anti-inflation legislative programs and expressed his desire to cooperate with any legislative proposals approving, regulating or rejecting the seizure of the steel mills. Consequently, there is no evidence whatever of any Presidential purpose to defy Congress or act in any way inconsistent with the legislative will. . . .

In this case, there is no statute prohibiting the action taken by the President in a matter not merely important, but threatening the very safety of the Nation. Executive inaction in such a situation, courting national disaster, is foreign to the concept of energy and initiative in the Executive as created by the Founding Fathers. The Constitution was itself adopted in a period of grave emergency. . . . While emergency does not create power, emergency may furnish the occasion for the exercise of power.

The Framers knew, as we should know in these times of peril, that there is real danger in Executive weakness. There is no cause to fear Executive tyranny so long as the laws of Congress are being faithfully executed. Certainly there is no basis for fear of dictatorship when the Executive acts, as he did in this case, only to save the situation until Congress could act. . . .

When the President acted on April 8, he had exhausted the procedures for settlement available to him. . . . Faced with immediate national peril through stoppage in steel production, on the one hand, and faced with destruction of the wage and price legislative programs, on the other, the President took temporary possession of the steel mills as the only course open to him consistent with his duty to take care that the laws be faithfully executed. . . .

The broad executive power granted by Article II to an officer on duty 365 days a year cannot, it is said, be invoked to avert disaster. Instead, the President must confine himself to sending a message to Congress recommending action. Under this messenger-boy concept of the Office, the President cannot even act to preserve legislative programs from destruction so that Congress will have something left to act upon. There is no judicial finding that the executive action was unwarranted because there was, in fact, no basis for the President's finding of the existence of an emergency for, under this view, the gravity of the emergency and the immediacy of the threatened disaster are considered irrelevant as a matter of law.

Seizure of plaintiffs' property is not a pleasant undertaking. Similarly unpleasant to a free country are the draft which disrupts the home and military procurement which causes economic dislocation and compels adoption of price controls, wage stabilization and allocation of materials. The President informed Congress that even a temporary Government operation of plaintiffs' properties was "thoroughly distasteful" to him, but was necessary to prevent immediate paralysis of the mobilization program. Presidents have been in the past, and any man worthy of the Office should be in the future, free to take at least interim action necessary to execute legislative programs essential to survival of the Nation. A sturdy judiciary should not be swayed by the unpleasantness or unpopularity of necessary executive action, but must independently determine for itself whether the President was acting, as required by the Constitution, to "take Care that the Laws be faithfully executed."

*   *   *   *   *   *

POSTSCRIPT

As soon as the Court's ruling was announced, the steelworkers went out on strike. Truman and the Congress had several options available to them. The president could invoke the Taft-Hartley Act and compel labor to return to work for a period of time while the unions and management searched for an agreement. Alternatively, the president could request that Congress pass legislation authorizing him to seize the steel mills for a limited period of time. Truman refused to invoke Taft-Hartley because it would be "unwise, unfair, and quite possibly ineffective," and announced to Congress that it was "squarely up to [them]" to resolve the standoff by enacting "fair and effective legislation." Congress, in turn, requested Truman to invoke the law already on the books, Taft-Hartley. With Congress and the president unable to reach agreement, the strike stretched on for nearly eight weeks.

In defending his seizure of the steel mills, Truman had pointed to the dire consequences that would result if there were even a temporary halt in the production of steel. It turned out, however, that there were substantial steel reserves and that the industries that used steel were able to operate largely at full capacity throughout the nearly two months that the steelworkers were on strike. However, as the strike continued into its second month, the administration became increasingly concerned that the work stoppage was placing the nation's economy and war effort in grave danger. The secretary of defense held a press conference in which he suggested that the strike "had probably caused more damage" to the nation's defenses "than any enemy bombing attack could have inflicted." The administration let it be known that it was ready to use the Selective Service Act to seize control of the steel industry, and on July 24 the leaders of the two sides came to the White House to negotiate a settlement. By the end of the day the two sides had at last reached an agreement, and Truman was able to announce to the nation that the strike was finished. The following day the steelworkers returned to work.

14

United States v. Reynolds (1953)

On October 6, 1948, a B-29 bomber took off from Robins Air Force Base in Georgia; its mission to test secret military equipment. Aboard were eight crew members as well as five civilian engineers involved in the research and development. About 170 miles southeast of Robins Air Force Base, one of the plane's engines caught fire, a second failed, and the plane quickly spiraled out of control. Looking skyward, reported the *Waycross Journal-Herald*, townspeople "stood frozen as bodies and plane parts hurtled downward." Four of those on board managed to parachute to safety, but five of the crew members died as did four of the civilians.

The widows of three of those civilians—Patricia Reynolds, Elizabeth Palya, and Phyllis Brauner—brought suit against the government for wrongful death. Their lawyer requested that the air force provide his clients with its investigative report as well as the statements of the three surviving crew members. The air force refused. Secretary of the Air Force Thomas Finletter explained to the district court that the plane and its crew "were engaged in a highly secret mission" and that release of the report "would not be in the public interest." The air force's top legal official, the judge advocate general, concurred that to release the report would "seriously hamper . . . national security." The judge was prepared to be persuaded and decided that he would make his ruling after reviewing the report in private. However, the government refused to allow even the judge to see the report. Since the government would not cooperate, the judge found in favor of the widows.

The air force could have left matters there, paying out the relatively paltry sum of $225,000 and keeping the report secret. But instead the air force appealed the judgment to the Court of Appeals for the Third Circuit. A three-judge panel heard the case and unanimously upheld the position of the lower court judge. The judiciary, not the executive, the appeals court ruled, had the final say in deciding whether a document should be privileged information and thus unavailable to a plaintiff or defendant in a legal proceeding. To allow the government to be the judge in its own case was a perversion of the rule of law. The court, moreover, found no danger in allowing federal judges to review classified materials in private (*in camera*); if additional information was necessary for a judge to understand the materials' import then the government was free to provide a judge with that background information as well.

Again the government appealed, this time to the Supreme Court. The government argued that it was well within its rights to refuse to divulge state secrets. If that meant the three widows could not win their case of wrongful death, then that was the price the nation paid for ensuring national security. The lawyer for the widows insisted that justice required the government to offer something more than mere assertion to justify its claim that the report would compromise the nation's defenses. The oral argument was heard in October 1952, and in March of the following year the Supreme Court rendered its verdict.

In a 6–3 ruling, the Court sided with the government. The majority opinion was authored by Chief Justice Fred M. Vinson, who had been on the losing side in the *Youngstown* case that had been decided the year before. The three dissenting judges in *Reynolds*—Felix Frankfurter, Robert Jackson, and Hugo Black—indicated only that they dissented "substantially for the reasons set forth in the opinion of Judge Maris," who had penned the Court of Appeals opinion.

*   *   *   *   *   *

Mr. Chief Justice Vinson delivered the opinion of the Court.

We have had broad propositions pressed upon us for decision. On behalf of the Government, it has been urged that the executive department heads have power to withhold any documents in their custody from judicial view if they deem it to be in the public interest. Respondents have asserted that the executive's power to withhold documents was waived by the Tort Claims Act.[1] Both positions have constitutional overtones which we find it unnecessary to pass upon, there being a narrower ground for decision. . . .

When the Secretary of the Air Force lodged his formal "Claim of Privilege," he attempted therein to invoke the privilege against revealing military secrets, a privilege which is well established in the law of evidence. The existence of the privilege is conceded by the court below, and, indeed, by the most outspoken critics of governmental claims to privilege.

Judicial experience with the privilege which protects military and state secrets has been limited in this country. English experience has been more extensive, but still relatively slight compared with other evidentiary privileges. Nevertheless, the principles which control the application of the privilege emerge quite clearly from the available precedents. The privilege belongs to the Government, and must be asserted by it. . . .

It is not to be lightly invoked. There must be a formal claim of privilege, lodged by the head of the department that has control over the matter, after actual personal consideration by that officer. The court itself must determine whether the circumstances are appropriate for the claim of privilege, and yet do so without forcing a disclosure of the very thing the privilege is designed to protect. The latter requirement is the only one that presents real difficulty. As to it, we find it helpful to draw upon judicial experience in dealing with an analogous privilege, the privilege against self-incrimination.

The privilege against self-incrimination presented the courts with a similar sort of problem. Too much judicial inquiry into the claim of privilege would force disclosure of the thing the privilege was meant to protect, while a complete abandonment of judicial control would lead to intolerable abuses. Indeed, in the earlier stages of judicial experience with the problem, both extremes were advocated, some saying that the bare assertion by the witness must be taken as conclusive, and others saying that the witness should be required to reveal the matter behind his claim of privilege to the judge for verification. Neither extreme prevailed, and a sound formula of compromise was developed. . . . There are differences in phraseology, but, in substance, it is agreed that the court must be satisfied from all the evidence and circumstances, and "from the implications of the question, in the setting in which it is asked, that a responsive answer to the question or an explanation of why it cannot be answered might be dangerous because injurious disclosure could result." If the court is so satisfied, the claim of the privilege will be accepted without requiring further disclosure.

Regardless of how it is articulated, some like formula of compromise must be applied here. Judicial control over the evidence in a case cannot be abdicated to the caprice of executive officers. Yet we will not go so far as to say that the court may automatically require a complete disclosure to the judge before the claim of privilege will be accepted in any case. It may be possible to satisfy the court, from all the circumstances of the case, that there is a reasonable danger that compulsion of the evidence will expose military matters that, in the interest of national security, should not be divulged. When this is the case, the occasion for the privilege is appropriate, and the court should not jeopardize the security that the privilege is meant to protect by insisting upon an examination of the evidence, even by the judge alone, in chambers.

In the instant case, we cannot escape judicial notice that this is a time of vigorous preparation for national defense. Experience in the past war has made it common knowledge that air power is one of the most potent weapons in our scheme of defense, and that newly developing electronic devices have greatly enhanced the effective use of air power. It is equally apparent that these electronic devices must be kept secret if their full military advantage is to be exploited in the national interests. On the record before the trial court, it appeared that this accident occurred to a military plane that had gone aloft to test secret electronic equipment. Certainly there was a reasonable danger that the accident investigation report would contain references to the secret electronic equipment which was the primary concern of the mission. . . .

In each case, the showing of necessity that is made will determine how far the court should probe in satisfying itself that the occasion for invoking the privilege is appropriate. Where there is a strong showing of necessity, the claim of privilege should not be lightly accepted, but even the most compelling necessity cannot overcome the claim of privilege if the court is ultimately satisfied that military secrets are at stake. . . .

There is nothing to suggest that the electronic equipment, in this case, had any causal connection with the accident. Therefore, it should be possible for respondents to adduce the essential facts as to causation without resort to material touching upon military secrets. Respondents were given a reasonable opportunity to do just that when petitioner formally offered to make the surviving crew members available for examination. We think that offer should have been accepted.

Respondents have cited to us those cases in the criminal field, where it has been held that the Government can invoke its evidentiary privileges only at the price of letting the defendant go free. The rationale of the criminal cases is that, since the Government which prosecutes an accused also has the duty to see that justice is done, it is unconscionable to allow it to undertake prosecution and then invoke its governmental privileges to deprive the accused of anything which might be material to his defense. Such rationale has no application in a civil forum. . . .

* * * * * *

POSTSCRIPT

In 1996, the air force declassified accident reports for thousands of air crashes that occurred between 1918 and 1955. Among the declassified reports was the one that Patricia Reynolds, Elizabeth Palya, and Phyllis

Brauner had tried so hard to obtain. Although nobody in the government informed the surviving family members that the report was now publicly available, Judith Loether—who was barely a month and half old at the time her father, Albert Palya, had died in the 1948 crash—fortuitously came across a Web site in February 2000 that was selling these newly released reports for a small fee. Within two weeks she had the 220-page accident report that the government, a half-century earlier, had refused to allow a judge to read.

Loether was stunned to find the report contained only a few passing references to secret equipment and little that she didn't already know from reading the contemporary news accounts. Those few places where the report revealed genuinely secret information—for instance, the name of the secret mission and its general purpose—could readily have been redacted by the government or the judge. If the report revealed next to nothing about state secrets it revealed everything about why the plane had crashed. The report found that the crew had never flown together before, that significant "confusion [existed] among the pilot, copilot and engineer," and that they made several crucial errors, including shutting off the fuel for the second engine when it was the first engine that was on fire. The report also suggested that the crew were slow to open the bomb bay doors, and as a result most of those on board were unable to parachute from the plane. In addition, according to air force investigators, the civilian engineers had not been given instructions about emergency procedures, including how to use a parachute. Most important, the investigators concluded that two air force orders to modify the exhaust system "for the purpose of eliminating a definite fire hazard" had been ignored; and it was the exhaust system that was at fault for the fire. In addition, the report found that this particular plane had required "more than the normal amount of maintenance." In fact in the six months prior to the crash the plane had been out of commission more than half of the time. In short, what the report revealed was not state secrets but rather negligence and malfeasance on the part of the government. Had the government released the report in 1952, it is hard to see how the three widows could have failed to win their case.

Wanting to set the record straight and hold her government accountable for its cover-up, Judith sued, claiming that the government had won its case by deceiving the courts. For Judith and the other family members who joined the suit—including the only surviving widow, Patricia Herring (formerly Reynolds), the two daughters of Phyllis Brauner, and Judith's two brothers—this seemed a simple matter of redressing a terrible injustice. The government had concealed its misdeeds and mistakes under a cloak of official secrecy. Surely in a proud democracy this fraudulent activity could not be tolerated. But Judith and the other family members were in for a shock, as the courts once again sided with the government.

First, the family members petitioned the Supreme Court "to set things right," but the Court refused to hear the case. They filed next in district court and lost again. They then appealed to the Third Circuit Court of Appeals with the same disappointing result. Finally, the Supreme Court refused to hear their appeal.

The Third Circuit explained that the principle of the "finality of a judgment" was so important to the judicial process that the plaintiffs faced a near impossible burden of proof: "not just a high hurdle to climb but a steep cliff-face to scale." The misleading statements made by the government, the court found, did not rise to the level of "egregious misconduct . . . such as bribery of a judge or jury or fabrication of evidence by counsel," and only such egregious misconduct could qualify as the sort of "intentional fraud" that would warrant reopening the case. Both the district court and the court of appeals expressed extreme reluctance to substitute their own judgment about what did or did not infringe on national security for the judgment of executive branch officials fifty years earlier. As the Third Circuit expressed it, in an opinion written by Ruggero Aldisert, an eighty-six-year-old justice who had served as a major in the Marine Corps during World War II: there was a "near impossibility of determining with any level of certainly what seemingly insignificant pieces of information would have been of keen interest to a Soviet spy fifty years ago." The district court judge put the same position even more strongly: "In all likelihood, fifty years ago the government had a more accurate understanding 'on the prospect of danger to [national security] from the disclosure of secret or sensitive information' than lay persons could appreciate or than hindsight now allows." Even seemingly innocuous information, the district judge reasoned, might be of use to a "sophisticated intelligence analyst" in uncovering national security secrets.

Judicial reluctance to second guess the executive's assertion of the state secrets privilege has encouraged the executive branch to invoke the privilege with increasing frequency, particularly in recent years. The Bush administration has successfully invoked the state secrets privilege to block suits challenging the National Security Agency's program of secretly eavesdropping on Americans' telephone conversations without a court warrant as well as to stymie legal claims brought by individuals who had been secretly abducted by the Central Intelligence Agency (CIA) and sent to other countries to be tortured and interrogated.

In May 2006, for instance, a federal district judge dismissed a lawsuit against the CIA filed by Khaled El-Masri, a German citizen who had been abducted by the CIA in Macedonia and flown to Afghanistan where he was secretly imprisoned and allegedly beaten. The U.S. government freed El-Masri in May 2004 after they realized he was a victim of mistaken identity, and in December 2005 El-Masri, with the help of the American Civil

Liberties Union (ACLU), filed suit against the government. In throwing out the case, the district judge called the state secrets privilege "a privilege of the highest dignity and significance," a privilege that is "derived from the President's constitutional authority over the conduct of this country's diplomatic and military affairs and [that] therefore belongs exclusively to the Executive Branch." Relying heavily on *Reynolds*—the judge cited the case nine times in his seventeen-page opinion—the judge noted that unlike other privileges, the state secrets privilege was "absolute and therefore once a court is satisfied that the claim is validly asserted, the privilege is not subject to a judicial balancing of the various interests at stake."

The Fourth Circuit Court of Appeals affirmed the district judge's ruling and echoed his reasoning. Although cognizant that cases involving state secrets pit "the judiciary's search for truth against the Executive's duty to maintain the nation's security," the Fourth Circuit held that if a court believed there was "a reasonable danger" that revealing information could compromise national security then the court was "obliged to honor the Executive's assertion of the privilege." Once the court determined that there was a reasonable chance that revealing such information could be injurious to the national interest then, "under the state secrets doctrine" articulated in *Reynolds*, "it is absolutely protected from disclosure—even for the purpose of *in camera* examination by the court." Indeed according to the Fourth Circuit, there were "certain circumstances" in which even asking the executive to explain "why a question cannot be answered would itself create unacceptable danger of injurious disclosure." In such cases the court "is obliged to accept the executive branch's claim of privilege without further demand."

In October 2007 the Supreme Court refused to hear El-Masri's appeal. El-Masri had been defeated in his effort to bring suit against the U.S. government for the harms he had suffered because the party being sued—the government—asserted that to reveal information about El-Masri's abduction and detention, even to a judge in the privacy of his chambers, would endanger national security. Forged in the Cold War, the state secrets privilege had become one of the executive branch's most favored weapons in the war on terror.

NOTE

1. The Tort Claims Act was enacted in 1946 as a way of reducing the amount of time Congress spent considering private claims against the federal government. Rather than have these claims take up valuable legislative time, the act authorized federal agencies and the courts to settle claims against the United States that were "caused by the negligent or wrongful act or omission of any employee of the Government while acting within the scope of his office or employment."

Wartime and Emergency Powers
The War on Terror

15

Hamdan v. Rumsfeld (2006)

"9/11 changed everything." The United States now faced a "new kind of war" and "a new kind of enemy." As President George W. Bush explained in a July 2005 speech, this new kind of enemy "hides in caves and plots in shadows, and then emerges to strike and kill in cold blood in our cities and communities." In this new kind of war—what the president called the "war on terror"—the old rules no longer applied, old laws were no longer adequate, and old ways of thinking and acting were downright dangerous.

There were two ways for President Bush to fight this new kind of war. He could press Congress to enact laws that would endow him with new authority. Or he could bypass Congress, ignoring the outmoded laws and precedents while donning the mantle of commander in chief and appealing to military exigency. Passage of the Patriot Act, which gave the executive new powers to combat terrorism, was an example of the former approach of updating laws to reflect new realities. Often, however, the Bush administration preferred to act unilaterally without congressional authorization. For instance, the president bypassed Congress when he secretly directed the National Security Agency to conduct electronic surveillance of American citizens on American soil in a manner that was plainly not in accordance with the procedures laid down in the Foreign Intelligence Surveillance Act of 1978.

Congress, of course, never declared a war on terror or even on Afghanistan or Iraq. Each of those wars, like the wars in Vietnam and Korea, were initiated by the president, not by Congress. However, President Bush did seek and get from Congress an Authorization for Use of Military Force (AUMF) a week after al Qaeda's murderous attacks killed nearly three thousand people, more than 90 percent of whom were Americans. The resolution authorized the president "to use all necessary and appropriate force against those nations, organizations, or persons he determines planned, authorized, committed, or aided the terrorist attacks that occurred on September 11, 2001, or harbored such organizations or persons, in order to prevent any future acts of international terrorism against the United States by such nations, organizations or persons." To the president's defenders, this joint resolution, passed on September 18, 2001, provided a broad warrant for all the president's antiterror policies, even those taken without Congress's knowledge or consent. Bush's critics, meanwhile, argued that many of the administration's actions extended well beyond what Congress had in mind when it passed that resolution, particularly the invasion of Iraq since Saddam Hussein's regime neither planned nor authorized nor aided the attacks of September 11. Nor, prior to the administration's invasion of Iraq, did Hussein's regime harbor al Qaeda terrorists.

Both defenders and critics of the Bush administration would agree, however, that the congressional resolution of September 18 was intended to authorize military action against the Taliban regime in Afghanistan, which was directly aiding and harboring members of al Qaeda. Congress clearly wanted the president to use all necessary and appropriate force to capture or kill those who were responsible for the September 11 attacks. And that is exactly what the administration did when it captured Salim Ahmed Hamdan in late November 2001 as U.S. forces fought to take Kandahar, the Taliban's last stronghold in Afghanistan. More precisely, Hamdan was captured by Afghan warlords, hogtied with electrical wire, and then handed over to the American forces for a $5,000 bounty.

Hamdan, the Americans soon discovered, had ties with Osama bin Laden. A Yemeni citizen and a part-time taxi driver, Hamdan was recruited in 1996 to join the small Islamic insurgency fighting against the Russian-backed government in Tajikistan. A six-month journey was in vain, however, when Hamdan and his fellow jihadists were turned away at the Tajikistan border. Unsure what to do next, they decided to visit Osama bin Laden, who had recently set up shop in Afghanistan after being expelled from Sudan. For the next five years Hamdan worked for bin Laden, largely as a driver and auto mechanic.

Hamdan was not a big fish in al Qaeda, yet he would become the first "enemy combatant" to be tried by the special military tribunals that Bush had established by military order on November 13, 2001.[1] All the rules that would govern these special tribunals—from the standard of evidence to the definition of war crimes—were written by the administration without consulting or seeking approval from Congress. Contested verdicts were to be reviewed not by a federal court of appeals but by a panel selected by the secretary of defense, thereby excluding the judiciary as well.

The government acknowledged that Hamdan had no role in planning or carrying out any al Qaeda actions, but charged him with conspiracy, which it defined as having "joined an enterprise of persons who shared a common criminal purpose." The military trial began in late August 2004 before a panel of five government-selected military officers, including the commanding officer of a marine who had been killed in al Qaeda's attack on the World Trade Center, an officer responsible for sending those captured in Afghanistan to Guantanamo Bay, and a third who "could not say with certainty what the Geneva Conventions are." Hamdan's lawyers filed for a writ of habeas corpus in federal district court, arguing that the presidentially constituted military commissions lacked the authority to try him. The lawyers put forward two main arguments: (1) the procedures governing the military commissions violated fundamental principles of military and international law, including that a defendant has the right to be present at his trial and to see the evidence presented against him; (2) conspiracy is not a crime that violates the law of war and so cannot be tried by military commission.

A federal judge and Clinton appointee, James Robertson, agreed with Hamdan's lawyers, bringing the military trial to a dramatic and abrupt halt. Robertson ruled that the United States was obliged to treat Hamdan as a prisoner of war; he could then be tried for war crimes but only by a regular court martial. Article 5 of the Third Geneva Convention, Robertson argued, required the administration to bring Hamdan before a special tribunal to determine whether he was a prisoner of war. Only if that tribunal found that Hamdan was not a prisoner of war could the administration then try him before a military commission. The president could not make this determination unilaterally. The Bush administration immediately appealed, objecting—in the words of a Justice Department spokesperson—that the judge "has put terrorism on the same legal footing as legitimate methods of waging war." The Geneva Conventions, the administration argued, did not apply to the war on terror. Indeed the president had issued an executive order in February 2002 that declared that the Geneva Conventions did not to apply to any Taliban and al Qaeda prisoners.

On July 25, a three-judge panel of the D.C. Circuit Court of Appeals overturned Robertson's ruling. Among the three judges was John G. Roberts, who only six days earlier had been nominated by President Bush to a seat on the Supreme Court. All three judges were Republican appointees:

Roberts had been elevated to the D.C. Court of Appeals by Bush in 2001, the opinion writer Arthur Randolph had been appointed by George H. W. Bush in 1990, and Stephen Williams was picked by President Reagan in 1986. The panel sided with the Bush administration on virtually every important point. Now it was Hamdan's turn to appeal. On November 7, 2005, the Supreme Court agreed to hear his case.

As soon as the Court agreed to hear *Hamdan*, South Carolina senator Lindsey Graham attached an amendment to a defense-authorization bill, which declared that "no court, justice, or judge shall have jurisdiction to hear or consider" habeas corpus petitions filed by detainees in Guantanamo Bay. Graham's original language would have specifically forbid courts from hearing pending cases, but Michigan Democrat Carl Levin persuaded Graham to alter the amendment's wording so that pending cases could proceed. The act as passed made no mention of pending cases, and the administration argued that the new law—part of the Detainee Treatment Act—meant that the Supreme Court should dismiss the case.

At least four important questions faced the justices. First, did the Court have the legal right to rule on Hamdan's case? Second, could the president establish military commissions without congressional authorization? Third, did the procedures adopted by the military commissions violate the Geneva Conventions or the Uniform Code of Military Justice passed by Congress in 1950? Finally, the Court was asked to decide whether conspiracy was an offense against the law of war that could be tried by a military commission?

The multifaceted character of the case and the ideological divisions on the court helped to produce a fractured court, in which six of the eight justices (Roberts recused himself) wrote opinions. The three most conservative justices—Samuel Alito, Antonin Scalia, and Clarence Thomas—each wrote dissenting opinions. Writing for the Court's majority was Justice John Paul Stevens.

*   *   *   *   *   *

Justice Stevens . . . delivered the opinion of the Court [Justice Kennedy did not join Part V and two paragraphs in Part VI].

For the reasons that follow, we conclude that the military commission convened to try Hamdan lacks power to proceed because its structure and procedures violate both the UCMJ [Uniform Code of Military Justice] and the Geneva Conventions. Four of us also conclude . . . that the offense with which Hamdan has been charged is not an "offens[e] that by . . . the law of war may be tried by military commissions." . . .

IV

The military commission, a tribunal neither mentioned in the Constitution nor created by statute, was born of military necessity. . . . "The occasion for the military commission arises principally from the fact that the jurisdiction of the court-martial proper . . . is restricted by statute almost exclusively to members of the military force and to certain specific offences defined in a written code."

Exigency alone, of course, will not justify the establishment and use of penal tribunals not contemplated by Article I, §8 and Article III, §1 of the Constitution unless some other part of that document authorizes a response to the felt need. And that authority, if it exists, can derive only from the powers granted jointly to the President and Congress in time of war.

The Constitution makes the President the "Commander in Chief" of the Armed Forces, but vests in Congress the powers to "declare War . . . and make Rules concerning Captures on Land and Water," to raise and support Armies," to "define and punish . . . Offences against the Law of Nations," and "To make Rules for the Government and Regulation of the land and naval Forces." The interplay between these powers was described by Chief Justice Chase in the seminal case of *Ex parte Milligan*:

> The power to make the necessary laws is in Congress; the power to execute in the President. Both powers imply many subordinate and auxiliary powers. Each includes all authorities essential to its due exercise. But neither can the President, in war more than in peace, intrude upon the proper authority of Congress, nor Congress upon the proper authority of the President. . . . Congress cannot direct the conduct of campaigns, nor can the President, or any commander under him, without the sanction of Congress, institute tribunals for the trial and punishment of offences, either of soldiers or civilians, unless in cases of a controlling necessity, which justifies what it compels.

Whether Chief Justice Chase was correct in suggesting that the President may constitutionally convene military commissions "without the sanction of Congress" in cases of "controlling necessity" is a question this Court has not answered definitively, and need not answer today. For we held in [*Ex parte*] *Quirin* that Congress had, through Article of War 15, sanctioned the use of military commissions in such circumstances. ("By the Articles of War, and especially Article 15, Congress has explicitly provided, so far as it may constitutionally do so, that military tribunals shall have jurisdiction to try offenders or offenses against the law of war in appropriate cases"). Article 21 of the UCMJ, the language of which is substantially identical to the old Article 15, . . . was preserved by Congress after World War II.

We have no occasion to revisit *Quirin*'s controversial characterization of Article of War 15 as congressional authorization for military commissions. Contrary to the Government's assertion, however, even *Quirin* did not view the authorization as a sweeping mandate for the President to "invoke military commissions when he deems them necessary." Rather, the *Quirin* Court recognized that Congress had simply preserved what power, under the Constitution and the common law of war, the President had had before 1916 to convene military commissions—with the express condition that the President and those under his command comply with the law of war. . . .

The Government would have us dispense with the inquiry that the *Quirin* Court undertook and find in either the AUMF [Authorization for Use of Military Force] or the DTA [Detainee Treatment Act of 2005] overriding authorization for the very commission that has been convened to try Hamdan. Neither of these congressional Acts, however, expands the President's authority to convene military commissions. First, while we assume that the AUMF activated the President's war powers, see *Hamdi v. Rumsfeld* (2004), and that those powers include the authority to convene military commissions in appropriate circumstances, there is nothing in the text or legislative history of the AUMF even hinting that Congress intended to expand or alter the authorization set forth in Article 21 of the UCMJ.

Likewise, the DTA cannot be read to authorize this commission. Although the DTA, unlike either Article 21 or the AUMF, was enacted after the President had convened Hamdan's commission, it contains no language authorizing that tribunal or any other at Guantanamo Bay. . . .

Together, the UCMJ, the AUMF, and the DTA at most acknowledge a general Presidential authority to convene military commissions in circumstances where justified under the "Constitution and laws," including the law of war. Absent a more specific congressional authorization, the task of this Court is, as it was in *Quirin*, to decide whether Hamdan's military commission is so justified. It is to that inquiry we now turn.

V

Quirin is the model the Government invokes most frequently to defend the commission convened to try Hamdan. That is both appropriate and unsurprising. Since Guantanamo Bay is neither enemy-occupied territory nor under martial law, the law-of-war commission is the only model available. At the same time, no more robust model of executive power exists; *Quirin* represents the high-water mark of military power to try enemy combatants for war crimes. . . .

The question is whether the preconditions designed to ensure that a military necessity exists to justify the use of this extraordinary tribunal have been satisfied here.

The charge against Hamdan . . . alleges a conspiracy extending over a number of years, from 1996 to November 2001. All but two months of that more than 5-year-long period preceded the attacks of September 11, 2001, and the enactment of the AUMF—the Act of Congress on which the Government relies for exercise of its war powers and thus for its authority to convene military commissions. Neither the purported agreement with Osama bin Laden and others to commit war crimes, nor a single overt act, is alleged to have occurred in a theater of war or on any specified date after September 11, 2001. None of the overt acts that Hamdan is alleged to have committed violates the law of war.

These facts alone cast doubt on the legality of the charge and, hence, the commission; . . . the offense alleged must have been committed both in a theater of war and during, not before, the relevant conflict. But the deficiencies in the time and place allegations also underscore—indeed are symptomatic of—the most serious defect of this charge: The offense it alleges is not triable by law-of-war military commission.

There is no suggestion that Congress has, in exercise of its constitutional authority to "define and punish . . . Offences against the Law of Nations," positively identified "conspiracy" as a war crime. As we explained in *Quirin*, that is not necessarily fatal to the Government's claim of authority to try the alleged offense by military commission; Congress, through Article 21 of the UCMJ, has "incorporated by reference" the common law of war, which may render triable by military commission certain offenses not defined by statute. When, however, neither the elements of the offense nor the range of permissible punishments is defined by statute or treaty, the precedent must be plain and unambiguous. To demand any less would be to risk concentrating in military hands a degree of adjudicative and punitive power in excess of that contemplated either by statute or by the Constitution. . . .

This high standard was met in *Quirin*; the violation there alleged was, by "universal agreement and practice" both in this country and internationally, recognized as an offense against the law of war. . . .

At a minimum, the Government must make a substantial showing that the crime for which it seeks to try a defendant by military commission is acknowledged to be an offense against the law of war. That burden is far from satisfied here. The crime of "conspiracy" has rarely if ever been tried as such in this country by any law-of-war military commission not exercising some other form of jurisdiction, and does not appear in either the Geneva Conventions or the Hague Conventions—the major treaties on the law of war. . . .

The charge's shortcomings are not merely formal, but are indicative of a broader inability on the Executive's part here to satisfy the most basic precondition—at least in the absence of specific congressional authorization—for establishment of military commissions: military necessity. Hamdan's tribunal was appointed not by a military commander in the field of battle, but by a retired major general stationed away from any active hostilities. Hamdan is charged not with an overt act for which he was caught red-handed in a theater of war and which military efficiency demands be tried expeditiously, but with an agreement the inception of which long predated the attacks of September 11, 2001 and the AUMF. That may well be a crime, but it is not an offense that "by the law of war may be tried by military commissio[n]." None of the overt acts alleged to have been committed in furtherance of the agreement is itself a war crime, or even necessarily occurred during time of, or in a theater of, war. Any urgent need for imposition or execution of judgment is utterly belied by the record; Hamdan was arrested in November 2001 and he was not charged until mid-2004. These simply are not the circumstances in which, by any stretch of the historical evidence or this Court's precedents, a military commission established by Executive Order under the authority of Article 21 of the UCMJ may lawfully try a person and subject him to punishment.

VI

The conflict with al Qaeda is not, according to the Government, a conflict to which the full protections afforded detainees under the 1949 Geneva Conventions apply because Article 2 of those Conventions (which appears in all four Conventions) renders the full protections applicable only to "all cases of declared war or of any other armed conflict which may arise between two or more of the High Contracting Parties." Since Hamdan was captured and detained incident to the conflict with al Qaeda and not the conflict with the Taliban, and since al Qaeda, unlike Afghanistan, is not a "High Contracting Party"—*i.e.*, a signatory of the Conventions, the protections of those Conventions are not, it is argued, applicable to Hamdan.

We need not decide the merits of this argument because there is at least one provision of the Geneva Conventions that applies here even if the relevant conflict is not one between signatories. Article 3, often referred to as Common Article 3 because, like Article 2, it appears in all four Geneva Conventions, provides that in a "conflict not of an international character occurring in the territory of one of the High Contracting Parties, each Party to the conflict shall be bound to apply, as a minimum," certain provisions protecting "persons taking no active part in the hostilities, including members of armed forces who have laid down their arms and those placed *hors de combat* by . . . detention." One such provision prohibits "the passing of sentences and the carrying out of executions without previous judgment pronounced by a regularly constituted court affording all the judicial guarantees which are recognized as indispensable by civilized peoples."

The Court of Appeals thought, and the Government asserts, that Common Article 3 does not apply to Hamdan because the conflict with al Qaeda, being "international in scope," does not qualify as a "conflict not of an international character." That reasoning is erroneous. . . .

Common Article 3, then, is applicable here and, as indicated above, requires that Hamdan be tried by a "regularly constituted court affording all the judicial guarantees which are recognized as indispensable by civilized peoples." . . . The commentary accompanying a provision of the Fourth Geneva Convention . . . defines "regularly constituted" tribunals to include "ordinary military courts" and "definitely exclud[e] all special tribunals." . . .

Inextricably intertwined with the question of regular constitution is the evaluation of the procedures governing the tribunal and whether they afford "all the judicial guarantees which are recognized as indispensable by civilized peoples." Like the phrase "regularly constituted court," this phrase is not defined in the text of the Geneva Conventions. But it must be understood to incorporate at least the barest of those trial protections that have been recognized by customary international law.

We agree with Justice Kennedy that the procedures adopted to try Hamdan deviate from those governing courts-martial in ways not justified by any "evident practical need," and for that reason, at least, fail to afford the requisite guarantees.[2] We add only that . . . various provisions of Commission Order No. 1 dispense with the principles, articulated in Article 75 and indisputably part of the customary international law, that an accused must, absent disruptive conduct or consent, be present for his trial and must be privy to the evidence against him. That the Government has a compelling interest in denying Hamdan access to certain sensitive information is not doubted. But, at least absent express statutory provision to the contrary, information used to convict a person of a crime must be disclosed to him.

Common Article 3 obviously tolerates a great degree of flexibility in trying individuals captured during armed conflict; its requirements are general ones, crafted to accommodate a wide variety of legal systems. But *requirements* they are nonetheless. The commission that the President has convened to try Hamdan does not meet those requirements.

VII

We have assumed, as we must, that the allegations made in the Government's charge against Hamdan are true. We have assumed, moreover, the truth of the message implicit in that charge—viz., that Hamdan is a dangerous individual whose beliefs, if acted upon, would cause great harm and even death to innocent civilians, and who would act upon those beliefs if given the opportunity. It bears emphasizing that Hamdan does not challenge, and we do not today address, the Government's power to detain him for the duration of active hostilities in order to prevent such harm. But in undertaking to try Hamdan and subject him to criminal punishment, the Executive is bound to comply with the Rule of Law that prevails in this jurisdiction.

The judgment of the Court of Appeals is reversed, and the case is remanded for further proceedings.

*   *   *   *   *   *

Justice Breyer, with whom Justice Kennedy, Justice Souter, and Justice Ginsburg join, concurring.

The Court's conclusion ultimately rests upon a single ground: Congress has not issued the Executive a "blank check." Indeed, Congress has denied the President the legislative authority to create military commissions of the kind at issue here. Nothing prevents the President from returning to Congress to seek the authority he believes necessary.

Where, as here, no emergency prevents consultation with Congress, judicial insistence upon that consultation does not weaken our Nation's ability to deal with danger. To the contrary, that insistence strengthens the Nation's ability to determine—through democratic means—how best to do so. The Constitution places its faith in those democratic means. Our Court today simply does the same.

*   *   *   *   *   *

Justice Kennedy, with whom Justice Souter, Justice Ginsburg, and Justice Breyer join as to Parts I and II, concurring in part.

Military Commission Order No. 1, which governs the military commission established to try petitioner Salim Hamdan for war crimes, exceeds limits that certain statutes, duly enacted by Congress, have placed on the President's authority to convene military courts. This is not a case, then, where the Executive can assert some unilateral authority to fill a void left by congressional inaction. It is a case where Congress, in the proper exercise of its powers as an independent branch of government, and as part of a long tradition of legislative involvement in matters of military justice, has considered the subject of military tribunals and set limits on the President's authority. Where a statute provides the conditions for the exercise of governmental power, its requirements are the result of a deliberative and reflective process engaging both of the political branches. Respect for laws derived from the customary operation of the Executive and Legislative Branches gives some assurance of stability in time of crisis. The Constitution is best preserved by reliance on standards tested over time and insulated from the pressures of the moment. . . .

Trial by military commission raises separation-of-powers concerns of the highest order. Located within a single branch, these courts carry the risk that offenses will be defined, prosecuted, and adjudicated by executive officials without independent review. Concentration of power puts personal liberty in peril of arbitrary action by officials, an incursion the Constitution's three-part system is designed to avoid. It is imperative, then, that when military tribunals are established, full and proper authority exists for the Presidential directive.

The proper framework for assessing whether Executive actions are authorized is the three-part scheme used by Justice Jackson in his opinion in *Youngstown Sheet & Tube Co. v. Sawyer* (1952). "When the President acts pursuant to an express or implied authorization of Congress, his authority is at its maximum, for it includes all that he possesses in his own right plus all that Congress can delegate." "When the President acts in absence of either a congressional grant or denial of authority, he can only rely upon his own independent powers, but there is a zone of twilight in which he and Congress may have concurrent authority, or in which its distribution is uncertain." And "when the President takes measures incompatible with the expressed or implied will of Congress, his power is at its lowest ebb."

In this case, as the Court observes, the President has acted in a field with a history of congressional participation and regulation. In the Uniform Code of Military Justice (UCMJ), which Congress enacted, building on earlier statutes, in 1950, Congress has set forth governing principles for military courts. . . . While these laws provide authority for certain forms of military courts, they also impose limitations. . . . If the President has exceeded these limits, this becomes a case of conflict between Presidential and congressional action—a case within Justice Jackson's third category, not the second or first.

At a minimum a military commission like the one at issue—a commission specially convened by the President to try specific persons without express congressional authorization—can be "regularly constituted" by the standards of our military justice system only if some practical need explains deviations from court-martial practice. . . . Relevant concerns . . . relate to logistical constraints, accommodation of witnesses, security of the proceedings, and the like, not mere expedience or convenience. This determination, of course, must be made with due regard for the constitutional principle that congressional statutes can be controlling, including the congressional direction that the law of war has a bearing on the determination. . . .

To begin with, the structure and composition of the military commission deviate from conventional court-martial standards. . . . These structural differences between the military commissions and courts-martial— the concentration of functions, including legal decision making, in a single executive official; the less rigorous standards for composition of the tribunal; and the creation of special review procedures in place of institutions created and regulated by Congress—remove safeguards that are important to the fairness of the proceedings and the independence of the court. Congress has prescribed these guarantees for courts-martial; and no evident practical need explains the departures here. For these reasons the commission cannot be considered regularly constituted under United

States law and thus does not satisfy Congress' requirement that military commissions conform to the law of war.

Apart from these structural issues, moreover, the basic procedures for the commissions deviate from procedures for courts-martial. [For instance,] the order imposes just one evidentiary rule: "Evidence shall be admitted if . . . the evidence would have probative value to a reasonable person." . . . The rule here could permit admission of multiple hearsay and other forms of evidence generally prohibited on grounds of unreliability. Indeed, the commission regulations specifically contemplate admission of unsworn written statements; and they make no provision for exclusion of coerced declarations save those "established to have been made as a result of torture." Besides, even if evidence is deemed nonprobative by the presiding officer at Hamdan's trial, the military-commission members still may view it. In another departure from court-martial practice the military commission members may object to the presiding officer's evidence rulings and determine themselves, by majority vote, whether to admit the evidence.

In sum, as presently structured, Hamdan's military commission exceeds the bounds Congress has placed on the President's authority in . . . the UCMJ. Because Congress has prescribed these limits, Congress can change them, requiring a new analysis consistent with the Constitution and other governing laws. At this time, however, we must apply the standards Congress has provided. By those standards the military commission is deficient.

*   *   *   *   *   *

Justice Scalia, with whom Justice Thomas and Justice Alito join, dissenting.

On December 30, 2005, Congress enacted the Detainee Treatment Act (DTA). It unambiguously provides that, as of that date, "no court, justice, or judge" shall have jurisdiction to consider the habeas application of a Guantanamo Bay detainee. Notwithstanding this plain directive, the Court today concludes that, on what it calls the statute's *most natural* reading, *every* "court, justice, or judge" before whom such a habeas application was pending on December 30 has jurisdiction to hear, consider, and render judgment on it. This conclusion is patently erroneous. . . .

The DTA provides: "No court, justice, or judge shall have jurisdiction to hear or consider an application for a writ of habeas corpus filed by or on behalf of an alien detained by the Department of Defense at Guantanamo Bay, Cuba." This provision "t[ook] effect on the date of the enactment of this Act, which was December 30, 2005. As of that date, then, *no* court had jurisdiction to "hear or consider" the merits of petitioner's habeas application. This repeal of jurisdiction is simply not ambiguous as between pending and future cases. It prohibits *any* exercise of jurisdiction, and it became effective as to *all* cases last December 30. . . .

Though it does not squarely address the issue, the Court hints ominously that "the Government's preferred reading" would "rais[e] grave questions about Congress' authority to impinge upon this Court's appellate jurisdiction, particularly in habeas cases." It is not clear how there could be any such lurking questions, in light of the aptly named *"Exceptions* Clause" of Article III, §2, which, in making our appellate jurisdiction subject to "such Exceptions, and under such Regulations as the Congress shall make," explicitly permits exactly what Congress has done here. . . .

    *   *   *   *   *   *

Justice Thomas, with whom Justice Scalia joins, and with whom Justice Alito joins in all but Part [I], . . . dissenting.

For the reasons set forth in Justice Scalia's dissent, it is clear that this Court lacks jurisdiction to entertain petitioner's claims. The Court having concluded otherwise, it is appropriate to respond to the Court's resolution of the merits of petitioner's claims because its opinion openly flouts our well-established duty to respect the Executive's judgment in matters of military operations and foreign affairs. The Court's evident belief that *it* is qualified to pass on the "military necessity" of the Commander in Chief's decision to employ a particular form of force against our enemies is so antithetical to our constitutional structure that it simply cannot go unanswered. I respectfully dissent.

I

Our review of petitioner's claims arises in the context of the President's wartime exercise of his commander-in-chief authority in conjunction with the complete support of Congress. Accordingly, it is important to take measure of the respective roles the Constitution assigns to the three branches of our Government in the conduct of war.

As I explained in *Hamdi v. Rumsfeld,* the structural advantages attendant to the Executive Branch—namely, the decisiveness, "'activity, secrecy, and dispatch'" that flow from the Executive's "'unity,'" (quoting The Federalist No. 70)—led the Founders to conclude that the "President has primary responsibility—along with the necessary power—to protect the national security and to conduct the Nation's foreign relations." Consistent with this conclusion, the Constitution vests in the President "the executive Power," provides that he "shall be Commander in Chief" of the Armed Forces, and places in him the power to recognize foreign governments. This Court has observed that these provisions confer upon the President broad constitutional authority to protect the Nation's security in the manner he deems fit.

Congress, to be sure, has a substantial and essential role in both foreign affairs and national security. But "Congress cannot anticipate and legislate with regard to every possible action the President may find it necessary to take or every possible situation in which he might act," and "such failure of Congress does not, 'especially . . . in the areas of foreign policy and national security,' imply 'congressional disapproval' of action taken by the Executive." *Dames & Moore v. Regan* (1981). Rather, in these domains, the fact that Congress has provided the President with broad authorities does not imply—and the Judicial Branch should not infer—that Congress intended to deprive him of particular powers not specifically enumerated. . . .

When "the President acts pursuant to an express or implied authorization from Congress," his actions are "supported by the strongest of presumptions and the widest latitude of judicial interpretation, and the burden of persuasion rest[s] heavily upon any who might attack it." (*Youngstown Sheet & Tube Co. v. Sawyer*, [1952] [Jackson, J., concurring]). Accordingly, in the very context that we address today, this Court has concluded that "the detention and trial of petitioners—ordered by the President in the declared exercise of his powers as Commander in Chief of the Army in time of war and of grave public danger—are not to be set aside by the courts without the clear conviction that they are in conflict with the Constitution or laws of Congress constitutionally enacted." *Ex parte Quirin* (1942).

Under this framework, the President's decision to try Hamdan before a military commission for his involvement with al Qaeda is entitled to a heavy measure of deference. In the present conflict, Congress has authorized the President "to use all necessary and appropriate force against those nations, organizations, or persons *he determines* planned, authorized, committed, or aided the terrorist attacks that occurred on September 11, 2001 . . . in order to prevent any future acts of international terrorism against the United States by such nations, organizations or persons." . . .

II

The plurality concludes that the legality of the charge against Hamdan is doubtful because "Hamdan is charged not with an overt act for which he was caught red-handed in a theater of war . . . but with an *agreement* the inception of which long predated . . . the [relevant armed conflict]." The plurality's willingness to second-guess the Executive's judgments in this context, based upon little more than its unsupported assertions, constitutes an unprecedented departure from the traditionally limited role of the courts with respect to war and an unwarranted intrusion on executive authority. . . .

Ultimately, the plurality's determination that Hamdan has not been charged with an offense triable before a military commission rests not upon any historical example or authority, but upon the plurality's raw judgment of the "inability on the Executive's part here to satisfy the most basic precondition . . . for establishment of military commissions: military necessity." This judgment starkly confirms that the plurality has appointed itself the ultimate arbiter of what is quintessentially a policy and military judgment, namely, the appropriate military measures to take against those who "aided the terrorist attacks that occurred on September 11, 2001." The plurality's suggestion that Hamdan's commission is illegitimate because it is not dispensing swift justice on the battlefield is unsupportable. Even a cursory review of the authorities confirms that law-of-war military commissions have wide-ranging jurisdiction to try offenses against the law of war in exigent and nonexigent circumstances alike. Traditionally, retributive justice for heinous war crimes is as much a "military necessity" as the "demands" of "military efficiency" touted by the plurality, and swift military retribution is precisely what Congress authorized the President to impose on the September 11 attackers in the AUMF.

Today a plurality of this Court would hold that conspiracy to massacre innocent civilians does not violate the laws of war. This determination is unsustainable. The judgment of the political branches that Hamdan, and others like him, must be held accountable before military commissions for their involvement with and membership in an unlawful organization dedicated to inflicting massive civilian casualties is supported by virtually every relevant authority, including all of the authorities invoked by the plurality today. It is also supported by the nature of the present conflict. We are not engaged in a traditional battle with a nation-state, but with a worldwide, hydra-headed enemy, who lurks in the shadows conspiring to reproduce the atrocities of September 11, 2001, and who has boasted of sending suicide bombers into civilian gatherings, has proudly distributed videotapes of beheadings of civilian workers, and has tortured and dismembered captured American soldiers. But according to the plurality, when our Armed Forces capture those who are plotting terrorist atrocities like the bombing of the Khobar Towers, the bombing of the USS *Cole,* and the attacks of September 11—even if their plots are advanced to the very brink of fulfillment—our military cannot charge those criminals with any offense against the laws of war. Instead, our troops must catch the terrorists "red-handed," in the midst of *the attack itself,* in order to bring them to justice. Not only is this conclusion fundamentally inconsistent with the cardinal principal of the law of war, namely protecting non-combatants, but it would sorely hamper the President's ability to confront and defeat a new and deadly enemy.

After seeing the plurality overturn longstanding precedents in order to seize jurisdiction over this case, and after seeing them disregard the clear prudential counsel that they abstain in these circumstances from using equitable powers, it is no surprise to see them go on to overrule one after another of the President's judgments pertaining to the conduct of an ongoing war. Those Justices who today disregard the commander-in-chief's wartime decisions, only 10 days ago deferred to the judgment of the Corps of Engineers with regard to a matter much more within the competence of lawyers, upholding that agency's wildly implausible conclusion that a storm drain is a tributary of the waters of the United States. It goes without saying that there is much more at stake here than storm drains. The plurality's willingness to second-guess the determination of the political branches that these conspirators must be brought to justice is both unprecedented and dangerous.

*   *   *   *   *   *

POSTSCRIPT

Four months after the Court's ruling and less than three weeks before the 2006 midterm elections, President George W. Bush appeared at a White House signing ceremony, affixing his signature to the Military Commissions Act of 2006, a law he said that would help the government "deliver justice to the terrorists we have captured." The act not only authorized the use of military tribunals but stripped courts of the power to hear appeals from enemy combatants who were not American citizens. It also empowered the president to determine what the Geneva Conventions meant and how they should be applied. In addition, the act broadened the definition of "unlawful enemy combatant" to include all those who have "purposefully and materially supported hostilities against the United States." Congress did succeed in getting the White House to accept some provisions in the final bill that the administration initially resisted, including giving the defendant the right to be present at the military trial. Overall, though, the bill emphatically enhanced the president's power in the war on terrorism.

There was less agreement, not surprisingly, on whether this bill was a step forward or backward. Critics contended that the law was a dangerous attack on civil liberties and an unconstitutional assault on judicial independence. Defenders claimed that the bill erases all doubts about the constitutionality of the president's actions since he was now clearly operating with the imprimatur of Congress. One thing is certain: immediately after the bill became law the Bush administration rushed to put it to use. The Justice Department promptly informed the federal courts that they no longer had the power to hear lawsuits that had been filed on behalf of enemy combatants held at Guantanamo Bay. The U.S. District Court in Washington, D.C., was instructed that it no longer had jurisdiction over nearly two hundred pending habeas corpus cases.

In the spring of 2007, the administration put Hamdan on trial again, charging him with conspiracy and with "providing material support for terrorism." The charges were initially dismissed on the grounds that the Combatant Status Review Tribunal had found that Hamdan was an enemy combatant but not an unlawful enemy combatant. Since the 2006 act gave military commissions the power to try only unlawful combatants, the military commission lacked jurisdiction to try Hamdan. In a subsequent hearing in December 2007, however, Hamdan was determined to be an illegal enemy combatant, allowing his military trial to begin, at last, in July 2008—the first trial by a military commission since the close of World War II.

Hamdan was charged by the government with conspiring to commit terrorist acts and with "providing material support for terrorism." Fourteen witnesses were called by the prosecution, four of whom remained anonymous. The defense called eight witnesses, including two who were compelled to give their testimony in a secret, closed session. Among those testifying on behalf of Hamdan was Khalid Sheik Mohammed, the self-described mastermind of the September 11, 2001, attacks, who described Hamdan as a "primitive" man who was "not fit to plan or execute" a terrorist attack. Hamdan, Mohammed stressed, was only "fit to change trucks' tires, change oil filters, wash and clean cars, and fasten cargo in pick up trucks." While the defense portrayed Hamdan as a low-level employee with no ideological commitment to al Qaeda, the prosecution painted Hamdan as a member of bin Laden's inner circle who had taken a personal oath of allegiance to al Qaeda's leader. The government argued that, even if only a driver, Hamdan had helped bin Laden to carry out acts of terrorism and to avoid capture. As one prosecution witness put it, "Without people like Mr. Hamdan, bin Laden would enjoy no support, enjoy no protection, and would probably have been unable to elude capture up until this point."

On August 6, 2008, a military jury made up of six unidentified military officers (selected from a pool of thirteen officers chosen by the Pentagon) delivered its verdict. Hamdan, the jury found, was not guilty of conspiracy. The government had failed to demonstrate that Hamdan had any role in the planning or execution of terrorist attacks. However, the jury also found that Hamdan had indeed been a driver for bin Laden and that he continued to work for bin Laden even after he knew that bin Laden was responsible for terrorist acts and that he therefore was guilty of providing material support for terrorism. The government refused to make public the precise vote count in the two decisions, but a guilty verdict required a two-thirds vote.

The government pressed the jury to provide "a very long sentence" for this "hardened al-Qaeda member." At least thirty years and preferably life in prison was necessary, the government prosecutor told the court, because "anyone who provides material support for terrorism is a serious war criminal and a continuing threat to our society." The jury should use Hamdan's sentence to "send a message to others that if anyone thinks of providing material support to the sword of terrorism . . . there will be painful consequences." The defense pressed the jury to consider a sentence of forty-five months or less in recognition of Hamdan's cooperation with U.S. officials, his peripheral involvement in al Qaeda's terrorist activities, and his expressions of regret at his involvement with bin Laden. The jury refused to send the message sought by the government, deciding instead that Hamdan should serve fifty-five months in prison. Since the judge had already granted a defense motion—fiercely resisted by the government's lawyers—giving Hamdan credit for the five years and one month that he had already served in Guantanamo since being formally charged in 2003, the jury's verdict meant that Hamdan would have to serve only five additional months in prison.

After the jury had issued its guilty verdict the government crowed that the case demonstrated that the military commission system was, in the words of the Deputy White House press secretary, "a fair and appropriate legal process for prosecuting detainees alleged to have committed crimes against the United States or our interests." Pentagon spokesman Bryan Whitman was quoted as saying that Hamdan was "no longer considered an enemy combatant" but was instead "a convicted war criminal." The relatively light sentence, however, brought a more subdued reaction from government officials. Whitman now reminded reporters that as soon as Hamdan completed his prison sentence he would revert to being an "enemy combatant" and could be held by the government indefinitely until such time as a military administrative review board determined he was no longer an enemy combatant.

Critics of the military commission system were cheered by the relatively light sentence but the outcome did not dim their criticisms of what Hamdan's attorney, Charles D. Swift, derided as "a made-up tribunal to try anybody we don't like." Among the objections raised by Hamdan's team of lawyers was that providing "material support" was well below the level that had historically been required to convict someone of a war crime, which is why Hitler's driver was not prosecuted as a war criminal at Nuremburg. Therefore, according to the defense, under international law, Hamdan's offense should not have been prosecuted before a military commission but rather in a regular court. Moreover, the defense attorneys pointed to the many ways that the military commissions failed to provide the protections afforded a defendant in a regular trial. True, the presiding judge in the military commission had excluded statements Hamdan made to interrogators in late 2001 because of the "highly coercive" conditions of those interrogations, but the judge also ruled that Hamdan was not entitled to the Fifth Amendment protections against self-incrimination. Defense attorneys objected too that much of the testimony was given in secret and that they were prevented from speaking about certain issues. They were forbidden, for instance, from mentioning the Central Intelligence Agency or its treatment of Hamdan in 2001. Although the defense attorneys had top-secret security clearances, they were not allowed to see the reports from CIA interrogations or talk to the CIA agents involved in the interrogations. Citing these and other shortcomings of the military commission system, Hamdan's attorney promised to appeal the verdict in the federal courts, all the way back to the U.S. Supreme Court if necessary.

In the final week of November 2008, with only one month left to run in Hamdan's sentence, the government announced that it was sending Hamdan back to his home country of Yemen to serve the remaining month of his sentence in a Yemeni prison. On December 27, under the terms of the agreement reached with the Yemeni government, Hamdan would be freed and reunited with his wife and family.

NOTES

1. The order on the "Detention, Treatment, and Trial of Certain Non-Citizens in the War Against Terrorism" defined "enemy combatant" as "an individual who was part of or supporting Taliban or al Qaeda forces, or associated forces that are engaged in hostilities against the United States or its coalition partners."

2. Kennedy did not join this paragraph or the preceding one.

Wartime and Emergency Powers
The War on Terror

16

Boumediene v. Bush (2008)

S alim Hamdan was not a typical detainee at Guantanamo Bay; he was one of the select few to be formally charged and brought to trial before a military commission. As of March 2008, according to a report by the *New York Times*, only 10 of the 385 prisoners at Guantanamo had been charged with a crime and designated for trial. More typical was Lakhdar Boumediene, an Algerian-born Bosnian citizen who was brought to Guantanamo in January 2002.

In October 2001, Boumediene and five other men were arrested by Bosnian police at the request of the U.S. government, who suspected the men of plotting to blow up the American embassy in Sarajevo. The police investigation turned up insufficient evidence to hold the men, in the opinion of the Bosnian Supreme Court, which ordered them to be freed. Upon their release from prison in January 2002, however, the men were immediately seized by the U.S. military and flown to Guantanamo Bay, where they have been ever since.

Lawyers for Boumediene promptly filed a petition for a writ of habeas corpus, but the district court agreed with the government that Boumediene had no grounds to challenge his detention in federal court since he was not a U.S. citizen and was not being held in the United States. The Court of Appeals agreed. The U.S. Supreme Court, however, did not, ruling in *Rasul v. Bush* (2004) that foreign nationals held at Guantanamo could challenge their detention in federal court. The Defense Department responded by establishing a system of Combatant Status Review Tribunals (CSRT) in which detainees would be provided an opportunity to challenge their designation as an enemy combatant.

Boumediene's CSRT hearing took place on September 21, 2004. The government did not allege that Boumediene had any designs on the American embassy in Sarajevo. Instead the government argued that Boumediene was properly classified as an enemy combatant because he was "a supporter of al Qaida." As evidence, the government pointed out that Boumediene was an Algerian native who had "repeatedly traveled to hotspots of regional conflict throughout the Middle East and Eastern Europe," including Pakistan, Yemen, Albania, and Bosnia. He had "on multiple occasions provided subsistence" to Bensayah Belkacem, who was "a known al Qaida operative," and that Boumediene had given "conflicting statements" about the nature of his association with Belkacem. Moreover, Boumediene had retained and financed legal representation for another known al Qaeda operative who had been arrested for terrorist activities. Upon the evidence provided by the government, the CSRT determined that Boumediene had been correctly designated as an enemy combatant.

Critics of the CSRT maintained that the new system of tribunals was heavily stacked against the detainees, who could not present witnesses or cross-examine the government's witnesses. Only about one in fifteen tribunals failed to uphold the government's initial designation of a detainee as an enemy combatant. In the eyes of critics, the Bush administration had failed to comply with the Court's holding in *Rasul v. Bush*. The government countered that CSRT gave detainees a fair opportunity to challenge their detention before an impartial tribune while still enabling the government to protect national security.

Boumediene and other detainees who had petitioned for a writ of habeas corpus continued their legal battle to challenge their detention in federal court. The Bush administration moved to close down this legal avenue by pressing Congress to pass the Detainee Treatment Act of 2005 (DTA), which provided that "no court, justice, or judge shall have jurisdiction to hear or consider . . . an application for a writ of habeas corpus filed by or on behalf of an alien detained by the Department of Defense at Guantanamo Bay, Cuba." Under the DTA, detainees could appeal their status as enemy combatants but only in the Court of Appeals for the District of Columbia Circuit, and the scope of that review was limited. The appeals court was required to defer to the CSRT's findings of fact and the detainee was not allowed to submit new evidence. In *Hamdan v. Rumsfeld* (2006), the Supreme Court sharply limited the scope of the DTA by ruling that it did not apply to those like Boumediene whose habeas petition was pending at the time the DTA was enacted. The Republican-controlled Congress responded by passing the Military Commissions Act of 2006

(MCA), which clarified its intent to withhold the privilege of habeas corpus from all Guantanamo detainees who had been designated as enemy combatants, "without exception."

Boumediene and his fellow detainees again appealed, arguing that this habeas-stripping provision was unconstitutional. Many lawmakers agreed, including some of those who voted for the MCA. Pennsylvania Republican Arlen Specter, who was then chairman of the Senate Judiciary Committee, declared that the provision was "patently unconstitutional." Oregon's Republican senator Gordon Smith declared the provision to be a "frontal attack on our judiciary . . . as well as our civil-rights laws." Both nonetheless voted for the bill, as did many Democrats who had similar misgiving about the provision's constitutionality. These members of Congress evidently hoped, as Specter put it, that the courts would "clean [the law] up."

The D.C. Circuit Court, however, refused to invalidate the work of Congress. In passing the MCA, the court ruled, Congress had clearly intended to stop petitions like Boumediene's from going forward. Under the statute, the circuit court was expressly forbidden from considering a writ of habeas corpus from Boumediene or any other alien held in Guantanamo Bay. Boumediene appealed to the Supreme Court, which initially declined to hear the case. Three months later, without explanation, the Court reversed itself and granted review. Oral arguments were heard on December 5, 2007, and on June 12, 2008, the Court announced its judgment.

*   *   *   *   *   *

Justice Kennedy delivered the opinion of the Court.

Petitioners present a question not resolved by our earlier cases relating to the detention of aliens at Guantanamo: whether they have the constitutional privilege of habeas corpus, a privilege not to be withdrawn except in conformance with the Suspension Clause, Art. I, §9, cl. 2. We hold these petitioners do have the habeas corpus privilege. Congress has enacted a statute, the Detainee Treatment Act of 2005 (DTA), that provides certain procedures for review of the detainees' status. We hold that those procedures are not an adequate and effective substitute for habeas corpus. Therefore §7 of the Military Commissions Act of 2006 (MCA) operates as an unconstitutional suspension of the writ. We do not address whether the President has authority to detain these petitioners nor do we hold that the writ must issue. These and other questions regarding the legality of the detention are to be resolved in the first instance by the District Court. . . .

We acknowledge . . . the litigation history that prompted Congress to enact the MCA. In *Hamdan* the Court found it unnecessary to address the petitioner's Suspension Clause arguments but noted the relevance of the clear statement rule in deciding whether Congress intended to reach pending habeas corpus cases. . . . This interpretive rule facilitates a dialogue between Congress and the Court. If the Court invokes a clear statement rule to advise that certain statutory interpretations are favored in order to avoid constitutional difficulties, Congress can make an informed legislative choice either to amend the statute or to retain its existing text. If Congress amends, its intent must be respected even if a difficult constitutional question is presented. The usual presumption is that Members of Congress, in accord with their oath of office, considered the constitutional issue and determined the amended statute to be a lawful one; and the Judiciary, in light of that determination, proceeds to its own independent judgment on the constitutional question when required to do so in a proper case.

If this ongoing dialogue between and among the branches of Government is to be respected, we cannot ignore that the MCA was a direct response to *Hamdan*'s holding that the DTA's jurisdiction-stripping provision had no application to pending cases. The Court of Appeals was correct to take note of the legislative history when construing the statute; and we agree with its conclusion that the MCA deprives the federal courts of jurisdiction to entertain the habeas corpus actions now before us.

In deciding the constitutional questions now presented we must determine whether petitioners are barred from seeking the writ or invoking the protections of the Suspension Clause either because of their status, *i.e.*, petitioners' designation by the Executive Branch as enemy combatants, or their physical location, *i.e.*, their presence at Guantanamo Bay. The Government contends that noncitizens designated as enemy combatants and detained in territory located outside our Nation's borders have no constitutional rights and no privilege of habeas corpus. Petitioners contend they do have cognizable constitutional rights and that Congress, in seeking to eliminate recourse to habeas corpus as a means to assert those rights, acted in violation of the Suspension Clause.

We begin with a brief account of the history and origins of the writ. Our account proceeds from two propositions. First, protection for the privilege of habeas corpus was one of the few safeguards of liberty specified in a Constitution that, at the outset, had no Bill of Rights. . . . Second, to the extent there were settled precedents or legal commentaries in 1789 regarding the extraterritorial scope of the writ or its application to enemy aliens, those authorities can be instructive for the present cases.

The Framers viewed freedom from unlawful restraint as a fundamental precept of liberty, and they understood the writ of habeas corpus as a vital instrument to secure that freedom. Experience taught, however, that the common-law writ all too often had been insufficient to guard against the abuse of monarchial power. That history counseled the necessity for specific language in the Constitution to secure the writ and ensure its place in our legal system. . . .

This history . . . no doubt [also] confirmed the [Framers'] view that pendular swings to and away from individual liberty were endemic to undivided, uncontrolled power. The Framers' inherent distrust of governmental power was the driving force behind the constitutional plan that allocated powers among three independent branches. This design serves not only to make Government accountable but also to secure individual liberty. Because the Constitution's separation-of-powers structure, like the substantive guarantees of the Fifth and Fourteenth Amendments, protects persons as well as citizens, foreign nationals who have the privilege of litigating in our courts can seek to enforce separation-of-powers principles, see, *e.g., INS v. Chadha* (1983).

That the Framers considered the writ a vital instrument for the protection of individual liberty is evident from the care taken to specify the limited grounds for its suspension: "The Privilege of the Writ of Habeas Corpus shall not be suspended, unless when in Cases of Rebellion or Invasion the public Safety may require it." Art. I, §9, cl. 2. . . .

Surviving accounts of the ratification debates provide . . . evidence that the Framers deemed the writ to be an essential mechanism in the separation-of-powers scheme. In a critical exchange with Patrick Henry at the Virginia ratifying convention Edmund Randolph referred to the Suspension Clause as an "exception" to the "power given to Congress to regulate courts." A resolution passed by the New York ratifying convention made clear its understanding that the Clause not only protects against arbitrary suspensions of the writ but also guarantees an affirmative right to judicial inquiry into the causes of detention. Alexander Hamilton likewise explained that by providing the detainee a judicial forum to challenge detention, the writ preserves limited government. As he explained in The Federalist No. 84:

> The practice of arbitrary imprisonments, have been, in all ages, the favorite and most formidable instruments of tyranny. The observations of the judicious Blackstone . . . are well worthy of recital: "To bereave a man of life . . . or by violence to confiscate his estate, without accusation or trial, would be so gross and notorious an act of despotism as must at once convey the alarm of tyranny throughout the whole nation; but confinement of the person, by secretly hurrying him to jail, where his sufferings are unknown or forgotten, is a less public, a less striking, and therefore a *more dangerous engine* of arbitrary government." And as a remedy for this fatal evil he is everywhere peculiarly emphatical in his encomiums on the *habeas corpus* act, which in one place he calls "the bulwark of the British Constitution."

The Suspension Clause . . . protects the rights of the detained by a means consistent with the essential design of the Constitution. It ensures that, except during periods of formal suspension, the Judiciary will have a time-tested device, the writ, to maintain the "delicate balance of governance" that is itself the surest safeguard of liberty. The Clause protects the rights of the detained by affirming the duty and authority of the Judiciary to call the jailer to account. . . . The separation-of-powers doctrine, and the history that influenced its design, therefore must inform the reach and purpose of the Suspension Clause.

The broad historical narrative of the writ and its function is central to our analysis, but we seek guidance as well from founding-era authorities addressing the specific question before us: whether foreign nationals, apprehended and detained in distant countries during a time of serious threats to our Nation's security, may assert the privilege of the writ and seek its protection. The Court has been careful not to foreclose the possibility that the protections of the Suspension Clause have expanded along with post–1789 developments that define the present scope of the writ. But the analysis may begin with precedents as of 1789, for the Court has said that "at the absolute minimum" the Clause protects the writ as it existed when the Constitution was drafted and ratified.

To support their arguments, the parties in these cases have examined historical sources to construct a view of the common-law writ as it existed in 1789. . . . The Government argues the common-law writ ran only to those territories over which the Crown was sovereign. Petitioners argue that jurisdiction followed the King's officers. Diligent search by all parties reveals no certain conclusions. In none of the cases cited do we find that a common-law court would or would not have granted, or refused to hear for lack of jurisdiction, a petition for a writ of habeas corpus brought by a prisoner deemed an enemy combatant, under a standard like the one the Department of Defense has used in these cases, and when held in a territory, like Guantanamo, over which the Government has total military and civil control. . . .

Petitioners argue the site of their detention is analogous to two territories outside of England to which the writ did run: the so-called "exempt jurisdictions," like the Channel Islands and (in former times) India. There are critical differences between these places and Guantanamo, however. . . . While not in theory part of the realm of England, [these areas] were nonetheless under the Crown's control. . . . Because the United States does not maintain formal sovereignty over Guantanamo Bay, the naval station there and the exempt jurisdictions discussed in the English authorities are not similarly situated. . . .

The Government argues . . . that Guantanamo is more closely analogous to Scotland and Hanover, territories that were not part of England but nonetheless controlled by the English monarch. Lord Mansfield can be cited for the proposition that, at the time of the founding, English courts lacked the "power" to issue the writ to Scotland and Hanover, territories Lord Mansfield referred to as "foreign." But what matters for our purposes is why common-law courts lacked this power. Given the English Crown's delicate and complicated relationships with Scotland and Hanover in the 1700's, we cannot disregard the possibility that the common-law courts' refusal to issue the writ to these places was motivated not by formal legal constructs but by what we would think of as prudential concerns. This appears to have been the case with regard to other British territories where the writ did not run. . . .

Even after the Act of Union [in 1707, through which the kingdoms of England and Scotland were merged politically], Scotland (like Hanover) continued to maintain its own laws and court system. Under these circumstances prudential considerations would have weighed heavily when courts sitting in England received habeas petitions from Scotland or the Electorate. Common-law decisions withholding the writ from prisoners detained in these places easily could be explained as efforts to avoid either or both of two embarrassments: conflict with the judgments of another court of competent jurisdiction; or the practical inability, by reason of distance, of the English courts to enforce their judgments outside their territorial jurisdiction. . . .

The prudential barriers that may have prevented the English courts from issuing the writ to Scotland and Hanover are not relevant here. We have no reason to believe an order from a federal court would be disobeyed at Guantanamo. No Cuban court has jurisdiction to hear these petitioners' claims, and no law other than the laws of the United States applies at the naval station. The modern-day relations between the United States and Guantanamo thus differ in important respects from the 18th-century relations between England and the kingdoms of Scotland and Hanover. This is reason enough for us to discount the relevance of the Government's analogy.

Each side in the present matter argues that the very lack of a precedent on point supports its position. The Government points out there is no evidence that a court sitting in England granted habeas relief to an enemy alien detained abroad; petitioners respond there is no evidence that a court refused to do so for lack of jurisdiction.

Both arguments are premised, however, upon the assumption that the historical record is complete and that the common law, if properly understood, yields a definite answer to the questions before us. There are reasons to doubt both assumptions. Recent scholarship points to the inherent shortcomings in the historical record. . . . And given the unique status of Guantanamo Bay and the particular dangers of terrorism in the modern age, the common-law courts simply may not have confronted cases with close parallels to this one. We decline, therefore, to infer too much, one way or the other, from the lack of historical evidence on point.

Drawing from its position that at common law the writ ran only to territories over which the Crown was sovereign, the Government says the Suspension Clause affords petitioners no rights because the United States does not claim sovereignty over the place of detention. . . .

The Government's formal sovereignty-based test raises troubling separation-of-powers concerns. . . . The political history of Guantanamo illustrates the deficiencies of this approach. The United States has maintained complete and uninterrupted control of the bay for over 100 years. At the close of the Spanish-American War, Spain ceded control over the entire island of Cuba to the United States and specifically "relinquishe[d] all claim[s] of sovereignty . . . and title." From the date the treaty with Spain was signed until the Cuban Republic was established on May 20, 1902, the United States governed the territory "in trust" for the benefit of the Cuban people. And although it recognized, by entering into the 1903 Lease Agreement, that Cuba retained "ultimate sovereignty" over Guantanamo, the United States continued to maintain the same plenary control it had enjoyed since 1898. Yet the Government's view is that the Constitution had no effect there, at least as to noncitizens, because the United States disclaimed sovereignty in the formal sense of the term. The necessary implication of the argument is that by surrendering formal sovereignty over any unincorporated territory to a third party, while at the same time entering into a lease that grants total control over the territory back to the United States, it would be possible for the political branches to govern without legal constraint.

Our basic charter cannot be contracted away like this. The Constitution grants Congress and the President the power to acquire, dispose of, and govern territory, not the power to decide when and where its terms apply. Even when the United States acts outside its borders, its powers are not "absolute and unlimited" but are subject "to such restrictions as are expressed in the Constitution." Abstaining from questions involving formal sovereignty and territorial governance is one thing. To hold the political branches have the power to switch the Constitution on or off at will is quite another. The former position reflects this Court's recognition that certain matters requiring political judgments are best left to the political branches. The latter would permit a striking anomaly in our tripartite system of government, leading to a regime in which Congress and the President, not this Court, say "what the law is." *Marbury v. Madison* (1803).

These concerns have particular bearing upon the Suspension Clause question in the cases now before us, for the writ of habeas corpus is itself an indispensable mechanism for monitoring the separation of powers.

The test for determining the scope of this provision must not be subject to manipulation by those whose power it is designed to restrain.

As we recognized in *Rasul*, the outlines of a framework for determining the reach of the Suspension Clause are suggested by the factors the Court relied upon in *Johnson v. Eisentrager* (1950). . . . The *Eisentrager* Court found relevant that each petitioner: "(a) is an enemy alien; (b) has never been or resided in the United States; (c) was captured outside of our territory and there held in military custody as a prisoner of war; (d) was tried and convicted by a Military Commission sitting outside the United States; (e) for offenses against laws of war committed outside the United States; (f) and is at all times imprisoned outside the United States."

Based on this language from *Eisentrager*, and the reasoning in our other extraterritoriality opinions, we conclude that at least three factors are relevant in determining the reach of the Suspension Clause: (1) the citizenship and status of the detainee and the adequacy of the process through which that status determination was made; (2) the nature of the sites where apprehension and then detention took place; and (3) the practical obstacles inherent in resolving the prisoner's entitlement to the writ.

Applying this framework, we note at the onset that the status of these detainees is a matter of dispute. The petitioners, like those in *Eisentrager*, are not American citizens. But the petitioners in *Eisentrager* did not contest, it seems, the Court's assertion that they were "enemy alien[s]." In the instant cases, by contrast, the detainees deny they are enemy combatants. They have been afforded some process in CSRT [Combatant Status Review Tribunals] proceedings to determine their status; but, unlike in *Eisentrager*, there has been no trial by military commission for violations of the laws of war. The difference is not trivial. The records from the *Eisentrager* trials suggest that, well before the petitioners brought their case to this Court, there had been a rigorous adversarial process to test the legality of their detention. The *Eisentrager* petitioners were charged by a bill of particulars that made detailed factual allegations against them. To rebut the accusations, they were entitled to representation by counsel, allowed to introduce evidence on their own behalf, and permitted to cross-examine the prosecution's witnesses.

In comparison the procedural protections afforded to the detainees in the CSRT hearings are far more limited, and, we conclude, fall well short of the procedures and adversarial mechanisms that would eliminate the need for habeas corpus review. Although the detainee is assigned a "Personal Representative" to assist him during CSRT proceedings, the Secretary of the Navy's memorandum makes clear that person is not the detainee's lawyer or even his "advocate." The Government's evidence is accorded a presumption of validity. The detainee is allowed to present "reasonably available" evidence, but his ability to rebut the Government's evidence against him is limited by the circumstances of his confinement and his lack of counsel at this stage. And although the detainee can seek review of his status determination in the Court of Appeals, that review process cannot cure all defects in the earlier proceedings.

As to the second factor relevant to this analysis, the detainees here are similarly situated to the *Eisentrager* petitioners in that the sites of their apprehension and detention are technically outside the sovereign territory of the United States. This is a factor that weighs against finding they have rights under the Suspension Clause. But there are critical differences between Landsberg Prison, circa 1950, and the United States Naval Station at Guantanamo Bay in 2008. Unlike its present control over the naval station, the United States' control over the prison in Germany was neither absolute nor indefinite. Like all parts of occupied Germany, the prison was under the jurisdiction of the combined Allied Forces. The United States was therefore answerable to its Allies for all activities occurring there. The Allies had not planned a long-term occupation of Germany, nor did they intend to displace all German institutions even during the period of occupation. The Court's holding in *Eisentrager* was thus consistent with the Insular Cases,[1] where it had held there was no need to extend full constitutional protections to territories the United States did not intend to govern indefinitely. Guantanamo Bay, on the other hand, is no transient possession. In every practical sense Guantanamo is not abroad; it is within the constant jurisdiction of the United States.

As to the third factor, we recognize, as the Court did in *Eisentrager*, that there are costs to holding the Suspension Clause applicable in a case of military detention abroad. Habeas corpus proceedings may require expenditure of funds by the Government and may divert the attention of military personnel from other pressing tasks. While we are sensitive to these concerns, we do not find them dispositive. Compliance with any judicial process requires some incremental expenditure of resources. Yet civilian courts and the Armed Forces have functioned along side each other at various points in our history. The Government presents no credible arguments that the military mission at Guantanamo would be compromised if habeas corpus courts had jurisdiction to hear the detainees' claims. And in light of the plenary control the United States asserts over the base, none are apparent to us.

The situation in *Eisentrager* was far different, given the historical context and nature of the military's mission in post-War Germany. When hostilities in the European Theater came to an end, the United States became responsible for an occupation zone encompassing over 57,000 square miles with a population of 18 million. In addition to supervising massive reconstruction and aid efforts, the American forces stationed in Germany faced potential security threats from a defeated enemy. In retrospect the post-War occupation may seem uneventful. But at the time *Eisentrager* was decided, the Court was right to be concerned about judicial interference with the military's efforts to contain "enemy elements [and] guerilla fighters."

Similar threats are not apparent here; nor does the Government argue that they are. The United States Naval Station at Guantanamo Bay consists of 45 square miles of land and water. The base has been used, at various points, to house migrants and refugees temporarily. At present, however, other than the detainees themselves, the only long-term residents are American military personnel, their families, and a small number of workers. The detainees have been deemed enemies of the United States. At present, dangerous as they may be if released, they are contained in a secure prison facility located on an isolated and heavily fortified military base.

There is no indication, furthermore, that adjudicating a habeas corpus petition would cause friction with the host government. No Cuban court has jurisdiction over American military personnel at Guantanamo or the enemy combatants detained there. While obligated to abide by the terms of the lease, the United States is, for all practical purposes, answerable to no other sovereign for its acts on the base. Were that not the case, or if the detention facility were located in an active theater of war, arguments that issuing the writ would be "impracticable or anomalous" would have more weight. Under the facts presented here, however, there are few practical barriers to the running of the writ. To the extent barriers arise, habeas corpus procedures likely can be modified to address them.

It is true that before today the Court has never held that noncitizens detained by our Government in territory over which another country maintains *de jure* sovereignty have any rights under our Constitution. But the cases before us lack any precise historical parallel. They involve individuals detained by executive order for the duration of a conflict that, if measured from September 11, 2001, to the present, is already among the longest wars in American history. The detainees, moreover, are held in a territory that, while technically not part of the United States, is under the complete and total control of our Government. Under these circumstances the lack of a precedent on point is no barrier to our holding.

We hold that Art. I, §9, cl. 2, of the Constitution has full effect at Guantanamo Bay. If the privilege of habeas corpus is to be denied to the detainees now before us, Congress must act in accordance with the requirements of the Suspension Clause. . . . This Court may not impose a *de facto* suspension by abstaining from these controversies. . . . The MCA does not purport to be a formal suspension of the writ; and the Government, in its submissions to us, has not argued that it is. Petitioners, therefore, are entitled to the privilege of habeas corpus to challenge the legality of their detention.

In light of this holding the question becomes whether the statute stripping jurisdiction to issue the writ avoids the Suspension Clause mandate because Congress has provided adequate substitute procedures for habeas corpus. The Government submits there has been compliance with the Suspension Clause because the DTA review process in the Court of Appeals provides an adequate substitute. . . .

The Court of Appeals, having decided that the writ does not run to the detainees in any event, found it unnecessary to consider whether an adequate substitute has been provided. In the ordinary course we would remand to the Court of Appeals to consider this question in the first instance. It is well settled, however, that the Court's practice of declining to address issues left unresolved in earlier proceedings is not an inflexible rule. Departure from the rule is appropriate in "exceptional" circumstances.

The gravity of the separation-of-powers issues raised by these cases and the fact that these detainees have been denied meaningful access to a judicial forum for a period of years render these cases exceptional. . . . While we would have found it informative to consider the reasoning of the Court of Appeals on this point, we must weigh that against the harms petitioners may endure from additional delay. And, given there are few precedents addressing what features an adequate substitute for habeas corpus must contain, in all likelihood a remand simply would delay ultimate resolution of the issue by this Court.

Under the circumstances we believe the costs of further delay substantially outweigh any benefits of remanding to the Court of Appeals to consider the issue it did not address in these cases.

Our case law does not contain extensive discussion of standards defining suspension of the writ or of circumstances under which suspension has occurred. This simply confirms the care Congress has taken throughout our Nation's history to preserve the writ and its function. Indeed, most of the major legislative enactments pertaining to habeas corpus have acted not to contract the writ's protection but to expand it or to hasten resolution of prisoners' claims. . . .

Here we confront statutes, the DTA and the MCA, that were intended to circumscribe habeas review. Congress' purpose is evident . . . from the unequivocal nature of MCA §7's jurisdiction-stripping language ("No court, justice, or judge shall have jurisdiction to hear or consider an application for a writ of habeas corpus . . ."). . . . In passing the DTA Congress did not intend to create a process that differs from traditional habeas corpus process in name only. It intended to create a more limited procedure. It is against this background that we must interpret the DTA and assess its adequacy as a substitute for habeas corpus.

We do not endeavor to offer a comprehensive summary of the requisites for an adequate substitute for habeas corpus. We do consider it uncontroversial, however, that the privilege of habeas corpus entitles the prisoner to a meaningful opportunity to demonstrate that he is being held pursuant to "the erroneous application or interpretation" of relevant law. And the habeas court must have the power to order the conditional release of an individual unlawfully detained—though release need not be the exclusive remedy and is not the appropriate one in every case in which the writ is granted. These are the easily identified attributes of any constitutionally adequate habeas corpus proceeding. But, depending on the circumstances, more may be required. . . .

The necessary scope of habeas review in part depends upon the rigor of any earlier proceedings. . . . Where a person is detained by executive order, rather than, say, after being tried and convicted in a court, the need for . . . review is most pressing. A criminal conviction in the usual course occurs after a judicial hearing before a tribunal disinterested in the outcome and committed to procedures designed to ensure its own independence. These dynamics are not inherent in executive detention orders or executive review procedures. In this context the need for habeas corpus is more urgent. The intended duration of the detention and the reasons for it bear upon the precise scope of the inquiry. Habeas corpus proceedings need not resemble a criminal trial, even when the detention is by executive order. But the writ must be effective. The habeas court must have sufficient authority to conduct a meaningful review of both the cause for detention and the Executive's power to detain. . . .

Petitioners identify what they see as myriad deficiencies in the CSRTs. The most relevant for our purposes are the constraints upon the detainee's ability to rebut the factual basis for the Government's assertion that he is an enemy combatant. As already noted, at the CSRT stage the detainee has limited means to find or present evidence to challenge the Government's case against him. He does not have the assistance of counsel and may not be aware of the most critical allegations that the Government relied upon to order his detention. The detainee can confront witnesses that testify during the CSRT proceedings. But given that there are in effect no limits on the admission of hearsay evidence—the only requirement is that the tribunal deem the evidence "relevant and helpful"—the detainee's opportunity to question witnesses is likely to be more theoretical than real. . . .

Although we make no judgment as to whether the CSRTs, as currently constituted, satisfy due process standards, we agree with petitioners that, even when all the parties involved in this process act with diligence and in good faith, there is considerable risk of error in the tribunal's findings of fact. . . . And given that the consequence of error may be detention of persons for the duration of hostilities that may last a generation or more, this is a risk too significant to ignore.

For the writ of habeas corpus, or its substitute, to function as an effective and proper remedy in this context, the court that conducts the habeas proceeding must have the means to correct errors that occurred during the CSRT proceedings. This includes some authority to assess the sufficiency of the Government's evidence against the detainee. It also must have the authority to admit and consider relevant exculpatory evidence that was not introduced during the earlier proceeding.

Consistent with the historic function and province of the writ, habeas corpus review may be more circumscribed if the underlying detention proceedings are more thorough than they were here. In two habeas cases involving enemy aliens tried for war crimes, *In re Yamashita* (1946) and *Ex parte Quirin* (1942), for example, this Court limited its review to determining whether the Executive had legal authority to try the petitioners by military commission. Military courts are not courts of record. And the procedures used to try General Yamashita have been sharply criticized by Members of this Court. See *Hamdan.* We need not revisit these cases, however. For on their own terms, the proceedings in *Yamashita* and *Quirin,* like those in *Eisentrager,* had an adversarial structure that is lacking here.

The extent of the showing required of the Government in these cases is a matter to be determined. We need not explore it further at this stage. We do hold that when the judicial power to issue habeas corpus properly is invoked, the judicial officer must have adequate authority to make a determination in light of the relevant law and facts and to formulate and issue appropriate orders for relief, including, if necessary, an order directing the prisoner's release.

We now consider whether the DTA allows the Court of Appeals to conduct a proceeding meeting these standards. . . .

The DTA does not explicitly empower the Court of Appeals to order the applicant in a DTA review proceeding released should the court find that the standards and procedures used at his CSRT hearing were insufficient to justify detention. This is troubling. Yet, for present purposes, we can assume congressional silence permits a constitutionally required remedy. In that case it would be possible to hold that a remedy of release is impliedly provided for. The DTA might be read, furthermore, to allow the petitioners to assert most, if not all, of the legal claims they seek to advance, including their most basic claim: that the President has no authority under the AUMF [Authorization for Use of Military Force] to detain them indefinitely. . . . At oral argument, the Solicitor General urged us to adopt both these constructions, if doing so would allow MCA §7 to remain intact.

The absence of a release remedy and specific language allowing AUMF challenges are not the only constitutional infirmities from which the statute potentially suffers, however. The more difficult question is whether the DTA permits the Court of Appeals to make requisite findings of fact. The DTA enables petitioners to request "review" of their CSRT determination in the Court of Appeals; but the "Scope of Review" provision confines the Court of Appeals' role to reviewing whether the CSRT followed the "standards and procedures" issued by the Department of Defense and assessing whether those "standards and procedures" are lawful. Among these standards is "the requirement that the conclusion of the Tribunal be supported by a preponderance of the evidence . . . allowing a rebuttable presumption in favor of the Government's evidence."

Assuming the DTA can be construed to allow the Court of Appeals to review or correct the CSRT's factual determinations, as opposed to merely certifying that the tribunal applied the correct standard of proof, we see no way to construe the statute to allow what is also constitutionally required in this context: an opportunity for the detainee to present relevant exculpatory evidence that was not made part of the record in the earlier proceedings.

On its face the statute allows the Court of Appeals to consider no evidence outside the CSRT record. In [*Bismullah v. Gates* (2008)], however, the Court of Appeals determined that the DTA allows it to order the production of all "reasonably available information in the possession of the U.S. Government bearing on the issue of whether the detainee meets the criteria to be designated as an enemy combatant," regardless of whether this evidence was put before the CSRT. . . . For present purposes . . . we can assume that the Court of Appeals was correct that the DTA allows introduction and consideration of relevant exculpatory evidence that was "reasonably available" to the Government at the time of the CSRT but not made part of the record. Even so, the DTA review proceeding falls short of being a constitutionally adequate substitute, for the detainee still would have no opportunity to present evidence discovered after the CSRT proceedings concluded.

Under the DTA the Court of Appeals has the power to review CSRT determinations by assessing the legality of standards and procedures. This implies the power to inquire into what happened at the CSRT hearing and, perhaps, to remedy certain deficiencies in that proceeding. But should the Court of Appeals determine that the CSRT followed appropriate and lawful standards and procedures, it will have reached the limits of its jurisdiction. There is no language in the DTA that can be construed to allow the Court of Appeals to admit and consider newly discovered evidence that could not have been made part of the CSRT record because it was unavailable to either the Government or the detainee when the CSRT made its findings. This evidence, however, may be critical to the detainee's argument that he is not an enemy combatant and there is no cause to detain him.

This is not a remote hypothetical. One of the petitioners, Mohamed Nechla, requested at his CSRT hearing that the Government contact his employer. The petitioner claimed the employer would corroborate Nechla's contention he had no affiliation with al Qaeda. Although the CSRT determined this testimony would be relevant, it also found the witness was not reasonably available to testify at the time of the hearing. Petitioner's counsel, however, now represents the witness is available to be heard. If a detainee can present reasonably available evidence demonstrating there is no basis for his continued detention, he must have the opportunity to present this evidence to a habeas corpus court. Even under the Court of Appeals' generous construction of the DTA, however, the evidence identified by Nechla would be inadmissible in a DTA review proceeding. The role of an Article III court in the exercise of its habeas corpus function cannot be circumscribed in this manner.

By foreclosing consideration of evidence not presented or reasonably available to the detainee at the CSRT proceedings, the DTA disadvantages the detainee by limiting the scope of collateral review to a record that may not be accurate or complete. In other contexts, e.g., in post-trial habeas cases where the prisoner already has had a full and fair opportunity to develop the factual predicate of his claims, similar limitations on the scope of habeas review may be appropriate. In this context, however, where the underlying detention proceedings lack the necessary adversarial character, the detainee cannot be held responsible for all deficiencies in the record.

The Government does not make the alternative argument that the DTA allows for the introduction of previously unavailable exculpatory evidence on appeal. It does point out, however, that if a detainee obtains such evidence, he can request that the Deputy Secretary of Defense convene a new CSRT. Whatever the merits of this procedure, it is an insufficient replacement for the factual review these detainees are entitled to receive through habeas corpus. The Deputy Secretary's determination whether to initiate new proceedings is wholly a discretionary one. And we see no way to construe the DTA to allow a detainee to challenge the Deputy Secretary's decision not to open a new CSRT. . . . Congress directed the Secretary of Defense to devise procedures for considering new evidence, but the detainee has no mechanism for ensuring that those procedures are followed. . . .

We do not imply DTA review would be a constitutionally sufficient replacement for habeas corpus but for these limitations on the detainee's ability to present exculpatory evidence. For even if it were possible, as a textual matter, to read into the statute each of the necessary procedures we have identified, we could not overlook the cumulative effect of our doing so. To hold that the detainees at Guantanamo may, under the DTA, challenge the President's legal authority to detain them, contest the CSRT's findings of fact, supplement the record on review with exculpatory evidence, and request an order of release would come close to reinstating the §2241 habeas corpus process Congress sought to deny them.[2] The language of the statute, read in light of Congress' reasons for enacting it, cannot bear this interpretation. Petitioners have met their burden of establishing that the DTA review process is, on its face, an inadequate substitute for habeas corpus.

Although we do not hold that an adequate substitute must duplicate §2241 in all respects, it suffices that the Government has not established that the detainees' access to the statutory review provisions at issue is an adequate substitute for the writ of habeas corpus. MCA §7 thus effects an unconstitutional suspension of the writ. . . .

In light of our conclusion that there is no jurisdictional bar to the District Court's entertaining petitioners' claims the question remains whether there are prudential barriers to habeas corpus review under these circumstances. . . .

The real risks, the real threats, of terrorist attacks are constant and not likely soon to abate. The ways to disrupt our life and laws are so many and unforeseen that the Court should not attempt even some general catalogue of crises that might occur. Certain principles are apparent, however. Practical considerations and exigent circumstances inform the definition and reach of the law's writs, including habeas corpus. The cases and our tradition reflect this precept.

In cases involving foreign citizens detained abroad by the Executive, it likely would be both an impractical and unprecedented extension of judicial power to assume that habeas corpus would be available at the moment the prisoner is taken into custody. If and when habeas corpus jurisdiction applies, as it does in these cases, then proper deference can be accorded to reasonable procedures for screening and initial detention under lawful and proper conditions of confinement and treatment for a reasonable period of time. Domestic exigencies, furthermore, might also impose such onerous burdens on the Government that here, too, the Judicial Branch would be required to devise sensible rules for staying habeas corpus proceedings until the Government can comply with its requirements in a responsible way. Cf. *Ex parte Milligan* ("If, in foreign invasion or civil war, the courts are actually closed, and it is impossible to administer criminal justice according to law, *then*, on the theatre of active military operations, where war really prevails, there is a necessity to furnish a substitute for the civil authority, thus overthrown, to preserve the safety of the army and society; and as no power is left but the military, it is allowed to govern by martial rule until the laws can have their free course"). Here, as is true with detainees apprehended abroad, a relevant consideration in determining the courts' role is whether there are suitable alternative processes in place to protect against the arbitrary exercise of governmental power.

The cases before us, however, do not involve detainees who have been held for a short period of time while awaiting their CSRT determinations. Were that the case, or were it probable that the Court of Appeals could complete a prompt review of their applications, the case for requiring temporary abstention or exhaustion of alternative remedies would be much stronger. These qualifications no longer pertain here. In some of these cases six years have elapsed without the judicial oversight that habeas corpus or an adequate substitute demands. And there has been no showing that the Executive faces such onerous burdens that it cannot respond to habeas corpus actions. To require these detainees to complete DTA review before proceeding with their habeas corpus actions would be to require additional months, if not years, of delay. The first DTA review applications were filed over a year ago, but no decisions on the merits have been issued. While some delay in fashioning new procedures is unavoidable, the costs of delay can no longer be borne by those who are held in custody. The detainees in these cases are entitled to a prompt habeas corpus hearing.

Our decision today holds only that the petitioners before us are entitled to seek the writ; that the DTA review procedures are an inadequate substitute for habeas corpus; and that the petitioners in these cases need not exhaust the review procedures in the Court of Appeals before proceeding with their habeas actions in the District Court. The only law we identify as unconstitutional is MCA §7. Accordingly, both the DTA and the CSRT process remain intact. Our holding with regard to exhaustion should not be read to imply that a habeas court should intervene the moment an enemy combatant steps foot in a territory where the writ runs. The Executive is entitled to a reasonable period of time to determine a detainee's status before a court entertains that detainee's habeas corpus petition. The CSRT process is the mechanism Congress and the President set up to deal with these issues. Except in cases of undue delay, federal courts should refrain from entertaining an enemy combatant's habeas corpus petition at least until after the Department, acting via the CSRT, has had a chance to review his status.

Although we hold that the DTA is not an adequate and effective substitute for habeas corpus, it does not follow that a habeas corpus court may disregard the dangers the detention in these cases was intended to prevent. . . .

In considering both the procedural and substantive standards used to impose detention to prevent acts of terrorism, proper deference must be accorded to the political branches. See *United States v. Curtiss-Wright Export*

Corp. (1936). Unlike the President and some designated Members of Congress, neither the Members of this Court nor most federal judges begin the day with briefings that may describe new and serious threats to our Nation and its people. The law must accord the Executive substantial authority to apprehend and detain those who pose a real danger to our security. . . .

Security depends upon a sophisticated intelligence apparatus and the ability of our Armed Forces to act and to interdict. There are further considerations, however. Security subsists, too, in fidelity to freedom's first principles. Chief among these are freedom from arbitrary and unlawful restraint and the personal liberty that is secured by adherence to the separation of powers. It is from these principles that the judicial authority to consider petitions for habeas corpus relief derives.

Our opinion does not undermine the Executive's powers as Commander in Chief. On the contrary, the exercise of those powers is vindicated, not eroded, when confirmed by the Judicial Branch. Within the Constitution's separation-of-powers structure, few exercises of judicial power are as legitimate or as necessary as the responsibility to hear challenges to the authority of the Executive to imprison a person. Some of these petitioners have been in custody for six years with no definitive judicial determination as to the legality of their detention. Their access to the writ is a necessity to determine the lawfulness of their status, even if, in the end, they do not obtain the relief they seek.

Because our Nation's past military conflicts have been of limited duration, it has been possible to leave the outer boundaries of war powers undefined. If, as some fear, terrorism continues to pose dangerous threats to us for years to come, the Court might not have this luxury. This result is not inevitable, however. The political branches, consistent with their independent obligations to interpret and uphold the Constitution, can engage in a genuine debate about how best to preserve constitutional values while protecting the Nation from terrorism. . . .

It bears repeating that our opinion does not address the content of the law that governs petitioners' detention. That is a matter yet to be determined. We hold that petitioners may invoke the fundamental procedural protections of habeas corpus. The laws and Constitution are designed to survive, and remain in force, in extraordinary times. Liberty and security can be reconciled; and in our system they are reconciled within the framework of the law. The Framers decided that habeas corpus, a right of first importance, must be a part of that framework, a part of that law.

The determination by the Court of Appeals that the Suspension Clause and its protections are inapplicable to petitioners was in error. The judgment of the Court of Appeals is reversed. The cases are remanded to the

Court of Appeals with instructions that it remand the cases to the District Court for proceedings consistent with this opinion.

It is so ordered.

*　*　*　*　*　*

Justice Souter, with whom Justice Ginsburg and Justice Breyer join, concurring.

I join the Court's opinion in its entirety and add this afterword only to emphasize two things one might overlook after reading the dissents.

Four years ago, this Court in *Rasul v. Bush* (2004) held that statutory habeas jurisdiction extended to claims of foreign nationals imprisoned by the United States at Guantanamo Bay, "to determine the legality of the Executive's potentially indefinite detention" of them. Subsequent legislation eliminated the statutory habeas jurisdiction over these claims, so that now there must be constitutionally based jurisdiction or none at all. Justice Scalia is thus correct that here, for the first time, this Court holds there is (he says "confers") constitutional habeas jurisdiction over aliens imprisoned by the military outside an area of *de jure* national sovereignty. But no one who reads the Court's opinion in *Rasul* could seriously doubt that the jurisdictional question must be answered the same way in purely constitutional cases, given the Court's reliance on the historical background of habeas generally in answering the statutory question. Indeed, the Court in *Rasul* directly answered the very historical question that Justice Scalia says is dispositive; it wrote that "application of the habeas statute to persons detained at [Guantanamo] is consistent with the historical reach of the writ of habeas corpus." Justice Scalia dismisses the statement as dictum, but if dictum it was, it was dictum well considered, and it stated the view of five Members of this Court on the historical scope of the writ. Of course, it takes more than a quotation from *Rasul,* however much on point, to resolve the constitutional issue before us here, which the majority opinion has explored afresh in the detail it deserves. But whether one agrees or disagrees with today's decision, it is no bolt out of the blue.

A second fact insufficiently appreciated by the dissents is the length of the disputed imprisonments, some of the prisoners represented here today having been locked up for six years. Hence the hollow ring when the dissenters suggest that the Court is somehow precipitating the judiciary into reviewing claims that the military (subject to appeal to the Court of Appeals for the District of Columbia Circuit) could handle within some reasonable period of time. . . . These suggestions of judicial haste are all the more out of place given the Court's realistic acknowledgment that in periods of exigency the tempo of any habeas review must reflect the immediate peril facing the country.

It is in fact the very lapse of four years from the time *Rasul* put every-one on notice that habeas process was available to Guantanamo prisoners, and the lapse of six years since some of these prisoners were captured and incarcerated, that stand at odds with the repeated suggestions of the dis-senters that these cases should be seen as a judicial victory in a contest for power between the Court and the political branches. The several answers to the charge of triumphalism might start with a basic fact of Anglo-American constitutional history: that the power, first of the Crown and now of the Executive Branch of the United States, is necessarily limited by habeas corpus jurisdiction to enquire into the legality of executive deten-tion. And one could explain that in this Court's exercise of responsibility to preserve habeas corpus something much more significant is involved than pulling and hauling between the judicial and political branches. In-stead, though, it is enough to repeat that some of these petitioners have spent six years behind bars. After six years of sustained executive deten-tions in Guantanamo, subject to habeas jurisdiction but without any ac-tual habeas scrutiny, today's decision is no judicial victory, but an act of perseverance in trying to make habeas review, and the obligation of the courts to provide it, mean something of value both to prisoners and to the Nation.

*   *   *   *   *   *

Chief Justice Roberts, with whom Justice Scalia, Justice Thomas, and Jus-tice Alito join, dissenting.

Today the Court strikes down as inadequate the most generous set of procedural protections ever afforded aliens detained by this country as enemy combatants. The political branches crafted these procedures amidst an ongoing military conflict, after much careful investigation and thorough debate. The Court rejects them today out of hand, without both-ering to say what due process rights the detainees possess, without ex-plaining how the statute fails to vindicate those rights, and before a single petitioner has even attempted to avail himself of the law's operation. And to what effect? The majority merely replaces a review system designed by the people's representatives with a set of shapeless procedures to be de-fined by federal courts at some future date. One cannot help but think, af-ter surveying the modest practical results of the majority's ambitious opinion, that this decision is not really about the detainees at all, but about control of federal policy regarding enemy combatants.

The majority is adamant that the Guantanamo detainees are entitled to the protections of habeas corpus—its opinion begins by deciding that question. I regard the issue as a difficult one, primarily because of the unique and unusual jurisdictional status of Guantanamo Bay. I nonethe-less agree with Justice Scalia's analysis of our precedents and the pertinent history of the writ, and accordingly join his dissent. The important point for me, however, is that the Court should have resolved these cases on other grounds. Habeas is most fundamentally a procedural right, a mechanism for contesting the legality of executive detention. The critical threshold question in these cases, prior to any inquiry about the writ's scope, is whether the system the political branches designed protects whatever rights the detainees may possess. If so, there is no need for any additional process, whether called "habeas" or something else.

Congress entrusted that threshold question in the first instance to the Court of Appeals for the District of Columbia Circuit, as the Constitution surely allows Congress to do. But before the D.C. Circuit has addressed the issue, the Court cashiers the statute, and without answering this critical threshold question itself. The Court does eventually get around to asking whether review under the DTA is, as the Court frames it, an "adequate substitute" for habeas, but even then its opinion fails to determine what rights the detainees possess and whether the DTA system satisfies them. The majority instead compares the undefined DTA process to an equally undefined habeas right—one that is to be given shape only in the future by district courts on a case-by-case basis. This whole approach is misguided.

It is also fruitless. How the detainees' claims will be decided now that the DTA is gone is anybody's guess. But the habeas process the Court mandates will most likely end up looking a lot like the DTA system it replaces, as the district court judges shaping it will have to reconcile review of the prisoners' detention with the undoubted need to protect the American people from the terrorist threat—precisely the challenge Congress undertook in drafting the DTA. All that today's opinion has done is shift responsibility for those sensitive foreign policy and national security decisions from the elected branches to the Federal Judiciary.

I believe the system the political branches constructed adequately protects any constitutional rights aliens captured abroad and detained as enemy combatants may enjoy. I therefore would dismiss these cases on that ground. With all respect for the contrary views of the majority, I must dissent.

$$* \quad * \quad * \quad * \quad * \quad *$$

Justice Scalia, with whom the Chief Justice, Justice Thomas, and Justice Alito join, dissenting.

Today, for the first time in our Nation's history, the Court confers a constitutional right to habeas corpus on alien enemies detained abroad by our military forces in the course of an ongoing war. The Chief Justice's dissent, which I join, shows that the procedures prescribed by Congress in the Detainee Treatment Act provide the essential protections that habeas corpus guarantees; there has thus been no suspension of the writ, and no basis exists for judicial intervention beyond what the Act allows. My problem with today's opinion is more fundamental still: The writ of habeas corpus does not, and never has, run in favor of aliens abroad; the Suspension Clause thus has no application, and the Court's intervention in this military matter is entirely *ultra vires*.

I shall devote most of [my] opinion to the legal errors contained in the opinion of the Court. Contrary to my usual practice, however, I think it appropriate to begin with a description of the disastrous consequences of what the Court has done today.

America is at war with radical Islamists. The enemy began by killing Americans and American allies abroad: 241 at the Marine barracks in Lebanon, 19 at the Khobar Towers in Dhahran, 224 at our embassies in Dar es Salaam and Nairobi, and 17 on the USS Cole in Yemen. On September 11, 2001, the enemy brought the battle to American soil, killing 2,749 at the Twin Towers in New York City, 184 at the Pentagon in Washington, D.C., and 40 in Pennsylvania. It has threatened further attacks against our homeland; one need only walk about buttressed and barricaded Washington, or board a plane anywhere in the country, to know that the threat is a serious one. Our Armed Forces are now in the field against the enemy, in Afghanistan and Iraq. Last week, 13 of our countrymen in arms were killed.

The game of bait-and-switch that today's opinion plays upon the Nation's Commander in Chief will make the war harder on us. It will almost certainly cause more Americans to be killed. That consequence would be tolerable if necessary to preserve a time-honored legal principle vital to our constitutional Republic. But it is this Court's blatant *abandonment* of such a principle that produces the decision today. The President relied on our settled precedent in *Johnson v. Eisentrager* (1950), when he established the prison at Guantanamo Bay for enemy aliens. Citing that case, the President's Office of Legal Counsel advised him "that the great weight of legal authority indicates that a federal district court could not properly exercise habeas jurisdiction over an alien detained at [Guantanamo Bay]." Memorandum from Patrick F. Philbin and John C. Yoo, Deputy Assistant Attorneys General, Office of Legal Counsel, to William J. Haynes II, General Counsel, Dept. of Defense (Dec. 28, 2001). Had the law been otherwise, the military surely would not have transported prisoners there, but would have kept them in Afghanistan, transferred them to another of our foreign military bases, or turned them over to allies for detention. Those other facilities might well have been worse for the detainees themselves.

In the long term, then, the Court's decision today accomplishes little, except perhaps to reduce the well-being of enemy combatants that the

Court ostensibly seeks to protect. In the short term, however, the decision is devastating. At least 30 of those prisoners hitherto released from Guantanamo Bay have returned to the battlefield. Some have been captured or killed. But others have succeeded in carrying on their atrocities against innocent civilians. In one case, a detainee released from Guantanamo Bay masterminded the kidnapping of two Chinese dam workers, one of whom was later shot to death when used as a human shield against Pakistani commandoes. Another former detainee promptly resumed his post as a senior Taliban commander and murdered a United Nations engineer and three Afghan soldiers. Still another murdered an Afghan judge. It was reported only last month that a released detainee carried out a suicide bombing against Iraqi soldiers in Mosul, Iraq.

These, mind you, were detainees whom *the military* had concluded were not enemy combatants. Their return to the kill illustrates the incredible difficulty of assessing who is and who is not an enemy combatant in a foreign theater of operations where the environment does not lend itself to rigorous evidence collection. Astoundingly, the Court today raises the bar, requiring military officials to appear before civilian courts and defend their decisions under procedural and evidentiary rules that go beyond what Congress has specified. As The Chief Justice's dissent makes clear, we have no idea what those procedural and evidentiary rules are, but they will be determined by civil courts and (in the Court's contemplation at least) will be more detainee-friendly than those now applied, since otherwise there would no reason to hold the congressionally prescribed procedures unconstitutional. If they impose a higher standard of proof (from foreign battlefields) than the current procedures require, the number of the enemy returned to combat will obviously increase.

But even when the military has evidence that it can bring forward, it is often foolhardy to release that evidence to the attorneys representing our enemies. And one escalation of procedures that the Court *is* clear about is affording the detainees increased access to witnesses (perhaps troops serving in Afghanistan?) and to classified information. During the 1995 prosecution of Omar Abdel Rahman, federal prosecutors gave the names of 200 unindicted co-conspirators to the "Blind Sheik's" defense lawyers; that information was in the hands of Osama bin Laden within two weeks. In another case, trial testimony revealed to the enemy that the United States had been monitoring their cellular network, whereupon they promptly stopped using it, enabling more of them to evade capture and continue their atrocities.

And today it is not just the military that the Court elbows aside. A mere two Terms ago in *Hamdan v. Rumsfeld* (2006), when the Court held (quite amazingly) that the Detainee Treatment Act of 2005 had not stripped habeas jurisdiction over Guantanamo petitioners' claims, four Members of today's five-Justice majority joined an opinion saying the following: "Nothing prevents the President from returning to Congress to seek the authority [for trial by military commission] he believes necessary. Where, as here, no emergency prevents consultation with Congress, judicial insistence upon that consultation does not weaken our Nation's ability to deal with danger. To the contrary, that insistence strengthens the Nation's ability to determine—through democratic means—how best to do so. The Constitution places its faith in those democratic means." (Breyer, J., concurring).

Turns out they were just kidding. For in response, Congress, at the President's request, quickly enacted the Military Commissions Act, emphatically reasserting that it did not want these prisoners filing habeas petitions. It is therefore clear that Congress and the Executive—*both* political branches—have determined that limiting the role of civilian courts in adjudicating whether prisoners captured abroad are properly detained is important to success in the war that some 190,000 of our men and women are now fighting. As the Solicitor General argued, "the Military Commissions Act and the Detainee Treatment Act . . . represent an effort by the political branches to strike an appropriate balance between the need to preserve liberty and the need to accommodate the weighty and sensitive governmental interests in ensuring that those who have in fact fought with the enemy during a war do not return to battle against the United States."

But it does not matter. The Court today decrees that no good reason to accept the judgment of the other two branches is "apparent." "The Government," it declares, "presents no credible arguments that the military mission at Guantanamo would be compromised if habeas corpus courts had jurisdiction to hear the detainees' claims." What competence does the Court have to second-guess the judgment of Congress and the President on such a point? None whatever. But the Court blunders in nonetheless. Henceforth, as today's opinion makes unnervingly clear, how to handle enemy prisoners in this war will ultimately lie with the branch that knows least about the national security concerns that the subject entails.

The Suspension Clause of the Constitution provides: "The Privilege of the Writ of Habeas Corpus shall not be suspended, unless when in Cases of Rebellion or Invasion the public Safety may require it." Art. I, §9, cl. 2. As a court of law operating under a written Constitution, our role is to determine whether there is a conflict between that Clause and the Military Commissions Act. A conflict arises only if the Suspension Clause preserves the privilege of the writ for aliens held by the United States military as enemy combatants at the base in Guantanamo Bay, located within the sovereign territory of Cuba.

We have frequently stated that we owe great deference to Congress's view that a law it has passed is constitutional. That is especially so in the area of foreign and military affairs; "perhaps in no other area has the Court accorded Congress greater deference." Indeed, we accord great deference even when the President acts alone in this area.

In light of those principles of deference, the Court's conclusion that "the common law [does not] yiel[d] a definite answer to the questions before us," leaves it no choice but to affirm the Court of Appeals. The writ as preserved in the Constitution could not possibly extend farther than the common law provided when that Clause was written. The Court admits that it cannot determine whether the writ historically extended to aliens held abroad, and it concedes (necessarily) that Guantanamo Bay lies outside the sovereign territory of the United States. Together, these two concessions establish that it is (in the Court's view) perfectly ambiguous whether the common-law writ would have provided a remedy for these petitioners. If that is so, the Court has no basis to strike down the Military Commissions Act, and must leave undisturbed the considered judgment of the coequal branches.

How, then, does the Court weave a clear constitutional prohibition out of pure interpretive equipoise? The Court resorts to "fundamental separation-of-powers principles" to interpret the Suspension Clause. According to the Court, because "the writ of habeas corpus is itself an indispensable mechanism for monitoring the separation of powers," the test of its extraterritorial reach "must not be subject to manipulation by those whose power it is designed to restrain."

That approach distorts the nature of the separation of powers and its role in the constitutional structure. The "fundamental separation-of-powers principles" that the Constitution embodies are to be derived not from some judicially imagined matrix, but from the sum total of the individual separation-of-powers provisions that the Constitution sets forth. Only by considering them one-by-one does the full shape of the *Constitution*'s separation-of-powers principles emerge. It is nonsensical to interpret those provisions themselves in light of some general "separation-of-powers principles" dreamed up by the Court. Rather, they must be interpreted to mean what they were understood to mean when the people ratified them. And if the understood scope of the writ of habeas corpus was "designed to restrain" (as the Court says) the actions of the Executive, the understood *limits* upon that scope were (as the Court seems not to grasp) just as much "designed to restrain" the incursions of the Third Branch. "Manipulation" of the territorial reach of the writ by the Judiciary poses just as much a threat to the proper separation of powers as "manipulation" by the Executive. As I will show below, manipulation is what is afoot here. The understood limits upon the writ deny our jurisdiction over the habeas petitions brought by these enemy aliens, and entrust the President with the crucial wartime determinations about their status and continued confinement.

The Court purports to derive from our precedents a "functional" test for the extraterritorial reach of the writ, which shows that the Military Commissions Act unconstitutionally restricts the scope of habeas. That is remarkable because the most pertinent of those precedents, *Johnson v. Eisentrager*, conclusively establishes the opposite. There we were confronted with the claims of 21 Germans held at Landsberg Prison, an American military facility located in the American Zone of occupation in postwar Germany. They had been captured in China, and an American military commission sitting there had convicted them of war crimes—collaborating with the Japanese after Germany's surrender. Like the petitioners here, the Germans claimed that their detentions violated the Constitution and international law, and sought a writ of habeas corpus. Writing for the Court, Justice Jackson held that American courts lacked habeas jurisdiction: "We are cited to [*sic*] no instance where a court, in this or any other country where the writ is known, has issued it on behalf of an alien enemy who, at no relevant time and in no stage of his captivity, has been within its territorial jurisdiction. Nothing in the text of the Constitution extends such a right, nor does anything in our statutes.". . . *Eisentrager* thus held—*held* beyond any doubt—that the Constitution does not ensure habeas for aliens held by the United States in areas over which our Government is not sovereign. . . .

The Court tries to reconcile *Eisentrager* with its holding today by pointing out that in postwar Germany, the United States was "answerable to its Allies" and did not "pla[n] a long-term occupation." Those factors were not mentioned in *Eisentrager*. Worse still, it is impossible to see how they relate to the Court's asserted purpose in creating this "functional" test— namely, to ensure a judicial inquiry into detention and prevent the political branches from acting with impunity. Can it possibly be that the Court trusts the political branches more when they are beholden to foreign powers than when they act alone? . . .

No one looking for "functional" equivalents would put *Eisentrager* and the present cases in the same category, much less place the present cases in a preferred category. The difference between them cries out for lesser procedures in the present cases. The prisoners in *Eisentrager* were *prosecuted* for crimes after the cessation of hostilities; the prisoners here are enemy combatants *detained* during an ongoing conflict. . . .

By blatantly distorting *Eisentrager*, the Court avoids the difficulty of explaining why it should be overruled. The rule that aliens abroad are not constitutionally entitled to habeas corpus has not proved unworkable in practice; if anything, it is the Court's "functional" test that does not (and never will) provide clear guidance for the future. *Eisentrager* forms a coherent whole with the accepted proposition that aliens abroad have no substantive rights under our Constitution. Since it was announced, no relevant factual premises have changed. It has engendered considerable reliance on the part of our military. And, as the Court acknowledges, text and history do not clearly compel a contrary ruling. It is a sad day for the rule of law when such an important constitutional precedent is discarded without an *apologia*, much less an apology.

What drives today's decision is neither the meaning of the Suspension Clause, nor the principles of our precedents, but rather an inflated notion of judicial supremacy. The Court says that if the extraterritorial applicability of the Suspension Clause turned on formal notions of sovereignty, "it would be possible for the political branches to govern without legal constraint" in areas beyond the sovereign territory of the United States. That cannot be, the Court says, because it is the duty of this Court to say what the law is. It would be difficult to imagine a more question-begging analysis. "The very foundation of the power of the federal courts to declare Acts of Congress unconstitutional lies in the power and duty of those courts to decide cases and controversies *properly before them*." *United States v. Raines* (1960); emphasis added. Our power "to say what the law is" is circumscribed by the limits of our statutorily and constitutionally conferred jurisdiction. And that is precisely the question in these cases: whether the Constitution confers habeas jurisdiction on federal courts to decide petitioners' claims. It is both irrational and arrogant to say that the answer must be yes, because otherwise we would not be supreme.

But so long as there are *some* places to which habeas does not run—so long as the Court's new "functional" test will not be satisfied *in every case*—then there will be circumstances in which "it would be possible for the political branches to govern without legal constraint." Or, to put it more impartially, areas in which the legal determinations of the *other* branches will be (shudder!) *supreme*. In other words, judicial supremacy is not really assured by the constitutional rule that the Court creates. The gap between rationale and rule leads me to conclude that the Court's ultimate, unexpressed goal is to preserve the power to review the confinement of enemy prisoners held by the Executive anywhere in the world. The "functional" test usefully evades the precedential landmine of *Eisentrager* but is so inherently subjective that it clears a wide path for the Court to traverse in the years to come.

Putting aside the conclusive precedent of *Eisentrager*, it is clear that the original understanding of the Suspension Clause was that habeas corpus was not available to aliens abroad. . . .

The Suspension Clause reads: "The Privilege of the Writ of Habeas Corpus shall not be suspended, unless when in Cases of Rebellion or Invasion the public Safety may require it." U.S. Const., Art. I, §9, cl. 2. The proper course of constitutional interpretation is to give the text the meaning it was understood to have at the time of its adoption by the people. That course is especially demanded when (as here) the Constitution limits the power of Congress to infringe upon a pre-existing common-law right. The nature of the writ of habeas corpus that cannot be suspended must be defined by the common-law writ that was available at the time of the founding.

It is entirely clear that, at English common law, the writ of habeas corpus did not extend beyond the sovereign territory of the Crown. To be sure, the writ had an "extraordinary territorial ambit," because it was a so-called "prerogative writ," which, unlike other writs, could extend beyond the realm of England to other places where the Crown was sovereign.

But prerogative writs could not issue to foreign countries, even for British subjects; they were confined to the King's dominions—those areas over which the Crown was sovereign. . . .

The common-law writ was codified by the Habeas Corpus Act of 1679, which "stood alongside Magna Charta and the English Bill of Rights of 1689 as a towering common law lighthouse of liberty—a beacon by which framing lawyers in America consciously steered their course." The writ was established in the Colonies beginning in the 1690's and at least one colony adopted the 1679 Act almost verbatim. . . .

The Act did not extend the writ elsewhere, even though the existence of other places to which British prisoners could be sent was recognized by the Act. The possibility of evading judicial review through such spiriting-away was eliminated, not by expanding the writ abroad, but by forbidding (in Article XII of the Act) the shipment of prisoners to places where the writ did not run or where its execution would be difficult.

The Habeas Corpus Act, then, confirms the consensus view of scholars and jurists that the writ did not run outside the sovereign territory of the Crown. The Court says that the idea that "jurisdiction followed the King's officers" is an equally credible view. It is not credible at all. The only support the Court cites for it is a page in Boumediene's brief, which in turn cites this Court's dicta in *Rasul*, mischaracterizing Lord Mansfield's statement that the writ ran to any place that was "under the subjection of the Crown." It is clear that Lord Mansfield was saying that the writ extended outside the realm of England proper, not outside the sovereign territory of the Crown. . . .

In sum, *all* available historical evidence points to the conclusion that the writ would not have been available at common law for aliens captured and held outside the sovereign territory of the Crown. Despite three opening briefs, three reply briefs, and support from a legion of *amici*, petitioners have failed to identify a single case in the history of Anglo-American law that supports their claim to jurisdiction. The Court finds it significant that there is no recorded case *denying* jurisdiction to such prisoners either. But a case standing for the remarkable proposition that the writ could issue to a foreign land would surely have been reported, whereas a case denying such a writ for lack of jurisdiction would likely not. At a minimum, the absence of a reported case either way leaves unrefuted the voluminous commentary stating that habeas was confined to the dominions of the Crown. . . .

In sum, because I conclude that the text and history of the Suspension Clause provide no basis for our jurisdiction, I would affirm the Court of Appeals even if *Eisentrager* did not govern these cases.

Today the Court warps our Constitution in a way that goes beyond the narrow issue of the reach of the Suspension Clause, invoking judicially brainstormed separation-of-powers principles to establish a manipulable "functional" test for the extraterritorial reach of habeas corpus (and, no doubt, for the extraterritorial reach of other constitutional protections as well). It blatantly misdescribes important precedents, most conspicuously Justice Jackson's opinion for the Court in *Johnson v. Eisentrager*. It breaks a chain of precedent as old as the common law that prohibits judicial inquiry into detentions of aliens abroad absent statutory authorization. And, most tragically, it sets our military commanders the impossible task of proving to a civilian court, under whatever standards this Court devises in the future, that evidence supports the confinement of each and every enemy prisoner.

The Nation will live to regret what the Court has done today. I dissent.

$$ *\qquad*\qquad*\qquad*\qquad*\qquad* $$

POSTSCRIPT

The Supreme Court's decision in *Boumediene* was immediately met with strong reactions from both ends of the political spectrum. Liberals hailed it as a landmark ruling of "fundamental importance" that preserved a cornerstone of American liberty and vindicated the principle of the separation of powers. In championing the writ of habeas corpus, crowed Democratic Senator Patrick Leahy, the Court had dealt a "stinging rebuke" to the Bush administration's detention policies and had decisively repudiated the un-American idea that "the President—and the President alone—can decide the rights of Americans." Never mind that none of the petitioners in *Boumediene* were Americans and that the Court had struck down a statute passed by Congress.

Many conservatives expressed outrage at the Court's ruling. Republican presidential nominee John McCain assailed it as "one of the worst decisions in the history of this country." McCain, like many other Republicans, echoed Scalia's charge that the decision would cause "more Americans to be killed." According to McCain, thirty detainees who had been released from Guantanamo "have already tried to attack America again."

The Pentagon's own numbers, however, suggest that McCain's rhetoric exaggerates the danger the nation has faced so far from the release of Guantanamo detainees. A Pentagon "fact sheet" dated June 13, 2008, estimates that around 5 percent of Guantanamo detainees are either "confirmed or suspected" of having commenced "terrorist activities" after their release. Thirteen former Guantanamo prisoners have been "confirmed" as participating in terrorist-related activities. Among the thirteen are three Chechens who were sent to Russia and then arrested by Russian authorities. Also on this list of thirteen is a Kuwaiti citizen who carried out a suicide bomb attack in northern Iraq that killed seven people. None of these thirteen men are known to have killed Americans, but the Pentagon fact sheet does indicate that six of the former detainees have taken up arms against the United States or coalition forces either in Iraq or Afghanistan. The military's fact sheet provides no information about the activities of the other twenty-four men who are "suspected" of engaging in terrorist activities.

Lakhdar Boumediene and the five other Algerian-Bosnians held at Guantanamo finally received their day in federal court on November 6, 2008. Although they were not permitted to be present during their habeas hearing, they were authorized to listen to the opening statements via telephone, although a technical malfunction prevented them from hearing any part of the opening proceedings. In its opening statement, the defense urged federal district judge Richard J. Leon—a Bush appointee who in 2005 had ruled that the detainees had no right to a habeas corpus hearing—to release the men because the government had presented no evidence that the men qualified as enemy combatants. Lawyers for the government countered that the only reason the defendants had not reached Afghanistan was that the government had acted proactively and prevented the men from carrying out their plans of joining the insurgency in Afghanistan. "The fact that they were captured before they were allowed to attack or kill Americans in the present conflict," the government's lawyers insisted, "does not diminish the government's authority to detain them" as enemy combatants.

In its opening statement, the government promised the judge that it possessed "reliable information" to support the charges being leveled against the detainees but insisted that the evidence not be revealed in open court since it was classified. Sporting "a red and white bow tie set against a blue shirt that peeked through his robes," Judge Leon then closed the courtroom to the public and the detainees for the remainder of the hearing. Defense attorneys were permitted to view the classified information but they could not share or discuss it with the detainees. The government's attorneys also provided the judge with a sealed envelope, with instructions to open it only if the judge deemed the evidence provided in the closed hearings insufficient. The defense lawyers had no idea what was in the sealed envelope and the judge warned that should he need to open the sealed envelope it may very well be "too sensitive" to share with the defense.

On November 21, 2008, Judge Leon issued his ruling. He directed the government to release Boumediene and four of the other five Bosnian men. Only in the case of one of the detainees (Bensayah Belkacem) did the government prove to the judge's satisfaction that "a preponderance of the evidence" suggested that the prisoner had connections to al Qaeda that justified holding him as an enemy combatant. The case against the other five men, however, rested on allegations by a single unnamed source and without any corroborating evidence or information that would enable the judge to evaluate the reliability of the source. "Seven years of waiting for a legal system to give them an answer," Judge Leon explained, "is more than enough." It was time for the government to release Boumediene and the other four Bosnians.

NOTES

1. The Insular Cases were a series of early twentieth-century cases in which the Supreme Court laid out a framework for deciding whether Constitutional protections extended to areas under U.S. control, like Puerto Rico, Guam, and the Philippines.

2. Section 2241 of the U.S. Code specifies the judiciary's power to grant the writ of habeas corpus. See http://www.law.cornell.edu/uscode/28/2241.html.

Glossary of Legal Terms

affidavit–A written statement of facts made under oath or affirmation.

affirm–To uphold the judgment rendered by a lower court.

appeal–A request that a higher court review a decision reached by a lower court.

appellant–The party that initiates a legal appeal.

appellee–The party that is responding to the suit brought by the appellant; typically the party that prevailed in the court ruling that is being appealed.

brief–A legal argument that is written by an attorney and submitted to a court.

circuit court–Same as court of appeals (federal). Name formally changed from United States Circuit Court of Appeals to United States Court of Appeals in 1947.

civil lawsuit–Legal case in which a victim sues for monetary damages against a private party for physical or emotional harm suffered. Contrasted with criminal law, in which the government prosecutes individuals who have broken the law.

common law–Law that is based on custom and usage, as adopted by courts. Typically distinguished from statutory law.

concurring opinion–A written judicial opinion that accepts the majority's decision but provides a different or additional rationale for that decision.

court of appeals (United States)–An intermediate court in the U.S. federal court system that hears appeals from judgments rendered in U.S. district courts. Each court of appeals has jurisdiction over one of twelve regions, also known as circuits.

de facto–Existing in fact but not recognized in law; contrasted with de jure.

defendant–The party being sued in a civil trial or prosecuted for a crime in a criminal trial.

de jure–Mandated or recognized by law; contrasted with de facto.

deposition–Sworn testimony taken prior to the beginning of a trial that may supplement live testimony in court.

dicta–The parts of a court opinion that are not necessary to reaching the decision in the case and are therefore not considered precedent for future decisions.

discovery–Process prior to the start of a trial in which one litigant is given access to the information and documents possessed by the opposing litigant.

dissenting opinion–A written opinion in which the judge explains why he or she does not agree with the decision reached by the court's majority.

district court–The trial court in the U.S. federal judiciary. Each state has at least one district court; as of 2008 there were 94 federal judicial districts and about 270 district court judges.

due process–The principle that the government cannot adversely affect a person's rights or interests without providing advance notice and a fair hearing.

enjoin–For a court to order that a person or organization desist from or carry out a particular action.

ex parte–Judicial hearing or proceeding in which only one party to a suit is present; literally "one part only."

grand jury–A jury used in certain criminal proceedings that is assigned the task of determining whether there is sufficient evidence to indict an individual and bring them to trial.

habeas corpus, writ of–A legal directive requiring a prisoner be brought before a judge so that the judge can decide whether the prisoner is being held lawfully; literally "you have the body."

immunity–Exemption from prosecution.

in camera–Legal proceedings that take place in the privacy of a judge's chambers or in a courtroom from which the public and jurors have been excluded; literally "in chambers."

indictment–A felony charge issued by a grand jury.

injunction–A court order prohibiting a litigant from taking some action.

judicial review–The idea that courts have the power to decide upon the constitutionality of actions taken by the legislature and the executive.

jus belli–The law of war.

litigant–Any of the parties to a lawsuit.

motion–A formal request that a court or judge issue a particular ruling or judgment.

opinion of the court–The judicial opinion in which the judgment and reasoning of the court's majority are announced.

oral argument–A forum in which the lead attorneys on both sides of a case summarize their arguments before the Supreme Court and answer the justice's questions; oral argument before the Supreme Court typically lasts one hour.

petitioner–The party who files a petition seeking relief in court; also used to designate the appellant in the Supreme Court.

petit jury–An ordinary trial jury in either civil or criminal cases.

plaintiff–The party who files a civil lawsuit.

plurality opinion–A written opinion in which the court's judgment is announced even though the reasoning used to arrive at that judgment is accepted only by a plurality rather than a majority of the justices.

precedent–A court decision establishing a principle or rule that is followed in a subsequent case.

quash–To set aside or annul.

remand–To send a case back to a lower court for further action consistent with the superior court's ruling.

respondent–The party being sued who must answer the petitioner's complaint; also used to designate the appellee in the Supreme Court.

reverse–For an appellate court to reach a decision that changes the outcome reached by the lower court.

show cause–A court order mandating that a party appear in court and demonstrate why the court should not pursue a particular action.

standing (to sue)–The right to file a lawsuit; typically requires demonstrating that one has been or will be directly impacted by an action.

stare decisis–The legal doctrine positing that previously decided cases should serve as a precedent and bind future courts that are faced with the same legal question; literally "let the decision stand."

statutory law–Law made by the legislature; as distinct from common law or constitutional law.

stay–A court-ordered delay in a judicial proceeding.

subpoena–A court order for an individual to appear at a certain time and place in order to testify or turn over documents.

subpoena duces tecum–A court order requiring an individual to produce a document in a judicial or legislative hearing.

summary judgment–A judicial ruling made in the absence of a full trial or hearing. Typically used at the trial court level when the judge determines that there are no factual issues to be resolved.

ultra vires–Acts that go beyond the legal authority possessed by a particular person or agency; literally "beyond powers."

List of Cases

1. *Myers v. United States* 272 U.S. 52 (1926)
2. *Humphrey's Executor v. United States* 295 U.S. 602 (1935)
3. *United States v. Nixon* 418 U.S. 683 (1974)
4. *Nixon v. Fitzgerald* 457 U.S. 731 (1982)
5. *Clinton v. Jones* 520 U.S. 681 (1997)
6. *Immigration and Naturalization Service v. Chadha* 462 U.S. 919 (1983)
7. *Clinton v. City of New York* 524 U.S. 417 (1998)
8. *United States v. Curtiss-Wright Export Corp.* 299 U.S. 304 (1936)
9. *The Prize Cases* 67 U.S. 635 (1863)
10. *Ex parte Milligan* 71 U.S. 2 (1866)
11. *Ex parte Quirin* 317 U.S. 1 (1942)
12. *Korematsu v. United States* 323 U.S. 214 (1944)
13. *Youngstown Sheet & Tube Co. v. Sawyer* 343 U.S. 579 (1952)
14. *United States v. Reynolds* 345 U.S. 1 (1953)
15. *Hamdan v. Rumsfeld* 548 U.S. 557 (2006)
16. *Boumediene v. Bush* 553 U.S. (2008)

Suggested Further Reading

Myers v. United States (1926)

Corwin, Edward S. *The President's Removal Power Under the Constitution*. New York: National Municipal League, 1927.

Entin, Jonathan L. "The Pompous Postmaster and Presidential Power: The Story of *Myers v. United States*." November 2005, Case Legal Studies Research Paper No. 05-39. Available at http://ssrn.com/abstract=845026.

Humphrey's Executor v. United States (1935)

Leuchtenburg, William E. "The Case of the Contentious Commissioner." In *The Supreme Court Reborn: The Constitutional Revolution in the Age of Roosevelt*. New York: Oxford University Press, 1995, 52–81.

United States v. Nixon (1974)

Berger, Raoul. *Executive Privilege: A Constitutional Myth*. Cambridge, MA: Harvard University Press, 1974.

Rozell, Mark J. *Executive Privilege: The Dilemma of Secrecy and Democratic Accountability*. Baltimore: Johns Hopkins University Press, 1994.

Nixon v. Fitzgerald (1982)

Fitzgerald, A. Ernest. *The Pentagonists: An Insider's View of Waste, Mismanagement, and Fraud in Defense Spending.* Boston: Houghton Mifflin, 1989.

Clinton v. Jones (1997)

Gerstmann, Evan, and Christopher Shortell. "Executive Immunity for the Post-Clinton Presidency." In *The Presidency and the Law: The Clinton Legacy.* David Gray Adler and Michael A. Genovese, eds. Lawrence: University Press of Kansas, 2002, 108–34.

Immigration and Naturalization Service v. Chadha (1983)

Craig, Barbara Hinkson. *Chadha: The Story of an Epic Constitutional Struggle.* New York: Oxford University Press, 1988.

Fisher, Louis. "The Legislative Veto: Invalidated, It Survives." *Law and Contemporary Problems* (Autumn 1993): 273–92.

Clinton v. City of New York (1998)

Spitzer, Robert J. "The Constitutionality of the Presidential Line-Item Veto." *Political Science Quarterly* (Summer 1997): 261–83.

United States v. Curtiss-Wright Export Corp. (1936)

Divine, Robert E. "The Case of the Smuggled Bombers." In *Quarrels That Have Shaped the Constitution.* Revised and enlarged edition. John A. Garraty, ed. New York: Harper & Row, 1987, 253–65.

Fisher, Louis. "Presidential Inherent Power: The Sole Organ Doctrine." *Presidential Studies Quarterly* (March 2007): 139–52.

The Prize Cases (1863)

McGinty, Bruce. *Lincoln and the Court.* Cambridge, MA: Harvard University Press, 2008, chap. 5.

Ex parte Milligan (1866)

Neely Jr., Mark E. *The Fate of Liberty: Abraham Lincoln and Civil Liberties.* New York: Oxford University Press, 1991, chap. 8.

Nevins, Allan. "The Case of the Copperhead Conspirator." In *Quarrels That Have Shaped the Constitution.* Revised edition. John A. Garraty, ed. New York: Harper & Row, 1987, 101–18.

Ex parte Quirin (1942)

Dobbs, Michael. *Saboteurs: The Nazi Raid on America*. New York: Knopf, 2004.
Fisher, Louis. *Nazi Saboteurs on Trial: A Military Tribunal and American Law*. 2nd ed. Lawrence: University Press of Kansas, 2005.

Korematsu v. United States (1944)

Irons, Peter. *Justice at War: The Story of the Japanese Internment Cases*. New York: Oxford University Press, 1983.

Youngstown Sheet & Tube Co. v. Sawyer (1952)

Marcus, Maeva. *Truman and the Steel Seizure Case: The Limits of Presidential Power*. New York: Columbia University Press, 1977.

United States v. Reynolds (1953)

Fisher, Louis. *In the Name of National Security: Unchecked Presidential Power and the Reynolds Case*. Lawrence: University Press of Kansas, 2006.
Pallitto, Robert, and William G. Weaver. *Presidential Secrecy and the Law*. Baltimore: Johns Hopkins University Press, 2007, esp. chap. 2.

Hamdan v. Rumsfeld (2006)

Mahler, Jonathan. *The Challenge: Hamdan v. Rumsfeld and the Fight over Presidential Power*. New York: Farrar, Straus & Giroux, 2008.

Boumediene v. Bush (2008)

Mayer, Jane. *The Dark Side: The Inside Story of How the War on Terror Turned into a War on American Ideals*. New York: Doubleday, 2008.
Wax, Steven T. *Kafka Comes to America: Fighting for Justice in the War on Terror*. New York: Other Press, 2008.

Index

223

About the Author

Richard J. Ellis is the Mark O. Hatfield Professor of Politics at Willamette University in Salem, Oregon, where he has taught since 1990. In 2008 he was named the Carnegie Foundation for Advancement of Teaching Oregon Professor of the Year. His previous books include *Presidential Travel: The Journey from George Washington to George W. Bush* (2008); *To the Flag: The Unlikely History of the Pledge of Allegiance* (2005); *Democratic Delusions: The Initiative Process in America* (2002); and *Founding the American Presidency* (1999).